The Healing Buddha

[illegible]

The Healing Buddha

Raoul Birnbaum

Foreword by John Blofeld

1979
SHAMBHALA
Boulder

Shambhala Publications, Inc.
1123 Spruce Street
Boulder, Colorado 80302

Distributed in the United States by Random House
and in Canada by Random House of Canada Ltd.

Printed in the United States of America.

Library of Congress Cataloging in Publication Data
Birnbaum, Raoul.
The healing Buddha.

Bibliography: p.
1. Bhaiṣajyaguru (Buddhist deity) I. Title.
BQ4690.B5B57 294.3'4'21 78-12979
ISBN 0-87773-742-8 (Shambhala) ISBN 0-394-50764-9 (Random House)
ISBN 0-87773-746-0 pbk. ISBN 0-394-73729-6 pbk.

DEDICATED TO ELLEN AND WINN

Contents

PART ONE

The Divine Healer in Buddhism: A Study of the Lapis Lazuli Radiance Buddha, Master of Healing

PART TWO

Translations from the Chinese Buddhist Canon

APPENDICES

Plates appear between pages 76–77

Foreword

THIS work is a valuable contribution to our understanding of an aspect of Buddhism hitherto little known in the West. In Part One, Pāli, Sanskrit, Chinese, and Tibetan sources are drawn upon to provide a well-documented account of traditional Buddhist remedies for physical maladies and, much more important, for spiritual ills. Scholarly standards are maintained throughout; nevertheless, the material is so presented as to make it no less acceptable to practicing Mahāyāna Buddhists and other devotees of Eastern wisdom than to academics. The sections dealing with healing rites performed by Chinese and Tibetans—including *mantras,* invocations, visualizations, and the use of special *maṇḍalas*—will be found entirely satisfactory by both groups of readers. Of particular interest is the emphasis on the role of art and aesthetic experience in mental healing practice. Of even more importance is the principle embodied in the words: "It is seen that the Buddha of Healing is especially concerned with aiding beings to awaken to their past deeds and to seek to change their negative patterns. That is, he is especially concerned with prompting beings to a great awakening, a momentous turning point at which the drifting life is cast aside for one of spiritual dedication." That, in a nutshell, is the whole message of this book. Those healing practices which may seem too ritualistic to appeal to modern Westerners are explained by the observation: "What is by nature invisible and inconceivable is thus crystallized in a formal way and thus comprehensible to the human mind."

Part Two comprises translations from the Chinese of several complete *sūtras* pertaining to the Healing Tathāgatas that were not, until now, available in any Western language. Besides being of great interest to students of Buddhism, healing, psychology, and Chinese and Tibetan art, these careful renderings of *sūtras* will undoubtedly be a welcome addition to the libraries of sacred works being built up by Mahāyāna Buddhist communities recently established in the

West. At present, only tiny fractions of the Chinese and Tibetan versions of the *Tripiṭaka* are to be found in English; therefore, every such addition is greatly prized in Western Buddhist circles.

It will be seen from this book that the Buddhist concept of healing marvelously anticipates the growing realization in the West that most illnesses, however physical their symptoms, are in fact psychosomatic disorders, or arise therefrom. To a Buddhist, the prime disease is ignorance of how to live sanely in this world and attune one's mind to the reality of existence; for this, the prime remedy is the intuitive wisdom that arises when delusion and consequent negativity are overcome. As the mind draws nearer to enlightenment, *karma*-forming propensities are reduced and bodily as well as spiritual ills relax their baneful grip. Meanwhile, visualization of the Healing Tathāgatas and recitation of their *mantras (properly used and understood)* will cure specific ills and lead to an upsurge of intuitive wisdom that will culminate in enlightenment and liberation.

Exponents of Tibetan tantric practice and of the Chinese/Japanese forms of Pure Land practice will recognize close affinities between what they have learned and what is advocated in these Healing Buddha *sūtras.* Those familiar with works about Kuan Yin (Avalokiteśvara, Chenresigs) will find that the powers attributed to the Healing Buddhas, and the reasons for those powers, are very similar in character to those attributed to that Bodhisattva. People who wrongly suppose that Pure Land Buddhism represents a turning away from the methods and values cherished by other schools such as Ch'an (Zen) will discover that this is far from being the case, since it can be confidently asserted that similar methods and values pertaining to the Healing Buddhas are accepted by the vast majority of Mahāyāna Buddhists, no matter to which school they belong.

To Western people eager to discover effective methods of spiritual as opposed to medical treatment of disease, the elaborately detailed rituals set forth in this book may seem too complicated and unsuited to a modern environment, but the principle underlying them should find many advocates in the West, once it is correctly understood. The essential practice arising from that principle consists of visualizing a radiant embodiment of the wisdom-compassion energy latent in Mind and drawing into one's own or another patient's body the rays emanating therefrom. Properly and regularly performed, this type of meditation is a sure means of cleansing mind and body; it reduces barriers to the influx of intuitive wisdom and may, in certain cases, produce spectacular cures of ills that are apparently physical in nature. I have known it to be used with extraordinary effect.

This book is also welcome as a further example of the tendency for Western scholars in the fields of Chinese and Tibetan studies to renounce the supercilious attitude of many of their predecessors. Earlier generations of scholars, being overconfident of the superiority of Western civilization to any other, whether past or present, did not always disguise their scornful skepticism as to the continuing value of the *content* of the ancient works on which they labored so diligently. To proclaim *acceptance* of the teachings of Chinese or Tibetan sages was to invite their scorn and probably arouse their doubts as to one's sanity. Now that Western man is no longer convinced of his innate superiority to the rest of the human race and more willing to see merits in other ways of life, sinologists such as Dr. Birnbaum approach the ancient works they translate in a spirit of respect and spiritual understanding. Among such scholars, there is now a readiness to concede that those works, besides adding to our scientific knowledge of the past, may indeed have much to contribute to the sum total of human wisdom. This new attitude is clearly discernible throughout the whole of Dr. Birnbaum's excellent book.

John Blofeld
Bangkok, Thailand
May, 1979

Preface

BUDDHISM is a way of life that emphasizes the development of mental faculties. The mind is trained to analyze and discriminate, to build up wholesome currents and tear away veils of negativity and ignorance. The Mahāyāna traditions especially emphasize the role of Divine beings—Buddhas and Bodhisattvas—in this task. Spiritual aspirants are taught to look to the Divine forces for aid, inspiration, and protection. In this way, their spiritual evolution can be immeasurably quickened.

In the living traditions of Mahāyāna Buddhism, devotees perceive these Divine beings as potent and vital forces, profoundly aware and ever responsive. The fundamental importance of Buddhas and Bodhisattvas to the daily practice of the Mahāyāna Buddhist way of life is well known: throughout the Far East there are temples large and small where worshippers bow before images and utter prayers, and the homes of devoted practitioners invariably have altars for daily meditation and worship.

I have sought in this book to discuss some of the traditions surrounding one of the most important deities of the Buddhist pantheon, the celestial Buddha known as Master of Healing, the Lapis Lazuli Radiance Buddha (in Sanskrit: Bhaiṣajya-guru vaiḍūrya-prabha tathāgata). The emphasis is on the Buddhist roots and the Buddhist manifestations of these traditions. For this reason, I have discussed concepts of healing in early Buddhism (both physical healing and spiritual healing) in the initial chapter, and I have sought to relate these concepts to the principles expressed in the texts and images central to the worship of the Healing Buddha.

According to the traditional life of Śākyamuni, the historical Buddha (ca. sixth century B.C.E.), the sight of a sick man was one of the catalytic events that awakened the young prince to the problem of human suffering and inspired him to begin his spiritual search. Śākyamuni's Four Noble Truths provide a key to the fundamental significance of healing in Buddhism, for they indicate that he who is not enlightened is by definition "ill."

In the early Buddhism of the Pāli Canon and later in the Mahāyāna teachings, one of the most important aspects of the healing process is the conversion of suffering into the aspiration to attain enlightenment. Time and time again, we read of instances where the experience of disease or disaster is transformed through new spiritual awareness into a fundamental event in which devotion arises and is intensified, energy is channeled into a sincere plea for aid, and the course of a life is profoundly changed. This is a special characteristic of Śākyamuni's treatments of ill monks recorded in the Pāli Canon, of Vimalakīrti's sage advice in the *Vimalakīrti-nirdeśa-sūtra,* and of the scriptures on the Healing Buddhas and Bodhisattvas.

The *Lotus Sūtra* equates the Healer with the Teacher of the Law, and the special scriptures on the Healing Buddhas and Bodhisattvas similarly hold that the most profound healing process is spiritual healing, taking place on an interior plane. This healing is the gradual elimination of the three inner "poisons" (lust, anger, and delusion), as well as the removal of the karmic veils or obstructions which have been built up through thoughts, words, and deeds of many lifetimes. Healing, in this sense, leads ultimately to direct apprehension of Reality, to the awakened state: enlightenment.

A potent aid in this healing process is the invisible assistance given by the Buddhas and Bodhisattvas of Healing. This assistance is often described as stemming from the force of their fundamental vows, which they made when they dedicated their lives to spiritual work. These vows to heal all beings and alleviate various sufferings served as special motivating factors in the spiritual development of the Buddhas and Bodhisattvas of Healing. Upon fruition of their spiritual work, when they attained their high evolutionary status as Buddhas and Bodhisattvas, they then truly became able to fulfill the vows.

If these beings can aid others, how can their help be sought for and received? The texts give several methods, the most fundamental being invocation of their spiritual force through recitation of their names. Special methods for the most part involve the use of images for invocation and worship of these deities. Thus, artists become involved and—though the most humble image can serve the profound purpose of invocation of a deity—some of the greatest works of Buddhist art and architecture have been dedicated to the Buddhas of Healing. Their symbolism can be seen as the concentrated essence of the teachings of the scriptures, the intent being to awaken the mind through spiritual experience to deeper levels of the Buddhist healing process and, ultimately, to enlightenment.

Three principal scriptures on the Healing Buddhas and Bodhisattvas, popular and influential for almost two millenia among the Asian Buddhist populace, have been translated here in full. These include: *Sūtra on the Contemplation of the Two Bodhisattvas, King of Healing and Supreme Healer* (from Chinese); *Sūtra on the Merits of the Fundamental Vows of the Master of Healing, the Lapis Lazuli Radiance Tathāgata* (from Chinese, with reference to the Sanskrit version); and the *Sūtra on the Merits of the Fundamental Vows of the Seven Masters of Healing, the Lapis Lazuli Radiance Buddhas* (from Chinese). I have also translated excerpts from a number of additional Chinese Buddhist texts, and these are included where relevant to this study. Based on the materials available to me, as far as I know, none of these principal texts have previously appeared in complete translation in any Western language. The only exception is the *Sūtra on the Merits of the Fundamental Vows of the Master of Healing, the Lapis Lazuli Radiance Tathāgata* (the *Bhaiṣajya-guru sūtra*), which was translated from a somewhat different Chinese text by Walter Liebenthal. (This English version was printed in Peking in 1936 in a limited edition and only recently has been reissued by the Hong Kong Book Distribution Press for The Buddhist Union, Singapore.)

One important aspect has only been touched on in this book, and that is the role of the Buddha of Healing in the history of Japanese religions. This I leave to specialists in that field, who can more fully describe the factors underlying the enduring popularity of the Buddha of Healing in Japanese religious practices.

I hope that in the future these and other aspects will be studied by additional scholars in order to round out our knowledge. What I seek to present here is an introduction to the Buddha of Healing and his companion deities, stressing the principles which they embody. It is my strong wish that this study be of special aid to all those interested in the principles of Eastern religions.

Raoul Oyang Birnbaum
New York City
February, 1978

Acknowledgments

I WOULD like to thank once again my teachers and mentors who aided me when I originally prepared this study in dissertation form at Columbia University: Professor Alex Wayman, who guided this study and also graciously permitted me to work with the draft manuscripts, iconographic illustrations, and Chinese texts from the collection of his teacher, the late Professor F. D. Lessing (these items being especially useful for my chapter four); Professor Yoshito S. Hakeda, who kindly read through the bulk of the translations, devoting many hours of his time to explicatory comments and corrections; Professor Pei-yi Wu, who aided me in initial Chinese readings in this area; and Professor Frederic B. Underwood, who guided my readings in the Pāli Canon and made many invaluable suggestions in the course of this study.

For knowledge regarding fundamental aspects of Pure Land practices, I wish to cite the special aid given by the Reverend Abbot Miao-ching during my visit in 1971 to the Monastery of the Eastern Grove, near Tsuen Wan in the New Territories sector of Hong Kong.

For insight into the spiritual principles of Buddhism, I wish to thank the Reverend Ellen Resch of the Temple for Buddhist Research and Learning (Weehawken, New Jersey), to whom this book is dedicated. To my guides and teachers of past and present, I express my deep gratitude. And to my wife, Celesta, goes heartfelt thanks for special aid and support.

I also wish to thank John Blofeld—author of many unusual books on Buddhism, Taoism, and Chinese culture—for contributing the foreword to this book. His kindness in encouraging my work by this means is deeply appreciated, as are his lucid remarks which place the principles of Buddhist healing in a modern context.

Mr. Long Tang kindly provided the Chinese characters included in the Appendices.

Finally, I would like to express my gratitude to Samuel Bercholz and the staff of the Shambhala Publications for their careful production of this book. Special thanks are due to Carolyn Rose and Jane Ellman, who provided editorial assistance and endless patience.

PART ONE

THE DIVINE HEALER IN BUDDHISM:

A STUDY OF THE LAPIS LAZULI RADIANCE BUDDHA, MASTER OF HEALING

I

Concepts of Healing in Early Buddhism

CONCEPTS of healing held a profound importance in the daily lives and spiritual work of the early Buddhist monks, according to the ancient texts of the Pāli Canon. The later Pāli texts and historical records expand on these concepts, indicating the increasing importance of healing activity within the Buddhist community. Mahāyāna texts of widespread popularity also discuss healing in some detail.

In these Buddhist texts healing is discussed from three points of view: (1) the cure of disease through healing agents (herbs and foods), surgery, and other physical means; (2) spiritual causes and cures of diseases; and (3) the healing process as a metaphor for spiritual growth, with the Buddha named as Supreme Physician and the Buddhist teachings termed the King of Medicines.

The symbolic and spiritual aspects of healing are especially fascinating in relation to the later worship of the Buddha of Healing, but physical healing is also of essential importance. In this initial chapter the early Buddhist attempts to grapple with this serious and sometimes dramatic aspect of human life can be seen.

A. HEALING AND THE MAINTENANCE OF LIFE IN EARLY BUDDHISM

1. Pāli Canon

The four requisites for life, stated repeatedly in the various texts of the Pāli Canon, are robes, food, lodging, and medicine. It is not surprising that medicine bears such significance, for surely great strains were placed upon the physical well-being of monks due to their austere life and strenuous meditative practices. Since illness and indisposition tend to weaken the mind, often causing it to lose its focus on its function as a liberating faculty, the prevention or proper treatment of illness held (and continues to hold) a great importance for the Buddhist monk. For those fully intent on achieving enlightenment, knowledge of how to prevent or cure serious illness was of utmost importance. Armed in this way, a monk would have some measure of defense against those life-destroying illnesses which might cause him to lose his grasp on human incarnation prior to achieving his spiritual goal.

According to Śākyamuni, the maintenance of health is especially related to proper diet. Certaiṇ foods were said by the Buddha to have unusually beneficial medicinal value, the chief of these being congee (or rice-milk) eaten with honey lumps. Eating this dish grants many healthful blessings:

> It confers ten things on him:
> Life and beauty, ease and strength;
> It dispels hunger, thirst, and wind,
> It cleanses the bladder, it digests food;
> This medicine is praised by the Well-farer.[1]

The Buddha advised against gluttony, suggesting to the king of Sāvatthī that moderating his intake of food would aid him in attaining a long and healthy span of life.[2] The prohibition of evening meals, a well-known feature of Buddhist monastic life, was instituted by Śākyamuni as a measure of preventative medicine:

> I, monks, do not eat a meal at night. Not eating a meal at night, I, monks, am aware of good health and of being without illness and of buoyancy and strength and living in comfort. Come, do you too, monks, not eat a meal at night.[3]

He sanctioned five principal medicines for use by monks. All of these were common dietary elements, including ghee (clarified butter), fresh butter, oil, honey, and molasses. The commentary in the *Suttavibhaṅga* section of the *Vinaya* indicates the exact nature of the five medicines:

> *Those medicines which are partaken of by ill monks* means: *ghee* is called ghee from cows or ghee from she-goats or ghee from buffaloes; ghee from

those whose meat is suitable. *Fresh butter* means: fresh butter from just these. *Oil* means: sesamun oil, oil of mustard seeds, oil containing honey, oil of the castor-oil plant, oil from tallow. *Honey* means: honey of bees. *Molasses* means: what is produced from sugar cane.[4]

Although the use of such substances as honey, oil, and butter as healing agents seems primitive at best, recent experiments by the pathologist and physician Guido Majno confirm the wisdom of prescribing these substances.[5]

In addition to the five standard medicines, the Buddha sanctioned use of a great variety of substances for special medicinal purposes. What amounts in effect to an entire *materia medica* can be found in the *Vinaya, Mahāvagga,* Section VI. A summary of that section is included here as Appendix I, "Healing Agents in the Pāli Canon."

In addition to healing by means of medicinal agents, various other methods are briefly mentioned. Surgical practices are apparently acceptable, since the only mention of them is to forbid treatments such as lancing "within a distance of two finger-breadths of the private parts."[6] Also, types of heat treatments were employed.[7]

An important passage in the *Dīgha-nikāya* lists a myriad of occupations forbidden by Śākyamuni as unacceptable means of livelihood. Among these occupations are quite a few pertaining to healing:

11–14. Administering emetics and purgatives.
15. Purging people to relieve the head (that is by giving drugs to make people sneeze).
16. Oiling people's ears (either to make them grow or to heal sores on them).
17. Satisfying people's eyes (soothing them by dropping medicinal oils into them).
18. Administering drugs through the nose.
19. Applying collyrium to the eyes.
20. Practicing as an oculist.
21. Practicing as a surgeon.
22. Practicing as a doctor for children.
23. Administering roots and drugs.
24. Administering medicines in rotation.[8]

Since many passages in the *Saṃyutta-nikāya* and the *Majjhima-nikāya* of the *Sutta* section and various books of the *Vinaya* section deal exclusively with the use and care of medicines and the practice of medical techniques, it is reasonable to assume that this is not a prohibition of the practice of medicine *per se.* Rather, it is a warning against habitual treatment of laymen (especially for the sake of alms); a warning against becoming a doctor rather than devoting time to the spiritual exercises of early Buddhist practices.

2. *Non-Canonical Pāli Texts, Historical Records, and Edicts*

Medical healing retained its importance in the later phase of early Buddhism, becoming a highly significant aspect in the lives of quite a few monks. For some, it was the focal point of contact with those outside the Order.

Pārapariyā, a monk who had studied under Śākyamuni, reveals in his lamenting verses the increase in healing activities carried on by monks in the years following the passing away of the Buddha:

> A thought came to the ascetic in the great wood, when it was in flower, when he was seated, intent, secluded, meditating:
>
> "The behavior of the bhikkhus now seems different from when the protector of the world, the best of men, was alive.
>
> "(There was) protection from the wind, a long-cloth as covering for their modesty; they ate moderately, satisfied with whatever came their way. . . .
>
> "They were not very eager for the necessities of life, for medicine and requisites, as they were for the annihilation of the *asavas* [outflows].
>
> "In the forest at the foot of trees, in caves and grottoes, devoting themselves to seclusion, they dwelt making that their aim,
>
> "Devoted to lowly things, of frugal ways, gentle, with unstubborn minds, uncontaminated, not garrulous, intent upon thinking about their goal.
>
> "Therefore their gait, eating, and practices were pious; their deportment was smooth, like a stream of oil.
>
> "Now those elders with all *asavas* completely annihilated, great meditators, great benefactors, are quenched. Now there are few such men. . . .
>
> "[The present members of the Order] . . . present clay, oil, and powder, water, lodgings, and food to householders, desiring more [in return].
>
> "Tooth-cleaner, and kapittha fruit, and flowers, and food to chew, palatable alms, and mangoes, and myrobalans [they give].
>
> "In medicines they are like doctors . . .
>
> "Running after pretexts, arrangements, stratagems, aiming at a livelihood they accumulate much wealth by a device."[9]

Thus, the Buddha's strict prohibition of medical practice by monks as a means of livelihood appears to have been disregarded within decades of his *parinirvāṇa,* his final passing away.

According to the historian A. L. Basham:

> We have no medical texts of the intervening period [between the *Vedas* and the texts of Caraka (first-second centuries C.E.) and Suśruta (fourth century C.E.)], but there is little doubt that two factors encouraged medical knowledge—the growth of interest in physiology through the phenomena of Yoga and mystical experience, and Buddhism. Like the Christian missionary of later times, the Buddhist monk often served as a doctor among the layfolk from whom he begged his food. . . .[10]

According to numerous passages in the *Vinaya,* the monks were expected to care for those among them who became ill, and, because of this, they became skilled in the fundamental practices of medicine. As has been noted, the extensive *materia medica* found in the *Mahāvagga* section of the *Vinaya* indicates the serious interest paid to the various remedies and treatments for the more common debilitating ailments. Seeing others ill and having the knowledge and means to cure those illnesses, certain compassionate monks took on the practice of aiding laymen, especially when they dwelt or wandered in outlying areas far from the centers of medical activity.

Some monk-physicians employed their healing abilities as a means of spreading the Dharma and converting non-believers. Certain monks from India and Central Asia, who traveled to China in the second through fourth centuries C.E., achieved great success in spreading the Dharma in part by means of their gifted healing activities, especially within aristocratic circles.[11]

Thus a monk might learn healing techniques to aid his fellow monks, to be of compassionate service to laymen, and as an expedient means for obtaining trust for the purpose of spreading the Buddhist teachings.

In addition to the monk-physicians, devout Buddhist rulers also saw the importance of compassionate healing activities, and they supported—as an aspect of their Buddhist practices—the building of hospitals and the dispensing of medicines. The great Buddhist king Aśoka, ruler of much of India in the third century B.C.E., had the following edict carved on a rock (Rock Edict #II, Girnar text):

Everywhere in the dominions of King Priyadarśi, Beloved of the Gods, and likewise in the bordering territories such as those of the Cholas and Pandyas as well as of the Satiyaputra and Keralaputra as far south as Tamraparni, and in the territories of the Yavana king Antiyoka and also the kings who are the neighbors of the said Antiyoka—everywhere King Priyadarśi, Beloved of the Gods, has arranged for two kinds of medical treatment, viz., medical treatment for men and medical treatment for animals. And, wherever there were no medicinal herbs beneficial to men and beneficial to animals, they have been caused to be imported and planted. On the roads, wells have been caused to be dug and trees have been caused to be planted for the enjoyment of animals and men.[12]

Many other Buddhist rulers continued such activities. For example, Duṭṭhagāmaṇi, devout Buddhist king of Ceylon, made a deathbed statement (177 C.E.) in which he listed the accomplishments of his reign. Among the many acts of devotion to the Buddha and the doctrine, the king states:

Constantly in eighteen places have I bestowed on the sick the foods for the sick and remedies, as ordered by the physicians.[13]

These activities have often been cited as evidence of the compassionate and benevolent influence which the Buddhist teachings exert on rulers who are faithful devotees. Through support of healing activities by rulers and through the actual practice of medicine by monks, the compassion generated by sincere practice of the Buddhist teachings could find expression.

3. Medicine in Early Mahāyāna Texts

The use of various medicines is discussed briefly in a wide range of early Mahāyāna texts. The extensive indices to the *Taishō Shinshū Daizōkyō* edition of the Chinese Buddhist Canon show that terms for "medicine" and various medicinal objects abound in a comprehensive range of scriptures.

As an example, we can cite an early Mahāyāna text that was quite popular in Central and East Asia, the heartlands of later worship of the Buddha of Healing. This text, the *Suvarṇaprabhāsa-sūtra* (or *The Sūtra of Golden Radiance*), contains two chapters on healing and medicine. It describes how Śākyamuni in a past life studied all the principles of medicine in order to aid his contemporaries.[14]

In recounting this story of an important past life of the Buddha, the general principles of Indian medicine are outlined. In so doing, the *sūtra* helps to establish medical study as appropriate for Buddhists. Since this text was revered in Central and East Asia, it strengthened the role of monk-physicians there and also communicated the essence of Indian medical principles to those regions.

B. SPIRITUAL CAUSES AND CURES OF DISEASE

1. Pāli Canon

In addition to diseases incurred through the weakening of the body due to old age or the physical strains of the difficult life led by members of the early Saṃgha, some illnesses are described which stem directly from karma of past or present lives. In one dramatic case, a monk repeatedly denounced two of the elders of the Order. The ferocity of his undermining and false accusations and the intensity of the multitude of negative thoughts motivating the statements were such that—by karmic repercussion—his entire body broke out in boils, discharging pus and thus causing death. The Buddha explained this karmic principle:

> In sooth to every man that's born
> A hatchet grows within his mouth,
> Wherewith the fool, whene'er he speaks
> And speaks amiss, doth cut himself . . .[15]

Now disease brought on by karma does not always lead to disaster. Sometimes it is the burning off of debts incurred in lives past; sometimes it is the catalytic factor which spurs the spiritually devoted onwards towards liberation.

The monk Samitigutta, confined to a monastic infirmary because of his hopeless case of leprosy, was given a meditative exercise on the contemplation of feeling. With profound effort, Samitigutta practiced this exercise and achieved liberation. In this process he gained knowledge of the negative actions in past lives which were the cause of his present disease. Being freed by insight (though still afflicted by the fatal disease), he said:

> Whatso of evil wrought in bygone days,
> In former births by me, just here and now.

'T is that whereby I lie and suffer sore
But other ground for ill exists no more.[16]

Śākyamuni Buddha is portrayed as a great healer in the Pāli Canon. His healing methods were twofold: healing through teaching, and psychic or "miraculous" healing. The Buddha taught patients according to the severity of the disease. Those with fatal diseases received lessons on impermanence, while those who could be cured were taught to meditate on the "seven limbs of enlightenment."

A number of patients received teachings on impermanence. For example, the Buddha once went to pay a call on an unknown novice who lay ill. Seeing that the man's distress was increasing, Śākyamuni posed successive questions on impermanence to him. In this way, being gradually led from realization to realization, finally:

> . . . in that brother arose the pure and flawless eye of the Norm, (so that he saw) "Whatsoever is of a nature to arise, all that is of a nature to cease."[17]

The Buddha aided the monk Assaji in a similar way. Lying grievously ill, Assaji told the Buddha that he could not enter into *jhāna* (meditative trance) because of breathing difficulties, and he was unable to attain balance of mind. With words of encouragement, Śākyamuni instructed him to dwell on thoughts of impermanence and non-self.[18] Now these teachings were not new to the venerable monk, for it was he who long before had succinctly summarized the Buddha's teachings on impermanence, in this way converting Sāriputta. The Buddha's emphasis on these teachings as final meditations in the earthly incarnation highlights their essential and fundamental importance as gateways to Liberation.

On occasions when the patient could be healed, the Buddha urged him to meditate on the seven limbs of enlightenment (seven *bojjhaṅgas;* Sanskrit *bodhyaṅgas*). These are:

1. mindfulness
2. investigation of things (*dharmas*)
3. striving
4. joy
5. tranquility
6. meditative trance (*samādhi*)
7. equanimity[19]

For example, once when the elder Kassāpa was ill, his pains increasing, the Buddha visited him and said:

> Kassāpa, these seven limbs of enlightenment fully expounded by myself, when cultivated and made much of, conduce to full comprehension, to the wisdom, to *Nibbāna.*[20]

Receiving and accepting the full teaching of the seven limbs, Kassāpa thereupon ". . . rose up from that sickness. There and then that sickness of the venerable Kassāpa the Great was abandoned."[21] Upon another occasion, Mogallāna was healed by similar instruction from the Buddha.[22]

To emphasize the potent healing power of this fundamental meditative exercise: once when the Buddha lay ill, Cunda (the younger brother of Sāriputta) visited him. The Buddha asked Cunda to recite the seven limbs of enlightenment to him. Upon hearing and approving both Cunda's recitation and the teaching itself, ". . . the Exalted One rose up from the sickness. There and then that sickness of the Exalted One was abandoned."[23]

These seven limbs are sometimes used as a *mātṛka,* a device for summarizing the Buddhist teachings. However, in the context of healing, it appears that they are used as successive steps in meditation. The prescription of meditative exercise as a cure for disease indicates that illnesses, from a Buddhist point of view, are intimately linked to mental states gone awry. If the mental currents of the patient can be clarified and rectified, then the cause of the illness will be removed, and the patient will be cured. This is not unrelated to the common modern belief that most diseases are psychological in origin, however real the manifested symptoms may be.

From a traditional Buddhist point of view, the meditation on the seven limbs of enlightenment can be seen as a method for overcoming the interior poisons often mentioned in the teachings—lust, anger, and delusion. These interior poisons are related to the three physiological poisons which, in imbalance, cause disease: lust generating too much wind; anger producing excess bile; and delusion yielding an overabundance of phlegm.

Although Śākyamuni generally healed through teaching, on rare occasions of dire need he exercised his spiritual ability to instantly heal those in distress. Generally these instances of "miraculous" healing involved devoted lay followers. For example, the laywoman Suppiya, who secretly cut off a section of her leg to provide a meat broth for an ill monk, was healed instantly by the Buddha (who then declared it a grave offense to eat human flesh).[24]

Importantly, in most of the incidents where Śākyamuni took the role of healer (either as teacher or miraculous physician), the experience of disease or injury served as a catalytic factor leading to new insight and—in some cases—to Liberation. So it is seen that while a disease or injury may appear to be a difficult manifestation of negative karma, it can have positive, liberating potential. This potential can be realized if the patient applies himself with whole-hearted effort to the appropriate teachings. In these cases, the Buddha treated the patient rather than the disease or wound, taking advantage of the opportunity to offer a cure for the more nagging disease: that of ignorance and craving.

2. *Non-Canonical Pāli Texts*

A special method for curing disease, although not mentioned in the Pāli Canon, is said by Nāgasena in the *Milindapañha*[25] to have been bequeathed by Śākyamuni himself. This method, called *parittā,* consists of recitations of various phrases and texts, thereby magically dispelling the disease. *Parittā* means "protection"; the Sinhalese equivalent, often used, is *pirit.* According to Nāgasena, the potent, protective strength of these invocatory formulae is of incalculable force:

> And when, O king, the voice of those who are repeating *parittā* is heard, the tongue may be dried up, and the heart beat but faintly, and the throat be hoarse, but by that repetition all diseases are allayed, all calamities depart.[26]

Nāgasena further discussed the ability *parittā* has to repel calamities:

> . . . And when *parittā* has been said over a man, a snake ready to bite will not bite him but will close his jaws—the club which robbers hold aloft to strike him with will never strike; they will let it drop and treat him kindly—the enraged elephant rushing at him will suddenly stop—the burning fiery conflagration surging towards him will die out—the malignant poison he has eaten will become harmless, and turn to food—assassins who have come to slay him will become as the slaves who wait upon him—and the trap into which he has trodden will hold him not.[27]

In discussing how *परित्ता* can cure diseases, Nāgasena touched on an important principle in Buddhist medicine: though various means can be of substantial aid in subduing disease, when the affliction is due to deeply-rooted karmic causes, it will take its determined toll:

> . . . There is no ceremony or artificial means, no medicine and no *parittā*, which can prolong the life of one whose allotted period has come to an end. All the medicines in the world are useless, O king, to such a one, but *parittā* is a protection and an assistance to those who have a period yet to live, who are full of life, and restrain themselves from the evil of Karma. And it is for that use that *parittā* was appointed by the Blessed One.[28]
>
> . . . *Parittā* [is] a protection to some and not to others. And there are reasons for its failure—the obstruction of Karma . . . That *parittā* which is a protection to beings loses its protecting power by acts done by those beings themselves.[29]

Parittā later became one of the chief healing ceremonies of Ceylonese Buddhism. It was officially sponsored by the state after its efficacious powers were demonstrated during the reign of Aggabodhi IV (reigned 658–674 C.E.).[30]

3. Spiritual Causes and Cures of Disease in Early Mahāyāna Texts

The sage Vimalakīrti discussed the experience of illness at great length. These fascinating passages are found in the *Vimalakīrti-nirdeśa-sūtra* (*Sūtra Spoken by Vimalakīrti*), chapter four. With many visitors assembled to inquire after his health, the infirm sage took the opportunity to speak out about the human body and its limitations:

> O virtuous ones, the wise do not rely upon the body. It is like a mass of froth which cannot be grasped, like a bubble which bursts in an instant. The body is like a flame arising from the thirst of love . . . like a shadow, appearing as a result of karma. It is like an echo, responding to causes and conditions . . . The body does not act of itself; but is spun around by the force of the winds [of passion].[31]

His own face gaunt and creased by illness, vividly impressing upon visitors the transitory nature of earthly existence, Vimalakīrti urged them to seek the "Buddha-body":

> . . . The *Tathāgata*-body arises from countless types of purities. O virtuous ones, if you desire to attain the Buddha-body and be rid of all the illnesses which beset living beings, you should aspire to attain perfect enlightenment.[32]

The sage's further comments, succinct and moving, indicate that his own illness stemmed from the burden which a Bodhisattva takes on when he pledges to save all beings:

> . . . I am ill because all sentient beings are ill. If the illnesses of all sentient beings were to come to an end, then my illness would be ended. Why is this so? Because when the Bodhisattva enters into the realm of birth and death for the sake of all beings, he becomes subject to the laws of this realm and thereupon becomes ill. If all sentient beings were to be cured of their diseases, then the Bodhisattva would never again be ill.
>
> It is like the rich man who only has one son. When this son becomes ill, his parents also become ill. If the son is cured of the disease, so also are the parents. It is the same for the Bodhisattva: he loves all beings as if each of them were his only son. When all beings are cured, then the Bodhisattva will be cured.[33]

Having spoken about those eminent ones, the highly-evolved Bodhisattvas who—within reach of *nirvāṇa*—turn back to aid all sentient beings, Vimalakīrti also spoke of those on the initial stages of the Bodhisattva Path. When such a person falls ill due to karmic repercussions, a friend should comfort him by speaking:

> . . . of the impermanence of the body, but not of the rejection of the body. He should tell him that having a body entails suffering, but he should not speak to him of the joys of *nirvāṇa.* He should speak to him about egolessness while retaining a body, about teaching and guiding all living beings. He should speak of the voidness of the body, but not of ultimate *nirvāṇa.* He should speak of the repentance of past faults, but not of brooding too deeply about them.[34]

Significantly, Vimalakīrti instructs Bodhisattvas to convert the experience of illness into something positive, to generate wholesome striving energy from this experience:

> Because of his own illness, he should take pity on all others who are sick. He should know of the sufferings of countless aeons of past lives, and because of this he should think of the welfare of all beings. He should be mindful of the pure life. Instead of generating grief and vexation, he should constantly give rise to striving energy. He should become a king of healing and cure all ills.[35]

For the Bodhisattva who follows Vimalakīrti's advice, the experience of illness will not be a hampering factor but rather a catalyst, the ultimate function of which is to stimulate renewed and increased dedication to spiritual work. Instead of causing the Bodhisattva to seek release from his bodily pains by entering into the bliss of *nirvāṇa,* illness for him should be a great leveller, reminding him of the essential brotherhood of man inherent in the shared suffering of disease. Conscious of his link to all beings, he should increase his resolve to come to their aid and succor.

C. THE HEALING PROCESS AS SPIRITUAL GROWTH

1. Pāli Canon

The Buddha frequently made analogies to disease and healing to explain various facets of his teaching. According to these teachings, a person who is not liberated, who is still subject to the sufferings brought on by insatiable craving, is considered "ill." Therefore the healing process is akin to the enlightenment process.

Śākyamuni once described a monk who became free of his karmic hindrances:

> Then just, O king, as if a man were a prey to disease, in pain, and very ill, and his food would not digest, and there was no strength left in him; then when he were to recover from that disease, and his food should digest, and his strength come back to him; then, when he realized his former and present state, he would be of good cheer at that, he would be glad of heart at that.[36]

In order to recover from a serious disease, one usually needs a physician to diagnose the disease and prescribe a treatment, one needs the systematic healing treatment itself, and one needs attendants to give aid. In the Pāli Canon, the Supreme Physician is the Buddha; the healing treatment—the medicine and therapeutic regimen—is the Dharma; and the attendants are the members of the Order.[37]

An important passage in the *Majjhima-nikāya* indicates the method of treatment employed by such a Healer. In this passage, the Buddha emphasizes the unavoidably painful aspects of spiritual work:

> . . . It is as if a man were pierced by an arrow that was thickly smeared with poison. And because he has felt that arrow he might experience a feeling that was painful, severe, sharp. His friends and acquaintances, kith and kin might procure a physician and surgeon. That physician and surgeon might cut round the opening of his wounds with a knife, but on account of cutting round the opening of his wounds with the knife the man might experience a feeling that was painful, severe, sharp. That

physician and surgeon might probe him for the arrow with a (surgeon's) probe, but on account of his being probed for the arrow with the surgeon's probe he might also experience a feeling that was painful, severe, sharp. That physician and surgeon might extract the arrow from him, but on account of having the arrow extracted he might also experience a feeling that was painful, severe, sharp. The physician and surgeon might dress the opening of his wound with medicinal powder, but on account of having the opening of the wound dressed with medicinal powder he might also experience a feeling that was painful, severe, sharp. After a time when the skin had healed on the wound he would be well, at ease, independent, his own master, going wherever he liked.[38]

Commenting on a similar passage, the Buddha explained the symbolism: the wound represents the six inner sense-fields, the poison represents ignorance, the arrow is craving, the surgeon's knife symbolizes pure insight, the surgeon's probe represents mindfulness, and the physician and surgeon is the Tathāgata himself.[39]

Again and again, the Buddha reminds his disciples that they are ill, that they should diligently seek to be healed, and that they can turn to the King of Medicines (the Dharma) and the Supreme Physician for aid and relief:

> Full rare and seldom are the wakened seen.
> Of those rare men, seen seldom in the world,
> Lo! I am one, physician without peer . . .[40]

2. *Non-Canonical Pāli Texts*

Monks who were direct disciples of Śākyamuni commonly referred to him as a Supreme Physician. For example, Adhimutta said:

> My teacher is the Conqueror knowing all
> And seeing all, the Master infinite
> In pity, all the world's physician, he.[41]

Telakām, referring to the "dart that springs from self," asked: who could "draw out this shaft that's stuck within my heart"? Answering his own question, he said:

> Master of Dhamma, he, the Best
> Who can the venom's fever-scathe disperse . . .[42]

The epithet of the Supreme Healer and Physician is used throughout a wide range of texts, including *The Questions of King Milinda*. In this text, Nāgasena also speaks of the "medicine bazaar of the Blessed One," in which there are medicines offered by the Buddha which can cure gods and men. These medicines are revealed as the thirty-seven items leading to enlightenment, the thirty-seven *bodhipakkhiya dhammas* (Skt. *bodhipakṣya dharmas*). With these medicines, the Buddha can purge all the negatives, removing all evil.[43]

In addition to discussing the healing qualities of the teachings, Nāgasena also compares medicine to an exalted state of mind:

> Just, O king, as vermin are not produced in medicine; just so, O king, should no evil dispositions be allowed to arise in the mind of the strenuous Bhikshu, earnest in effort . . .
>
> And again, O king, just as medicine is an antidote to whatever poison may have been imparted by bites or contact, by eating or by drinking in any way; just so, O king, should the strenuous Bhikshu, earnest in effort, counteract in himself the poison of lusts, and malice, and dullness, and pride, and wrong belief . . . For it was said, O king, by the Blessed One, the god over all the gods:
>
> The strenuous recluse who longs to see
> Into the nature and the meaning of the true,
> Of the constituent elements of things,
> Must as it were an antidote become,
> To the destruction of all evil thoughts.[44]

This continual emphasis on the Supreme Physician and his Medicine indicates a fundamental attitude of Buddhism: dispassionate compassion. The great physician, a model of selfless compassion, devotes his life to easing the pain of others. Retaining an attitude of detachment, he does not allow his emotions to become tangled in his work, and he cures his patients in an efficacious manner. Similarly, the Buddhist retains an attitude of detachment and observes his various flaws or "illnesses." Using the medicine prescribed by the master healer, the teachings bequeathed by the Buddha, he is able to root out the diseases in a dispassionate manner, retaining compassion for the patient (himself), yet showing no mercy for the disease.

3. Parables in Early Mahāyāna Texts: the Lotus Sūtra

The Buddha's role as a healer is asserted in the oft-quoted parable of the physician, found in the *Saddharma-puṇḍarīka-sūtra.* Explaining to the Bodhisattvas why the appearance of a Buddha in the world is a rare event, and why Buddhas do not dwell constantly in the world, Śākyamuni compared himself to an excellent physician:

. . . who, wise and astute, brilliant in the dispensing of medicines, is adept at healing all illnesses. He has many sons, ten, twenty, perhaps a hundred or more. Having some matter to attend to, he goes abroad to a distant land. Afterwards, his sons eat some poisonous medicines, causing stupefaction, confusion, and collapse.

At this point their father returns home. Of all the sons who have eaten the poison, some have lost their minds while others are still overjoyed to see him. Kneeling and making obeisance, they ask him: "How good it is that you have returned safely! We have foolishly swallowed poisonous medicines by mistake. We beg you to save and cure us. Give us back our lives!"

Seeing his sons' calamity and relying on the standard prescriptions, the father seeks out excellent medicinal herbs altogether perfect in color, scent, and flavor. He pounds, strains, and mixes them, and orders his sons to take their dosage, saying: "This is a supreme medicine, with color, scent, and flavor altogether perfect. If you partake of it, you will quickly be rid of your distress, and these sufferings will not recur."

Among the sons, those who are sane, seeing this excellent medicine with color and scent both good, take it immediately and are totally healed of their disease. However, when the others who have lost their senses see their father approach, even though they also rejoice, salute him, and ask him to cure their disease, still they do not dare take his medicine.

Why is this so? Because the poisonous essences have penetrated deeply, they have taken leave of their senses. Thus, seeing this medicine of excellent color and fragrance, they call it vile.

The father reflects: "Alas, for these sons whose minds have been turned upside down in the throes of this poison. Even though they are glad to see me and implore me to heal them, they do not take a medicine as excellent as this. I will have to devise an expedient means to induce them to take the medicine."

Then he says to them: "You should know that I am now in my old age, and the time of my death has arrived. This excellent medicine I bequeath to you. You may take it and be assured that you will be healed."

After these instructions, he departs again for another land where he then dispatches a messenger to return with the words: "Your father is dead."

When these sons hear of their father's death, their minds are greatly distraught. They reflect: "If our father were here, he would feel compassion and pity for us, and we would be able to be saved and protected. Now he has abandoned us, dead in a far-distant land. We are only young orphans, never again having someone to depend on."

Immersed in constant grief and sorrowful emotions, their minds awake.

They recognize the color, scent, beauty, and taste of the medicine. Then they take it, and the illness caused by the poison is completely cured.

When the father hears that the sons have all recovered, he seeks for an opportunity to return so that they all may see him.[45]

It is relevant that the three Mahāyāna texts mentioned in this chapter—those which especially highlight healing and healers—were quite popular among laymen as well as monks in Central and East Asia, for lay Buddhist worship was a fundamental factor in the spread of popularity of the Healing Buddha. Although certain topics may appeal only to those trained in meditative or philosophical practices, illness is an experience to which all beings in this world are subject, and the topic of healing strikes a universal chord bearing an importance to laymen and monks alike.

In concluding this introductory chapter, it should be noted that all the principal aspects of healing discussed in these earlier texts—physical healing of bodily ills, spiritual healing of bodily ills, and the healing of inner ills through spiritual work and insight—find special expression in the texts and traditions of the Healing Bodhisattvas and Healing Buddhas. Having established that these topics were of unusual concern for the early Buddhist authors, we can see the Buddhist roots of the healing deities.

1. I. B. Horner, trans., *The Book of the Discipline (Vinaya-piṭaka)*, vol. IV (*Mahāvagga*) (London: 1951), p. 302. (Hereafter referred to as *Vinaya: Mahāvagga.*)
2. Caroline Rhys Davids, trans., *The Book of the Kindred Sayings (Saṃyutta-nikāya)*, vol. I (London: 1971 reprint of 1917 ed.), p. 108. (Hereafter referred to as *Saṃyutta-nikāya.*)
3. *Vinaya: Mahāvagga*, pp. 269–270.
4. I. B. Horner, trans., *The Book of the Discipline (Vinaya-piṭaka)*, vol. II (*Suttavibhaṅga*) (London: 1940), pp. 131–132.
5. Guido Majno, *The Healing Hand* (Cambridge, Mass.: 1975), pp. 115–120. According to Dr. Majno, honey is "practically harmless to the tissues, aseptic, antiseptic, and antibiotic" (p. 118). It does not support bacterial growth for several reasons: (1) It is extremely hypertonic and draws water from bacterial cells, causing them to shrivel and die; (2) an enzyme secreted by the pharyngeal glands of the bee—

glucose oxidase—reacts to form hydrogen peroxide (the common disinfectant) and gluconic acid, a mild antibiotic. This antibiotic mechanism is active in dilutions as low as thirteen per cent; and (3) A sticky material called propolis is used to patch cracks in the hive, and thus becomes mixed with the honey itself. It is antibiotic, and its main active ingredient, galangine, is now patented in the United States as a food preservative.

According to written records, honey has been used as a primary component in wound dressings from the time of the ancient Egyptians to the modern era. In addition to its aseptic, antiseptic, and antibiotic qualities, "the main advantage seems to be mechanical. Despite its own stickiness it prevents the dressing from sticking to the wound, because it draws out a large amount of fluid, and this is said to have a cleansing effect, especially useful on dirty or infected wounds" (p. 118).

The addition of grease, oil, or butter gives the honey a more soothing consistency, and is proven to be effective as a wound salve. This honey-butter preparation was often used on wounds in ancient India (p. 273).

6. *Vinaya: Mahāvagga,* p. 295.

7. I. B. Horner, trans., *The Book of the Discipline (Vinaya-piṭaka),* vol. I (*Suttavibhaṅga*) (London: 1938). p. 143.

8. T. W. Rhys Davids, trans., *Dialogues of the Buddha (Dīgha-nikāya)* vol. I (London: 1899), pp. 25–26. (Hereafter referred to as *Dīgha-nikāya.*)

9. K. R. Norman, trans., *The Elder's Verses,* vol. I (London: 1969), pp. 86–88.

10. A. L. Basham, *The Wonder That Was India* (New York: 1959), p. 449.

11. Cf. Erik Zürcher, *The Buddhist Conquest of China* (Leiden: 1972), 2 vols. Also Arthur F. Wright, "Fo-t'u-teng: a biography," *Harvard Journal of Asiatic Studies,* XI (1948), pp. 321–371.

The healing abilities of several of these monks helped to establish belief in the potency of Buddhism. Among the Central Asians were the Parthian An Shih-kao and Fo-t'u-teng, probably from Kucha. According to Fo-t'u-teng's biography in the *Kao-seng-chüan,* when he arrived in Loyang in 310 C.E., ". . . there was a chronic illness which no one was able to cure. When Teng treated the disease, it was immediately cured. Those whom he secretly treated and who benefited in silence were uncountable." (Wright, p. 340) Further, listing means by which Teng propagated Buddhism in China, the *Kao-seng-chüan* states, "Using secret spells, he saved those on the point of death; using the fragrance of incense, he rescued those on the verge of disaster." (Wright, p. 370)

Several other eminent monks of the fourth century, these of native Chinese origin, were also involved in medical work. For example, Chu Fa-k'uang (327–402 C.E.) "knew a great number of 'divine spells' of curative power, and healed many patients during a pestilence in the eastern provinces." (Zürcher, p. 145)

Yü Fa-k'ai (310–370 C.E.) and his disciple Yü Tao-sui (305–335 C.E.) were both able physicians, Fa-k'ai being one of the most famous physicians of his time. He justified his medical practice as a way of elucidating the Dharma and benefiting others (Zürcher, pp. 140–141). Chih Tun (314–366), another great teacher of that era, also practiced medicine, perhaps due in part to his great rivalry with Yü Fa-k'ai (Zürcher, p. 145).

12. D. C. Sircar, trans., *The Inscriptions of Aśoka* (Delhi: 1967), pp. 46–47.
13. Wilhelm Geiger, trans., *The Mahāvaṃsa, or The Great Chronicles of Ceylon* (London: 1964 reprint of 1912 ed.), p. 223.
14. This story is related in chapters 16 and 17 of some versions (e.g., the Khotanese version used by R. E. Emmerick in his translation *The Sutra of the Golden Light* [London: 1970]), while other versions condense the tale to one chapter.
15. *Saṃyutta-nikāya*, vol. 1, p. 191.
16. Caroline Rhys Davids, trans., *Psalms of the Early Buddhists*, vol. II (*Theragātha*) (London: 1964 reprint of 1913 ed.), p. 79. (Hereafter referred to as *Theragātha.*) Although a non-canonical text, quotes from the *Theragātha* are included here where they relate to the period of the Buddha's ministry.
17. F. L. Woodward, trans., *The Book of Kindred Sayings (Saṃyutta-nikāya)*, vol. IV (London: 1928), p. 23–25.
18. F. L. Woodward, trans., *The Book of Kindred Sayings (Saṃyutta-nikāya)*, vol. III (London: 1954 reprint of 1925 edition), pp. 106–7.
19. Cf. *Saṃyutta-nikāya*, vol. V, pp. 51–118.
20. Cf. *Saṃyutta-nikāya*, vol. III, p. 67.
21. Cf. *Saṃyutta-nikāya*, vol. III, p. 67.
22. Cf. *Saṃyutta-nikāya*, vol. III, p. 67.
23. Cf. *Saṃyutta-nikāya*, vol. III, p. 67.
24. *Vinaya: Mahāvagga*, pp. 297–298.
25. Dialogue between the Buddhist sage Nāgasena and Menander, ruler of Greek origins who controlled Bactria, a portion of Northwest India (reigned 163–150 B.C.E.). For more on Menander, see Étienne Lamotte's *Histoire du Bouddhisme Indien* (Louvain: 1958), pp. 461–469.

26. T. W. Rhys Davids, trans., *The Questions of King Milinda,* vol. I (New York: 1963 reprint of 1898 ed.), p. 215.
27. Rhys Davids, *The Questions of King Milinda,* p. 216.
28. Rhys Davids, *The Questions of King Milinda,* pp. 214–215.
29. Rhys Davids, *The Questions of King Milinda,* p. 218.
30. Walpola Rahula, *History of Buddhism in Ceylon* (Colombo: 1956), p. 107. According to Buddhist traditions in Ceylon, the origins of *parittā* are as follows: At one time the Buddha journeyed to Vesāli (Skt. Vaiśālī) upon the invitation of the Licchāvi princes during a period of famine and disease. In order to counteract tne malevolent influences, the Buddha recited the *Ratana-sutta* (found in the *Sutta-nipāta* and the *Kuddakapātha*). He taught it to his disciple Ānanda, and had him go around the city, accompanied by the princes, reciting the *sutta* and sprinkling water from the Buddha's alms bowl. By these actions the malevolent influences were dispelled.
31. I have translated all the excerpts from the *Vimalakīrti-sūtra* included here, basing them on Kumārajīva's Chinese version (translated into Chinese in 406 C.E.), *Wei-mo-chieh so-shuo ching,* T. XIV, 475. The Chinese passage for the above quote is found on page 539B. (Hereafter referred to as *Wei-mo-chieh so-shuo ching.*)
32. *Wei-mo-chieh so-shuo ching,* p. 539C.
33. *Wei-mo-chieh so-shuo ching,* p. 544B.
34. *Wei-mo-chieh so-shuo ching,* p. 544C.
35. *Wei-mo-chieh so-shuo ching,* p. 544C.
36. *Dīgha-nikāya,* vol. I, p. 83.
37. The fourth century C.E. sage Buddhaghosa approached the Four Noble Truths in a similar fashion, writing: "The truth of ill [*duḥkha,* suffering] is like a disease, the truth of the origin is like the cause of the disease, the truth of cessation is like the allaying of disease, the truth of the path is like the medicine." Cf. Pe Maung Tin, trans., *Buddhaghosa's Visuddhimagga, The Path of Purity* (London: 1971 reprint of 1923 ed.), p. 721.
38. I. B. Horner, trans., *Middle Length Sayings (Majjhima-nikāya),* vol. III (London: 1959), pp. 4–5. (Hereafter referred to as *Majjhima-nikāya.*)
39. *Majjhima-nikāya,* p. 44.
40. E. M. Hare, trans., *Woven Cadences of the Early Buddhists (Sutta-nipāta)* (London: 1944), p. 88.
41. *Theragātha,* p. 293.
42. *Theragātha,* pp. 300–302.

43. These thirty-seven items are: 1) *Four Stations of Mindfulness* (body, sensations, mind, things); 2) *Four Right Efforts* (to prevent negatives from arising, to forsake or uproot negative things already produced, to initiate that which is wholesome, to strengthen wholesome things already in existence); 3) *Four Bases of Psychic Strength* (concentration of will, concentration of mind, concentration of effort, concentration of analysis); 4) *Five Spiritual Faculties* (faith, striving, mindfulness, meditative trance, insight); 5) *Five Powers* (the development of the five spiritual faculties); 6) *Seven Limbs of Enlightenment* (mindfulness, investigation of things, striving, joy, tranquility, meditative trance, equanimity); 7) *Eightfold Noble Path* (right view, right intention, right speech, right conduct, right livelihood, right effort, right mindfulness, right meditation).

44. Rhys Davids, *The Questions of King Milinda,* pp. 218–219.

45. I have used Kumārajīva's Chinese version (translated into Chinese in 406 C.E.) as the basis for my translation of all excerpts from the *Lotus Sūtra* quoted here. Cf. *Miao-fa lien-hua ching,* T. IX. 262. (Hereafter referred to as *Miao-fa lien-hua ching.*) The parable of the physician is found on p. 43A–B of the Chinese text.

II

The Bodhisattvas of Healing

Two Bodhisattvas of Healing, the brothers King of Healing (Bhaiṣajya-rāja) and Supreme Healer (Bhaiṣajya-samudgata), are the first major deities to appear in Buddhist texts whose primary quality is the ability to heal. They are mentioned in a number of Mahāyāna texts, which were composed ca. the first century B.C.E. through the first century C.E.

Since many early versions of the name of the Buddha of Healing include the word "king" (*rāja*), there is a strong indication of an important connection to the earlier worship of the Bodhisattva King of Healing. That connection will be explored further in Chapter Three. In this chapter it will be important to consider the primary scriptural references to the Bodhisattvas of Healing and to analyze various aspects of these references in order to further draw out some sense of the meaning of healing in Mahāyāna Buddhism.

Before surveying some of the myriad appearances of these Bodhisattvas in various texts, it would be valuable to consider the use of the terms *bhaiṣajya-rāja* and *bhaiṣajya-samudgata* in earlier Mahāyāna works. These terms later became the evocative names of the two Bodhisattvas, and since such names emphasize the fundamental qualities of a being, the study of them may bring these qualities into sharper focus.

The term *bhaiṣajya-rāja* can be found in various *sūtras* to refer to a substance: the ultimate medicine. For example, in a *sūtra* translated quite early into Chinese, a Bodhisattva named "Heals Through Sight" is described by Ānanda as like Mount Sumeru, like the king of medicines (*bhaiṣajya-rāja*). Whoever sees this medicine will be cured of all diseases.[1] Further, in the *Ratnakūṭa sūtras,* there is a substance mentioned, a king of medicines named "All-Seeing" (or "Seen by All"). If a person with a pure mind ingests a dose of this medicine, all his defilements will be removed.[2]

It is apparent from these and other references, as well as from usage in the Pāli Canon, that the "king of medicines" is the Dharma, the Buddhist teachings in their fundamental and essential form.

A similar reference can be found in the *vīrya* (striving) chapter of the *Bodhisattva-piṭaka.* In addition to speaking of *bhaiṣajya-rāja* as a substance, this same text uses the term as an epithet. Here the Buddha relates to Śāriputra a tale about a hermit in the Himalayas who is described as a "great king of healing."[3]

In contrast to the widespread use of the term *bhaiṣajya-rāja* in a variety of contexts, *bhaiṣajya-samudgata* is found in the Chinese Buddhist Canon solely as the name of the Bodhisattva Supreme Healer.[4]

It seems likely that Bhaiṣajya-rāja emerged earlier in the pantheon than did Bhaiṣajya-samudgata, since he bears a more recognizable name, which was used as a term of considerable importance in early Buddhist traditions. This would also account for his prominent role without his brother in the early sections of the *Lotus Sūtra,* and for his further appearances without his brother in other Mahāyāna texts. This contrasts with the appearances of Bhaiṣajya-samudgata, who rarely is mentioned in a role independent of his brother. Importantly, King of Healing is always called the elder brother of Supreme Healer, further indicating an age-gap that may be historical as well as spiritual.

The two Bodhisattva brothers can be found in a wide range of Mahāyāna texts, the full extent of which is listed in Appendix II. They appear more frequently in the "esoteric" texts of the *Taishō Shinshū Daizōkyō,* which were composed at a later date than the bulk of the non-esoteric Mahāyāna *sūtras.*

There are three major types of appearances of these two Bodhisattvas. They appear as: (1) *Auditors*—where they are cited as present in the assembly of Bodhisattvas gathered to listen to an exposition of the Teachings. They appear in this role in a wide variety of Mahāyāna texts. (2) *Active participants*—where, as representatives of the Bodhisattva assembly, they ask the Buddha various questions and in return receive teachings on behalf of the entire assembly. King of Healing takes on this role, for example, in the earlier chapters of the *Lotus Sūtra,* generally believed to date to ca. first century B.C.E. (3) *Central figures*—where they either present a teaching, or their most significant past life is recounted by the Buddha. Passages of this sort can be found in the later chapters of the *Lotus Sūtra,* which probably date to the first or second century C.E.

A. LOTUS SŪTRA: THE TEACHER AS HEALER

Since King of Healing is prominently featured in the *Lotus Sūtra,* appearing in all three of the roles mentioned above, an analysis of these appearances will cast light upon the nature of this important Bodhisattva, and upon the deeper meanings of healing and the Healer in the Mahāyāna context. The *Lotus Sūtra* is a key text in the traditions of the Buddhist healing deities. Due to the popularity of the text in India and especially in Central and East Asia, knowledge of these healing deities was disseminated, thus widening the ranks of the manifold spiritual beings who, Buddhist devotees believe, compassionately seek to aid all sentient beings.

For the sake of analysis, the contents of the text can be assayed for three types of information: (1) Instances when Śākyamuni Buddha addresses Bhaiṣajya-rāja directly (in the King of Healing's role as a representative of the Bodhisattva assembly); (2) Instances when Bhaiṣajya-rāja speaks to Śākyamuni; and (3) Instances when Śākyamuni speaks of the past lives of Bhaiṣajya-rāja.

The analysis of the quotes amassed for each of these categories is based on the belief that the symbology of the *Lotus Sūtra* is precise and intentional, and that names of Buddhas and Bodhisattvas are highly relevant to the teachings that are addressed to them, or with which they are associated. In accordance with this belief, it is held that when Śākyamuni chooses to address certain teachings to Bhaiṣajya-rāja, it is because these teachings relate naturally to the function of healing. Similarly, that which Bhaiṣajya-rāja offers himself (through his own words) is seen as highly relevant to his healing function. Since the extraordinary devotion of Bhaiṣajya-rāja in past lives has led to his present high evolutionary status as a Bodhisattva, the three past lives discussed by Śākyamuni further amplify the meaning of healing and the

Healer in early Mahāyāna teachings. Although the later chapters that describe the past lives of the King of Healing are believed to date from the first and second centuries C.E., while the earlier chapters were probably written ca. first century B.C.E., the references to King of Healing in these later chapters amplify rather than transform the conception.

1. Śākyamuni Addresses Teachings to Bhaiṣajya-rāja

The Bodhisattva King of Healing is introduced in the first chapter as one of the leaders of the grand assembly of Bodhisattvas who have gathered—together with multitudes of monks, nuns, lay-disciples, and various spirit beings—to hear Śākyamuni teach at Vulture Peak. Such familiar stalwarts of the later Buddhist pantheon as Avalokiteśvara and Mañjuśrī also appear among the Bodhisattvas.

King of Healing rises to special prominence when the Buddha addresses the 80,000 Bodhisattvas by speaking at length to him. This occurs in chapter ten, "The Teacher of the Law." Here, as in previous chapters, the Buddha stresses the importance of the *Lotus Sūtra* teachings:

> King of Healing, now I say to you:
> Of all the *sūtras* I have preached,
> Among these *sūtras,*
> The Blossom of the Law is supreme.[5]

Praising those who delight in hearing the *sūtra* and those who pay it honor, the Buddha reserves special mention for the teachers of the Dharma. Those who expound upon the *Lotus Sūtra,* according to Śākyamuni, deserve the highest respect, for they transmit the supreme teachings of the Buddhas. Acting as representatives of those high teachings and their source, the teachers are mystically supported by the highest spiritual energies:

> O King of Healing, you should know that he who reads and recites the *sūtra* of the Blossom of the Law is adorned with the glorious adornments of the Buddha, and he is carried by the Tathāgata upon his shoulder.[6]

Since the *Lotus Sūtra* is the "treasury of the secret essence of the Buddhas . . . [which] is guarded and protected by the Buddhas,"[7] those who copy, keep, read and recite, worship, and explain the *sūtra* to others after Śākyamuni's *parinirvāṇa:*

Will be clothed by the Tathāgata with his robe, and will be protected by Buddhas presently abiding in other regions, and held in their thoughts. These persons shall have great powers of faith, the power of resoluteness, and the powers stemming from wholesome roots. You should know that these people shall dwell with the Tathāgata, and the Tathāgata shall place his hand upon their heads.[8]

Thus, the highest forces of the invisible realms respond to the teacher of the Law with incalculable protection, strength, and comfort. The teacher is especially cherished by those high forces for the difficult task of transmitting the teachings without the sustaining presence of an incarnate Buddha.

The teacher should expound to audiences without prejudice. Desiring to teach, he should take on the profound qualities of the Buddha, immersing himself in the Buddha's vibration:

He should enter into the Tathāgata's abode,
Don the Tathāgata's robes,
And be seated on the Tathāgata's throne . . .
Let him take compassion as his abode,
Gentleness and forbearance as his robes,
And the voidness of all things as his throne.
Dwelling in these, let him preach the Law.[9]

In response to the act of teaching, Śākyamuni pledges to send spirits to protect the teacher and to gather together beings to hear the Law. If the teacher dwells in solitude, various non-human beings such as *yakṣas* (fierce forest-dwelling spirits) and *nāga*-kings (serpent-like spirits dwelling in waters) will be sent to benefit from his teaching. Such a teacher will always be blessed with visions of the Tathāgata, who will supply words and phrases when the teacher's memory lapses:

That man will take joy in preaching the Law
And explain it without hindrance;
Because Buddhas hold him in their protective thoughts,
He can cause great multitudes to rejoice.[10]

This important chapter, known from Kumārajīva's Chinese version as "The Teacher of the Law," is expressly directed towards the Bodhisattva King of Healing, and it can be inferred that healing is equated with the teaching of Divine principles. Such an association, of course, has its roots in the Buddhist scriptures of the Pāli Canon. It is important to emphasize that it is the Law which heals, while the teacher remains the vessel conveying the

Law to those who are "ill." And because the teacher in his healing mission conveys this Divine medicine, this "treasury of the secret essence of the Buddhas," he is especially cherished and protected.

2. Bhaiṣajya-rāja Addresses Śākyamuni

Later in the narrative, in chapter thirteen, "Fortitude," it is apparent that King of Healing together with the Bodhisattva Great Eloquence and their retinue of twenty thousand Bodhisattvas have listened well to the Buddha's words, for they make the following vow before him:

> We sincerely wish, O Lord, that you not be concerned, for after your *parinirvāṇa* we will receive and keep, read, recite, and expound this scripture. In that later evil age the wholesome roots of all beings will increasingly diminish, and negativity shall flourish. Those beings will worship material goods and profit, their negative roots will increase, and they will be far removed from Liberation. Even though it may be difficult to teach and transform them, we will arouse the strength of great forbearance and read and recite this *sūtra*, keep, expound, and copy it, and worship it in every way, sparing not our bodies or lives.[11]

Bhaiṣajya-rāja further strengthens his special association with teachers of the Law when, in chapter twenty-six, "*Dhāraṇīs*," he vows before the Buddha to give teachers a mystic formula for their guard and protection. He said:

> O Lord, this sacred *dhāraṇī* has been spoken by Buddhas as numerous as 620 million times the number of grains of sand in the Ganges River. If anyone does violence to the teacher of the Law, then he will have done violence to these Buddhas.[12]

To summarize, it is seen in the preceding remarks that when the Buddha specifically singles out Bhaiṣajya-rāja to direct his words, rather than one of the 79,999 other Bodhisattvas present, the subject is the teacher, teaching, and the preservation of the Law. Again, when Bhaiṣajya-rāja speaks to the Buddha, it is on the subject of promulgating and preserving the Divine Principles, and protecting those others who choose such work. Thus, in the *Lotus Sūtra*, healing is intimately connected with teaching the Law.

3. Śākyamuni Relates Three Past Lives of Bhaiṣajya-rāja

One of the later chapters of the *Lotus Sūtra* (chapter twenty-three) is devoted to Śākyamuni's recounting of major events in the spiritual development of King of Healing. In this chapter, the key events of two related past lives of the Bodhisattva are discussed.

In the earlier life he was known as "He Whom All Beings Delight to See,"[13] and he was a disciple of the Buddha Pure and Bright Virtue of the Sun and Moon. Through devoted and zealous practice, the Bodhisattva attained a *samādhi* known as "Manifestation of All Form."

Seeking to pay homage to the Buddha and to the Lotus teaching by which he had attained this state, the Bodhisattva caused heavenly flowers and rare incense to rain down by means of his supernormal powers. Still, such offerings seemed superficial, and he decided to make an offering of his body. For 1,200 years he ate various kinds of incense and drank oil-essences of flowers. Then, anointing his body with perfumed unguents, wrapping himself in a garment bathed in perfumed oil, he burned his own body before the Buddha.

According to the tale, the brilliance of his flaming body illumined as many worlds as 800 million times the amount of sands in the Ganges River, and the Buddhas of these worlds responded, saying:

> Excellent, excellent, good son! This is true striving. It is called the Offering of the Genuine Law to the Tathāgatas. Offerings of flowers, scents, necklaces, burnt incense, powdered incense, perfumed unguents, banners and canopies of celestial silk, and incense of native sandalwood, offerings of such various things as these cannot equal it, nor even the bestowal of countries, cities, wives, and children. My good son, this is termed the supreme gift, the most honored and sublime gift of them all, for it is the offering of the Law to the Tathāgatas.[14]

His body was utterly consumed by the fire, which burned for twelve hundred years.

This Bodhisattva was then reborn as the son of the King of Pure Virtue in the same domain of that Buddha Pure and Bright Virtue of the Sun and the Moon. Having full and complete knowledge of his previous Law Offering and the attainments leading up to it, the Bodhisattva immediately returned to the Buddha to serve him. However, the time for that Buddha's *parinirvāṇa* had arrived, and he commanded the Bodhisattva to take his place as leader of the disciples, responsible for the Buddha-law, entrusted with the vast Buddha-land and the distribution of the Buddha's relics within it.

Mourning the passing of the Buddha, the Bodhisattva paid homage by erecting 84,000 *stūpas* (reliquary mounds), each of which contained a precious urn bearing relics of the Tathāgata's body. Desiring to pay further homage, he burned his arms before the 84,000 *stūpas*. The fire lasted for 72,000 years. By this worship offering, he:

> Caused the aspiration to attain perfect and complete enlightenment to be aroused in the minds of the numberless assembly of seekers after *śrāvaka*-ship, incalculable *asaṃkhyeyas* of people, causing them to abide in the *samādhi* of the Manifestation of All Form.[15]

Due to the Bodhisattva's virtue and wisdom, his arms were spontaneously restored. Thus the tale ends.

Since the traditional Buddhist prohibition against suicide is well known, the teachings contained in this chapter of the *Lotus Sūtra* may be rather surprising. Adding to the element of shock is the association of the King of Healing with seeming self-destruction. However, if this self-immolation is considered from a symbolic point of view, then the chapter takes on a meaning consonant with the general intent of the *sūtra*'s teachings.

This act can be seen as the ultimate in the practice of *dāna-pāramitā*, the "perfection of giving" which is described as the first of the perfections practiced by a Bodhisattva. In the example described above, the myriad Buddhas praise Bhaiṣajya-rāja for his act of homage, terming it far superior to any other type of worship offering. The "offering of the Genuine Law to the Tathāgatas" is the offering of the body or physical vehicle, the sacrifice of the self to the Buddhas.

Through eating the fragrant food of the subtle teachings—through eating incense and flower-essences for 1,200 years—the body is transformed until it reaches a highly inflammable state: it is extremely pure and needs but a final spark before it is subsumed in the Divine. At the moment of conflagration, at the moment when the body is given over as an offering to the Buddha, the scintillating radiance of the event is of such profound splendor that it is seen by innumerable Buddhas in their distant realms, causing them to exclaim in praise.

In this context, it is significant that the Bodhisattva's name refers to form (He Whom All Beings Delight to See) and the *samādhi* attained appears to be a culminating awareness of the material world (the *samādhi* of the Manifestation of All Form). Fully cognizant of the potentialities of the material world, the Bodhisattva presents the most personal and valuable form—his own—to the Buddhas.

A similar account in the *Samādhi-rāja-sūtra* (chapter thirty-three) further clarifies the meaning of this homage. In this account, the Bodhisattva Kṣemadatta burns his hand as an offering at a site where millions of people have placed lamps of worship offerings. The brilliant, fiery blaze of his offering, according to the text, made the millions of lamps seem faint by comparison.[16]

Though the others gave sincere offerings of objects—lamps—as devotions, Kṣemadatta sincerely offered himself: he literally became a living lamp, a torch of devotion. Just as the appearance of the radiant sun renders obscure the rays of the stars, so too does the supreme offering of one's own body far outshine and outdazzle the countless lamps. Here again, this episode refers to a supreme event in spiritual evolution: the sacrifice of self, rather than mundane and emotion-ridden self-sacrifice. It is significant in this context that the tale of Kṣemadatta's offering is identified as the recounting of a pivotal past life of Śākyamuni, the Supreme Physician: this giving over of self, the perfection of *dāna,* is linked to the selfless compassion required of any great physician.

Seeking further Buddhist explanations for symbolic self-immolation, it is explained that a flaming body is an outer indication of the achievement of deep meditative trance. For example, Asaṅga, commenting in his *Samahitabhūmi* on the Second *Dhyāna,* wrote: "Here, the body has an outer light like a flame."[17] The body may appear to be flaming upon the attainment of significant stages of spiritual development. The third and fourth stages of the ten levels of development in the career of the Bodhisattva, according to the *Daśabhūmika-sūtra,* are named "Illuminating" and "Blazing."[18]

According to the sage Candrakīrti's discussion of the third stage:

On nomme cette terre le Lumineuse, parce que, en ce moment, apparait la lumière du feu, du savoir qui consume entièrement le combustible appélé "connaissable."[19]

Here, the Bodhisattva especially cultivates the perfection of forbearance and is especially concerned with promoting the welfare of others.[20]

The fourth stage is also described by Candrakīrti:

Alors, dans le fils du Sugata, par la culture extrème des auxiliaires de la parfaite illumination, nait un éclat qui est supérieur en resplendissement du cuivre . . . Par conséquent, produisant le rayon de feu du savoir parfait, cette terre du bodhisattva est appélé *Arciṣmati.*[21]

At this stage, the Bodhisattva especially cultivates striving-energy, acquiring inexhaustible energy and a special ardor and zeal for the instruction and aid of all beings.[22] Though these stages and meditative states may not fully correspond to the fundamental deeds of Kṣemadatta and Sarvasattva-priyadarśana, they further indicate that the flaming body is a potent symbol of high spiritual attainment.

Despite the apparent symbolic intent of these stories of self-immolation, this act was taken in a literal sense by some East Asian Buddhists. The chapter on Bhaiṣajya-rāja served for some as justification for actual suicide or for the offering of fingers to the Buddha.[23] It is also likely that the practice of burning incense on the freshly shaven scalps of Chinese Buddhist monks, as part of their initiation into the Order, stems from beliefs arising out of this chapter.

In addition to the two related past lives of Bhaiṣajya-rāja in which self-immolation was such an integral event, a third past life was revealed by the Buddha, this one in chapter twenty-seven of the *Lotus Sūtra.* In that life the Bodhisattva's name was Pure Matrix (or Pure Womb, Pure Embryo [Vimalagarbha]). He had a brother (Bhaiṣajya-samudgata) who was known at that time as Pure Eye. The brothers worked particularly hard to persuade their parents (the monarchs of the realm) and the members of the court to become fellow disciples of their spiritual teacher, the Buddha of that age. It was said of the two brothers:

The Bodhisattva Pure Eye had for a long time thoroughly penetrated into the *samādhi* of the Blossom of the Law. The Bodhisattva Pure Matrix had for boundless hundreds of thousands of ten thousands of hundred thousands of aeons thoroughly penetrated into the *samādhi* of Freedom from Woesome Paths, and therefore he sought to lead all beings to freedom from their woesome paths.[24]

After 84,000 years of spiritual work, the king (their father) attained the *samādhi* of Adornment of All Merits, and he realized that:

These sons are my good friends, for out of a desire to develop the wholesome roots [planted] in my former lives and to benefit me, they came and were born in my home.[25]

This tale then emphasizes the long history of devotion and good deeds performed by the two Bodhisattva brothers, stretching back into far antiquity. It infers that their present state as great healers is based on rigorous cultivation of wholesome roots.

Thus, we have seen in this section that the *Lotus Sūtra* places significant emphasis on the role of the teacher of the Law as a spiritual healer, healing through teaching. It indicates that the sacrifice of self, resulting in a conflagration of spiritual radiance which illumines countless Buddha realms, is prerequisite for attaining these healing abilities. Further, it indicates the long history of zealous and devoted spiritual work necessary to attain such an exalted status.

B. ŚŪRAṂGAMA-SŪTRA: BODHISATTVAS OF HEALING AND THE PERFECTION OF TASTE

In chapter four, "Self-Enlightenment," of the *Śūraṃgama-sūtra,* Śākyamuni asked the assembled Bodhisattvas and arhats the following questions:

When you first aspired to attain enlightenment, realizing the eighteen sense-fields, which did you consider as perfectly penetrating? By what means did you enter into *samādhi*?[26]

One by one the various members of the assembly arose and recounted their personal experiences. The two Bodhisattvas King of Healing and Supreme Healer together responded to the Buddha's query:

Since time without beginning we have been skillful physicians in the world, and we have tasted with our own mouths [various kinds of] plants, trees, metals, and stones found in this world. Those that we can name number 108,000 in all. As a result, we know all of their tastes, whether they are bitter or sour, salty, bland, sweet, acrid, etc., as well as knowing the tastes of compounds of them or variations of them. With all of them we are able to differentiate whether they are cooling or heating, poisonous or non-poisonous. We received instructions from the Tathāgata and understood that the nature of taste is neither non-existent nor existent. It is neither body-mind nor is it separate from them. We accordingly achieved our awakening through differentiating the causes of taste. We two brothers received authentication of our awakening from the Buddha, who named us the Two Bodhisattvas, King of Healing and Supreme Healer. Now we are Princes of the Dharma within the assembly. Because of our awakening by means of taste, we have attained the Bodhisattva stage. In response to the Buddha's question about the best means to perfection, according to our experience, the supreme means for us is taste.[27]

Here it is made clear that according to the traditions of this *sūtra,* the two Bodhisattvas—in addition to being spiritual healers—were originally accomplished physicians. Through the subtle mastery of their healing art, attained through life after life of study and practice, they plunged into the depths of spiritual search and achieved a great awakening. This awakening was certified by the Buddha, who gave them initiation names consonant with their special healing abilities.

C. SŪTRA ON THE CONTEMPLATION OF THE TWO BODHISATTVAS, KING OF HEALING AND SUPREME HEALER

Kālayaśas, a monk from Central Asia, arrived in 424 C.E. at Chien-k'ang (now Nanking), the capital of the southern Liu Sung state. At the behest of Emperor Wen, he dwelt at the Tao-lin monastery, remaining in this region until 442.

His biography in the *Kao-seng-chuan (Lives of the Eminent Monks)* recounts that he had a clear understanding of the *sūtras* and was well acquainted with the *abhidharma* (metaphysics) and *vinaya* (moral regulations) of the scriptures. His special interest, however, was in *dhyāna,* meditation. According to the biography, he sometimes remained rapt in contemplation for seven days.

His meditative methods especially interested a number of monks. The monks Pao-chih and Seng-han are mentioned in the biography as having influenced him to translate two *sūtras* on meditation, Seng-han recording the translation as it was dictated by Kālayaśas.

Kālayaśas traveled to Szechüan in 442 to transmit his teachings on meditation, and he later returned to the Chien-k'ang region, where he died at age sixty.[28]

The two *sūtras* which he translated are the *Sūtra on the Contemplation of Amitāyus Buddha* (the *Kuan Wu-liang-shou-fo ching,* T. XII, 345), and the *Sūtra Spoken by the Buddha on the Contemplation of the Two Bodhisattvas, King of Healing (Bhaiṣajya-rājā) and Supreme Healer (Bhaiṣajya-samudgata)* (the *Fo-shuo kuan Yao-wang Yao-shang erh-p'u-sa ching.* T.XX, 1161). Though structurally quite different, both of these texts emphasize methods of visualization or contemplation upon the form of a Divine being. Successful practice of these meditative methods, it is stated, will result in unusual spiritual benefits.

The scripture on the contemplation of Amitāyus, the Buddha of Immeasurable Life, eventually became one of the fundamental texts of the Pure Land School, and as such has enjoyed a special popularity in China, Korea, and Japan. There are several English translations of the scripture, including versions by J. Takakusu and Charles Luk. The *sūtra* on the two Bodhisattvas, although also a significant work, did not attain a position of similar importance in the history of Buddhist literature. My translation included in this book is the first full translation of this work to appear in a Western language. Though it is said that several translations of the scripture on Amitāyus and one additional translation of the scripture on the Bodhisattvas of Healing were made in China, in both cases only the version by Kālayaśas has been preserved.[29]

Though by tradition these texts are said to be translated from Sanskrit, no Sanskrit versions of the texts have as yet been found. Due to this point and to the unusual nature of the contents of the scriptures, many scholars have speculated that the origin of the two texts is not India, holding that the scriptures were either composed in China or stem from a Central Asian source.[30]

These scriptures, though, are not isolated works. They appear to be related by theme and title—contemplation or visualization of radiant Buddhas or Bodhisattvas—to a number of additional *sūtras* also transmitted to China in the first half of the fifth century. The extant *sūtras* of this group include (in addition to the two already cited):

Sūtra on the Contemplation of the Bodhisattva Ākāśagarbha (*Kuan Hsü-k'ung-tsang p'u-sa ching,* T. XIII, 409). This was translated by Dharmamitra, a contemporary of Kālayaśas in the Liu Sung state.

Sūtra Spoken by the Buddha on the Method of Practice for the Contemplation of the Bodhisattva Samantabhadra (*Fo-shuo kuan P'u-hsien p'u-sa hsing-fa ching,* T. IX, 277). Also translated by Dharmamitra.

Sūtra Spoken by the Buddha on the Samādhi Sea Attained by Contemplation of the Buddha (*Fo-shuo kuan-fo san-mei-hai ching,* T. XV, 643). Translated by Buddhabhadra, active 398–421 in the E. Chin state.

Sūtra Spoken by the Buddha on the Contemplation of Maitreya Bodhisattva and Rebirth on High in the Tuṣita Heaven (*Fo-shuo kuan Mi-lo p'u-sa shang-sheng Tu-shi-t'ien ching,* T. XIV, 452). Translated in South China in 455 by the Prince of An-yang, exiled from the state of Northern Liang. This same prince is said to have translated the *Sūtra on the Contemplation of Avalokiteśvara (Kuan-shih-yin kuan ching),* now lost.[31]

In considering these six *sūtras* as a group, it is not unlikely that their common bond—the special practice of contemplation (and thus invocation) of individual Buddhas and Bodhisattvas—may stem from teachings especially popular in or near Kashmir in the third, fourth, and fifth centuries, thus stimulating the composition of these scriptures. According to the research of Julian F. Pas, who proposes Kashmir as the place of origin of these texts:

> The area in and around Kashmir seems the most probable choice: it is not pure accident that almost *all* the translators of the *Kuan Sūtras* are connected with Kashmir.
>
> Buddhabhadra studied there; Dharmamitra was born there; the Prince (or Marquis) of An-yang, while staying in Khotan, studied meditation under *dhyāna*-master Buddhasena, who came from Kashmir and was considered one of the most famous *dhyāna* teachers. About Kālayaśas we only know that he was from the Western Regions; but his specialty being meditation, it is not presumptuous to believe that he was in some way related to Kashmir.[32]

Analysis of the contents of the various *sūtras* of this group may point to other possible sources, though also fairly near to Kashmir (for example, Alexander Soper attributes the *Fo-shuo kuan-fo san-mei-hai ching* to southeast Afghanistan, perhaps the ancient pilgrimage center of Nagarahāra near modern Haḍḍa).[33] It does seem likely, at this stage of research, to hold that such texts were composed in the borderlands of the extreme northwest of India or in Central Asia.

In his extensive analysis of this group of texts, Pas proposes that they were variously composed between ca. 300 C.E. and ca. 400 C.E. Such a date would be reasonable for the scripture on the Bodhisattvas of Healing, which maintains in expanded fashion some of the traditions of these Bodhisattva brothers which are found in the *later* chapters of the *Lotus Sūtra* (generally dated no later than second century C.E.). Further research may eventually bring more precision to these dates.

The structure and contents of the scripture on the Bodhisattvas of Healing are perhaps of more interest than speculation about the origins of the text. The *sūtra* is a cohesive and well-planned balance of awesome and mind-dazzling visions, manifestations, and miraculous events, on one hand, and fundamental Mahāyāna teachings of the Bodhisattva Path, on the other. The primary concern is not philosophical speculation and analysis. Instead, the text stresses the cultivation of fundamental spiritual practices.

The *sūtra* is classified as "esoteric" in the Chinese Buddhist Canon (appearing in the Taishō Canon, vol. XXI, 1161). Its esoteric or secret nature is especially expressed by the emphasis on the two mystic invocations uttered by the Bodhisattvas. Since the complete translation of this scripture (included here as Translation I) is the first to appear in a Western language, I would like to summarize and discuss its contents. This summary is divided into sections for the sake of discussion, although the scripture itself has no chapters or subdivisions.

1. Introduction: Highlighting the Two Bodhisattvas

The teachings of this scripture were conferred by Śākyamuni Buddha at a great assembly held at the Blue Lotus Pond in the Monkey Grove at Vaiśālī. As is usual in Mahāyāna *sūtras,* the assembly included all classes of humans and spirits. These include among humans: monks, nuns, laymen, and laywomen; among spirits: *devas* (gods), *nāgas* (serpent-like spirits who dwell in waters), *yakṣas* (fierce forest-dwelling spirits), *gandharvas* (flying spirits who feed on incense and create celestial music), *asuras* (titan-like spirits whose great joy is to engage in battle), *garuḍas* (celestial birds, somewhat eagle-like), *kiṃnaras* (mountain spirits with human bodies and horse heads), and *mahoragas* (great serpent-like beings). When the various participants had gathered together and settled down, the Buddha entered into the *samādhi* of Universal Light, and various unusual "miraculous" events occurred.

The expression of mind-dazzling visual images—frequently employed in this text—at the outset of the teaching conveys a vivid sense of Divine realms freely conjoining and merging with the earthly plane. A direct quote from the text gives some of the essence of this important aspect of the *sūtra:*

At that time the Lord entered into the *samādhi* of Universal Light. All the pores of his body emitted multi-hued rays, illuminating the Markaṭa Grove with the colors of the seven precious substances. The light rising above the grove became a jeweled canopy, and various phenomena rare to the realms of the Ten Directions appeared within the canopy . . .

. . . the Buddha's eyes radiated light which illumined the foreheads of the two Bodhisattvas King of Healing and Supreme Healter. Above their foreheads, all the limitless Buddhas of the Ten Directions dazzlingly manifested like a diamond mountain, and all these Lords also emitted light from their eyes, which universally illumined the foreheads of all the Bodhisattvas [in the assembly]. Above the foreheads of the Bodhisattvas, all the Bodhisattva-mahāsattvas of the realms of the Ten Directions who had attained the *śūraṃgama samādhi* brilliantly appeared, resembling a lapis lazuli mountain.

At the manifestation of this form, a jeweled lotus blossom arose in the Markaṭa pond. It was the color of a white gem, but this color was a white so rare that there is nothing to which it can be compared.

Various manifested Buddhas were seated on the lotus blossom, their bodies subtle and sublime. They, too, entered into *samādhi.* Each radiated light from his eyes which illumined the foreheads of the two Bodhisattvas King of Healing and Supreme Healer, and further illumined the foreheads of all the Bodhisattvas.

At that time, the Lord withdrew from *samādhi.* With a subtle smile of radiant harmony, the Buddha exhaled through his mouth five-colored rays which completely illumined his full-moon-like face. Then there were numerous changing manifestations of light from the features of the Buddha's face, which appeared a million times more glorious than his ordinary appearance.[34]

In this impressive manner, the two Bodhisattvas of Healing are introduced.

2. The Names of the Two Bodhisattvas and Their Sacred Formulae

Responding to these manifold displays, a young layman, son of a wealthy leader of Vaiśālī, fervently requested the Buddha to reveal teachings about how one should prepare oneself to receive the names of the two Bodhisattvas who were highlighted in the preceding miraculous events. This emphasis on names is frequently stressed in the Mahāyāna teachings about Bodhisattvas and Buddhas; in these teachings, the names of great beings are held to be precious. By hearing the name of the great being, one can gain contact with his spiritual force and protection. A particularly important and popular method of invoking a great being—according to these texts—is through calling out or concentrating on the name of that being.

It should be noted that this young layman, named Jewel Heap (Ratnakūṭa or Ratnarāśi), appears in many Mahāyāna texts, such as the *Saddharma-puṇḍarīka-sūtra,* the *Śatasāhasrikā-prajñā-pāramitā-sūtra,* the *Vimalakīrti-nirdeśa-sūtra,* and many others. In these texts he often appears with a slightly different name (Ratnakāra, Jewel Mine), and very often he is considered to be a layman Bodhisattva.[35]

In response to Jewel Heap's request, the Buddha explained that a devotee may hear the names of the two Bodhisattvas if five prerequisites are met:

1. He must have unceasing compassion and uncompromising deportment.
2. He should practice filial piety and the ten wholesome precepts (abstention from the following wayward acts of body, speech, and mind: murder, theft, and adultery; lies, slander, use of harsh language, and frivolous talk; and covetous thoughts, malice, and heretical views).
3. He should have peace and quiescence of body and mind, with thoughts bound to that which is free from disorder.
4. He should listen to the *vaipulya sūtras* (the expanded teachings, the Mahāyāna) without harboring doubts or suspicions, neither drowning (in emotions), nor backsliding (in spiritual progress).
5. He should believe in the eternity of the Buddha, his mind

unceasingly flowing—like a running stream—towards ultimate truth.

Those who have perfected these five qualities will hear the names of the two Bodhisattvas, King of Healing and Supreme Healer, in incarnation after incarnation. Due to the awesome spiritual force mystically transmitted by the Bodhisattvas to those who hear the names, these people will be protected from sinking into the woesome paths of existence of the animals, hungry ghosts, or hell-dwellers. Thus, these names are treated as protective *mantras*, conferred only on those prepared through purification to receive them.

At this point in Śākyamuni's teaching, the two Bodhisattvas were mystically inspired by the Buddha to utter long *dhāraṇīs*, sacred formulae treasured and handed down by Buddhas of aeons long past. The *dhāraṇī* uttered by King of Healing especially confers purification of karmic fetters and defilements, leading to greater spiritual attainment. It also confers protection from various negative spirits and grants rebirth into a pure Buddha land. Supreme Healer's *dhāraṇī* subdues the sea of afflictions and confers ten special blessings, including the healing of disease.

The two Bodhisattvas then offered in worship necklaces of precious gems to the Buddha. These were magically transformed into mountains, where millions of sublime beings dwelt. Within a palace were Buddhas of the Ten Directions who, in unison, praised the two Bodhisattvas, confirming the antiquity and precious value of the *dhāraṇīs*.

3. *Prophecy of the Future Achievements of the Two Bodhisattvas*

Śākyamuni Buddha, after asking the great assembly to confirm as witnesses the devotion of the two Bodhisattvas, prophesied to Maitreya about their future. He declared that King of Healing would eventually become a Buddha named Pure Eye, and all the inhabitants of his Buddha-realm would be free from disease, both of body and mind. Following his elder brother, Supreme Healer would become a Buddha named Pure Matrix.

These names bear a strong connection to the teachings in the *Lotus Sūtra*, where in an important past life the two Bodhisattvas were named Pure Eye and Pure Matrix. In that time, of course, they bore those names prior to achieving their high status as Bodhisattva-mahāsattvas, not as Buddhas.

4. Contemplation on King of Healing

Having completed initial practices which qualify them to hear the names of these two Bodhisattvas and thus be connected to their spiritual force, devotees may learn to fix their thoughts on sole contemplation of the Bodhisattvas. Śākyamuni taught a two-stage contemplation on King of Healing in which the increasing purity and spiritual accomplishment of the devotee qualifies him for more profound revelations.

The prerequisite for the "initial contemplation of the meritorious form and appearance of the Bodhisattva King of Healing" is the successful cultivation of five meditations:

1. Meditation of stabilizing thoughts by counting breaths.
2. Meditation of pacifying and settling the mind.
3. Meditation of non-exhaling of breath.
4. Meditation of reflecting on Absolute Form.
5. Meditation of serene abiding in *samādhi*.

Cultivating these meditations, the devotee will have a glorious vision of King of Healing, in which healing of the 404 diseases that beset the body is granted, and various fundamental teachings are transmitted.

An interesting statement reveals that perception of the Bodhisattva varies from individual to individual: "This Bodhisattva is twelve *yojanas* tall, though in response to sentient beings he may appear to be either one hundred eighty or eight feet in height."[36] Taking this a step further, in describing the second contemplation, Śākyamuni reveals that "it is due to the conditioned thoughts [of sentient beings] that the Bodhisattva gloriously adorns himself."[37] Although the Bodhisattva dwells in spirit realms of principle rather than form, in response to the conditioned minds of devotees, he manifests in their visions in a manner suited to their abilities to comprehend him: in glorious human-like form.

A second, more complete vision of King of Healing also grants special purifications. Through the spiritual experience granted during the vision, the devotee is able to make great strides in his spiritual progress.

Even though the focus of the contemplation is on King of Healing, other high spiritual forces appear before the devotee as well. For example, the Buddhas and Bodhisattvas of the Ten Directions bring teachings to the devotee during this experience. By means of their spiritual force, they propel the devotee forward in his evolution.

This is a significant aspect, indicating the existence of an invisible spiritual brotherhood. Through contemplation and meditation on one member of this brotherhood, other potent energies and high spiritual forces are revealed. This could be compared to concentration on the water of a surging stream and contemplation of its unbroken path, leading to mighty rivers and finally to the great seas. Similarly, devoted contemplation on a great Bodhisattva reveals the vast, unfathomable spiritual hierarchies from which he cannot be separated.

5. *Contemplation on Supreme Healer*

Having revealed the twofold contemplation on King of Healing, Śākyamuni then described how to contemplate on Supreme Healer. Seven prerequisites were listed:

1. Constant delight in holding to the precepts.
2. Cultivation of the methods for living in the world and the methods for becoming free of the world.
3. Freedom from arrogance and pride, and compassion towards all beings.
4. Passionlessness.
5. Abode in undifferentiated truth.
6. Cultivation of discernment and calming the mind.
7. Freedom from fear or alarm upon attaining the perfection of insight.

Having thus established a strong spiritual foundation, the devotee will have a vision of Supreme Healer. All who have heard the name of the Bodhisattva and who contemplate his form will be enfolded in Supreme Healer's radiance. In coming to aid a devotee, the Bodhisattva may take up any suitable form: *deva, gandharva, kiṃnara,* or other spirit being; king, great minister, elder, monk, grandmother or grandfather, adept physician, or other human being. In the case of the Bodhisattva's assumption of the form of a wife, child, or king, etc., this may be interpreted as Divine inspiration flooding into these persons such that they may be of special aid or comfort to the devotee in a potent moment of need. It could also be understood more literally as the actual manifestation of the Bodhisattva in any appropriate form. This special aid is activated in the spirit realms of the dream states; for it is in his dreams that the devotee encounters these manifestations of the Bodhisattva. They recite to him the *dhāraṇīs* transmitted by King of Healing and Supreme Healer in a memorable experience, which is retained by the devotee to the end of his days.

In *samādhi* he then perceives the pure and sublime form of Supreme Healer, who reveals the names of the Fifty-three Buddhas of the Past. At this point, the Seven Buddhas of the (Immediate) Past will appear to speak in praise of the Fifty-three Buddhas.

Śākyamuni Buddha, who was revealing the progression of the contemplation, here interjected with a discussion of the role of the Fifty-three Buddhas in his own spiritual development. In an aeon long ago, he related, he heard the names of these Buddhas and transmitted them to 3,000 persons. These 3,000 revered and worshipped the Buddhas. Due to the mystical force these Buddhas issued in response to that devotion, the 3,000 made tremendous spiritual progress. According to Śākyamuni, the 3,000 persons are the beings now known as the 1,000 Buddhas of the past aeon (the age of "Glorious Adornment"), the 1,000 Buddhas of the present aeon ("Auspicious"), and the 1,000 Buddhas of the next age ("Stellar").

Śākyamuni said: "All the present Buddhas in the Ten Directions, those Tathāgatas of excellent virtue, each have achieved Buddhahood . . . because they also heard the names of the Fifty-three Buddhas."[38]

Alexander Soper wrote of the Fifty-three Buddhas:

> Their position is explained neither in time nor in space, but their importance is unmistakable; they constitute a mysterious source of the highest power.[39]

The Fifty-three Buddhas' fundamental spiritual influence on the development of the 3,000 Buddhas indicates the important role of Divine spirit forces for those on the spiritual path. Through the special aid of beings of advanced spiritual evolution, the devotee is propelled towards Buddhahood. Initiation into the Mysteries, and learning the names of the Buddhas and thus the method of invoking their spiritual aid, are both profound steps instrumental in the highest attainments of the spiritual path, according to these teachings of Śākyamuni.

The number fifty-three also appears in the *Gaṇḍa-vyūha-sūtra.* There, the searching youth Sudhāna, in a kind of "pilgrim's progress," embarks on a spiritual quest in which he receives instruction from fifty-three gurus. Although the gurus are not Buddhas, here again fifty-three figures confer initiatory knowledge essential for spiritual progress.[40]

Returning again to the contemplation on the two Bodhisattvas of Healing, Śākyamuni suggests that those who seek release from karmic faults should recite the *dhāraṇīs* of the two Bodhisattvas and worship the various Buddhas mentioned (the Fifty-three, the Seven, the Thousand of this age, and so on):

> Six times during the day and night, with heart and mind clear and keen like a flowing river, they should practice confession and repentance. Afterwards they should fix their thoughts on the pure forms of the two Bodhisattvas, King of Healing and Supreme Healer.[41]

In so doing, the devotee will also have visions of the Buddhas of the Ten Directions, who will bring him teachings and prophecy on his future attainment of Buddhahood. Various meditative states are then experienced, and the Buddhas convey more teachings (fundamentals such as the *pāramitās,* the *bodhipakṣya dharmas,* the twelve-fold chain of dependent origination, and so on).

It is interesting that here the Buddhas of the East are stressed, for the scriptures on the Buddha known as Master of Healing (to be discussed in chapter three) locate his paradise realm in the East. Perhaps this has to do with the dawning of spiritual accomplishment: healing as the awakening of a new dawn.

In any case, Śākyamuni concludes this section with discussion of the benefits to be gained from praising, recollecting, and cherishing the names of the two Bodhisattvas, from contemplation of their forms, and from recitation of their spiritual formulae. He said:

> If there is any being who merely hears the names of these two Bodhisattvas, he will obtain blessings which are limitless and inexhaustible. How

much more complete would these blessings be if he cultivates the practices which I have described![42]

6. Past Life of the Bodhisattvas

The disciple Ānanda, amazed at what he had learned that day in the Assembly, asked the Buddha to recount the fundamental past life of the two Bodhisattvas. This past life, in which the Bodhisattvas planted the seeds coming to fruition at the Assembly that day, is quite different from the past lives of the two Bodhisattvas discussed in chapters twenty-three and twenty-seven of the *Lotus Sūtra.*

The past life revealed on this occasion took place during the period of replica teachings (that is, during the first period of the decline of teachings after a Buddha's *parinirvāṇa,* when form, rather than content, is stressed) of the Buddha known as Shining Ray of Lapis Lazuli. It is notable that lapis lazuli is emphasized here as well as in the miraculous manifestations that introduce the *sūtra,* for the Buddha Master of Healing is especially associated with that gemstone (as will be discussed in chapters three and four).

In that past life, there was a great monk named Solar Womb, who wandered from place to place discoursing on the meritorious acts of the Bodhisattvas and on the supreme purity, equanimity, and wisdom of the Buddha. Through his discourse and his personal example, he inspired a wealthy layman named Star Light to offer *harītakī* (myrobalan) and other healing herbs and fruits to the Order. Star Light then expressed the aspiration to attain enlightenment—a fundamental moment in soul evolution which is the firm stepping onto the spiritual path—and vowed to attain the Buddha-wisdom. At that same time, he also vowed that when he attained enlightenment, he would heal all sentient beings from the three kinds of disease. These include the 404 physical diseases afflicting the body; the sufferings caused by false views, stupid doubts, and negative paths; and the sufferings caused by sinking into woesome modes of existence.

Star Light's younger brother Shining Lightning was inspired by his elder's example to also make a gift of healing herbs and substances. He, too, expressed the aspiration to attain enlightenment, and made vows similar to those of his brother. The only difference was that Shining Lightning's gift of medicines was not restricted to the Order, as was his elder brother's gift.

Due to the profound efficacy of the medicines presented by the two brothers, which cured both physical diseases and karmic obstructions, the two men were given new names by the Assembly of monks: King of Healing and Supreme Healer. King of Healing responded in this way:

> Monks of the Assembly of Great Virtue, you have conferred upon me the name "King of Healing." I now should take refuge in this name and establish its reality. If my giving accords with the Buddha Way, and I inevitably attain perfection, I vow that with my two hands I shall rain down all varieties of medicines, cleansing all beings and freeing them from all diseases . . .[43]

From a voice swelling out of a miraculously manifested canopy came a verse predicting King of Healing's future attainment of Buddha-hood: "As a Buddha," the voice intoned, "his name will be Pure Eye." Supreme Healer also responded with vows, including the bestowal to all beings of the medicine of the Supreme Teachings. Then, from a jeweled pavillion also appearing in the sky, another pure voice resonated, chanting the Supreme Healer's future attainment of Buddhahood: "At that time," the voice chanted, "he will be known as Pure Matrix."

7. Conclusion: Summary of Merits, Naming the Sūtra, Attaining Samādhi

Having recounted the tale, Śākyamuni once again emphasized the great merits to be gained by hearing, reciting, and holding to the names of the two Bodhisattvas, by uttering the spiritual formulae of the Bodhisattvas, and by contemplating their pure forms. In seeking to extract the essence of the teaching, the Buddha gave the scripture the following names:

1. Eliminating All the Faults and Fetters.
2. Spiritual Formula for the Confession and Repentance of Bad Deeds.
3. Sublime Medicine, the Sweet Dew Which Cures Afflictions and Diseases.

4. Contemplation on the Pure Forms of King of Healing and Supreme Healer.

After discussing the special benefits obtained by reading, reciting, and retaining this *sūtra,* the narrative concludes with a brief recitation of the various spiritual states achieved by those in the Assembly after having heard these teachings.

We have seen that many of the aspects of the Bodhisattvas of Healing build upon the foundation of principles elucidated in the Pāli Canon: the Buddha's teachings identified as the Supreme Medicine; the great teacher identified as a Supreme Healer; and the belief that diseases can be healed through meditation and contemplation. In addition, the expanded view of the Mahāyāna plays a significant role in the teachings associated with the Healing Bodhisattvas. Here and later, in the scriptures of the Healing Buddhas, there is a special emphasis on aid from spiritual realms to hasten this healing process. The vow to heal all beings becomes one of the great pledges made when a spiritual youth steps out upon the Bodhisattva Path. When this student achieves spiritual maturity as a Bodhisattva of advanced evolution, his invisible force directed by this vow can be invoked by those in need through mystic invocation using *dhāraṇīs,* meditations, and devotional rites.

1. Dharmarakṣa, trans., *Hui-shang p'u-sa wen ta-shan-ch'uan ching* ([*Upāyakauśalya*] *jñānottarabodhisattvaparipṛcchā*), T. XII, 345, p. 159B.
2. Bodhiruci, trans., *Ta-ch'eng fang-pien hui,* T. XI, 310, p. 599A. Similar examples can also be found, for example, in the *Shou-leng-yen san-mei ching,* or *Śūraṃgama-samādhi-sūtra* (Kumārajīva translation), T. XV, 642, p. 623B.
3. Hsüan-tsang, trans., *P'u-sa tsang* [*Bodhisattvapiṭaka*], T. XI, 310, p. 284A.
4. The only exception is the occasional mention of a Buddha named Supreme Healer. See Part One, chapter three, p. 55.
5. *Miao-fa lien-hua ching,* p. 31B.
6. *Maio-fa lien-hua ching,* p. 31A.

7. *Miao-fa lien-hua ching*, p. 31B.
8. *Miao-fa lien-hua ching*, p. 31C.
9. *Miao-fa lien-hua ching*, p. 32A.
10. *Miao-fa lien-hua ching*, p. 32B.
11. *Miao-fa lien-hua ching*, p. 36A.
12. *Miao-fa lien-hua ching*, p. 58C.
13. Although the literal translation from the Chinese would have it "Excellent to See," the name in the Sanskrit text is Sarvasattva-priyadarśana, hence, "He Whom All Beings Delight to See." As found in the Sanskrit text edited by U. Wogihara and C. Tsuchida, *Saddharma-puṇḍarīka-Sūtram* (Tokyo: 1958), p. 340.
14. *Miao-fa lien-hua ching*, p. 53B.
15. *Miao-fa lien-hua ching*, pp. 53C–54A.
16. As quoted in Jean Filliozat, "La mort volontaire par le feu et la tradition bouddhique indienne," *Journal Asiatique* 251 (1963), p. 26. This passage was apparently translated from the Sanskrit manuscript of the *Samādhi-rāja-sūtra* found at Gilgit.
17. Alex Wayman, "Aspects of meditation in the Theravāda and Mahīśāsaka Buddhist sects," *Studia Missionalia* XXIV (1975), p. 15.
18. Alex Wayman, "Buddhism," *Historia Religionum*, vol. II (Leiden: 1971), p. 440.
19. From the *Madhyāmakāvatāra*, as quoted by Har Dayal, *The Bodhisattva Doctrine in Buddhist Sanskrit Literature* (London: 1931), p. 286.
20. According to the *Mahāyāna-sūtrālaṃkāra*, as discussed by Har Dayal, *Bodhisattva Doctrine*, p. 287.
21. Quoted in Dayal, p. 287.
22. Discussed by Dayal, p. 288.
23. For more on this, see: Jacques Gernet, "Les suicides par le feu chez les bouddhistes chinois du Ve ou Xe siècle," *Mélanges publiés par l'Institut des Hautes Études Chinoises*. II (Paris: 1960), pp. 527–558. Jan Yün-hua, "Buddhist self-immolation in medieval China," *History of Religions* IV (1965), pp. 243–268. One of the foremost exponents of Ch'an in modern China, Hsü Yün, burned off his finger in sacrifice for the sake of his deceased mother in his fifty-eighth year. This is discussed in his autobiography translated by Charles Luk, *Empty Cloud: The Autobiography of the Chinese Zen Master Hsü Yün* (Rochester, New York: 1974), pp. 27–28.
24. *Miao-fa lien-hua ching*, p. 60B.
25. *Miao-fa lien-hua ching*, p. 60C.

26. Translated from Paramiti's Chinese version of the *Śūraṃgama-sūtra,* T, XIX, 945, p. 125C. (Hereafter referred to as *Śūraṃgama-sūtra*). This *sūtra,* quite different from the *Sūraṃgama-samādhi-sūtra* (T. XV, 642) cited in footnote 2 above, is said to have been translated by the North Indian monk Paramiti in 705. In recent decades many questions have been raised regarding the origins of the text, with many scholars of both Western and Asian traditions holding to the belief that the text is a native Chinese composition. Despite these questions, I have included this short section due to the intrinsic interest of the quoted passage, which may record a story of long-standing tradition.
27. *Śūraṃgama-sūtra,* p. 126A.
28. Hui-chiao, *Kao-seng-chuan,* T. L, 2059, p. 343C.
29. In the case of the scripture on the Bodhisattvas of Healing, the translation by Kālayaśas is said to be the second translation of the text into Chinese. See Bunyiu Nanjio, *A Catalogue of the Chinese Translations of the Buddhist Tripiṭaka* (Oxford: 1883), p. 79.
30. K. Fujita's article "The problem of compilation of the *Kuan Wu-liang-shou ching*" in *Indogaku Bukkyōgaku Kenkyū (Journal of Indian and Buddhist Studies)* 17 (1969), pp. 465–472, summarizes recent Japanese scholarship on this subject, indicating a continuing divergence of opinion as to Central Asian or Chinese origins for the text.
31. As stated in the *Chung-ching mu-lu,* T. LV, 2416. p. 1116c.
32. Julian F. Pas, "The *Kuan Wu-liang-shou-fo ching:* Its Origin and Literary Criticism," in Leslie Kawamura and Keith Scott, editors, *Buddhist Thought and Civilization* (Emeryville, Calif.: 1977), p. 203.
33. Alexander Coburn Soper, *Literary Evidence for Early Buddhist Art in China,* (Ascona, Switzerland: 1959), p. 185.
34. Part Two, *Translation I,* pp. 116–117.
35. For more detailed discussion, citations, etc., see Étienne Lamotte, *L'Enseignement de Vimalakīrti* (Louvain: 1962), p. 103, fn. 38.
36. Part Two, *Translation I,* p. 124.
37. Part Two, *Translation I,* p. 126.
38. Part Two, *Translation I,* p. 133.
39. Soper, *Literary Evidence for Early Buddhist Art in China,* p. 201.
40. The only other reference to the Fifty-three Buddhas of the Past that I have found occurs in the *Sūtra on the Contemplation of the Bodhisattva Womb of Space (Kuan Hsü-k'ung-tsang p'u-sa ching),* T. XIII, 409. This text was translated into Chinese by Dharmamitra, a monk from Kashmir, in the second quarter of the fifth century. In this reference, the names of the Fifty-three are identical—with the exception of two minor additions of characters—to the names of the

Buddhas listed in T. 1161. The literary style of this text is rather perfunctory and abrupt, with a few sentences added after the listing of the names of the Buddhas, indicating the benefits to be gained as a result of worshipping them. This passage is found on pp. 678C–679A.

These Fifty-three Buddhas are also listed in a sixth-century Chinese manuscript found at Tun-huang (now in the British Museum), the *Hsien-tsai shih-fang ch'ien-wu-pai fo-ming ping-tsa fo t'ung-hao.* This text is a *Buddhanāma* text, a composite of lists of names of Buddhas. The list of the Fifty-three seems to have been taken directly from T. 1161. See Lionel Giles, *Descriptive Catalog of the Chinese Manuscripts from Tun-huang in the British Museum* (London: 1957), #6411.

41. Part Two, *Translation I,* pp. 133–134.

42. Part Two, *Translation I,* pp. 135–136.

43. Part Two, *Translation I,* p. 141.

III

The Lapis Lazuli Radiance Buddha, Master of Healing, and His Buddha Brothers

A. BHAIṢAJYA-GURU AND THE BHAIṢAJYA-GURU SŪTRA

1. Origins

As the principles of Mahāyāna Buddhism became popular and found acceptance, various Buddhas and Bodhisattvas rose to special prominence among devotees. According to basic Mahāyāna teachings of the *Lotus Sūtra* and other texts that precede or are roughly contemporary with the emergence of worship of the Healing Buddha (as shall be discussed below), there are Buddhas dwelling in all the realms of the universe. Their number is as inconceivable as the number of stars in the sky, or grains of sand in the Ganges. Each of these Buddhas has a name, which often indicates his special spiritual emphasis, and each presides over a "pure land," a spirit realm described in paradisiacal terms, where all the inhabitants can concentrate on spiritual growth.

According to these texts, knowledge gained by humans of these celestial beings and their realms stems, in this age, from the revelations of Śākyamuni, the historical Buddha. He is thus a link between the earth and the myriad spiritual realms, the great spiritual master who reveals the potent Divine forces of the universe and initiates and instructs disciples on the methods of their invocation.

Here we have a significant historical problem. The composition of these Mahāyāna texts seems to have occurred four to seven centuries after the death of Śākyamuni, yet the texts purport to record his spoken teachings. From a Mahāyāna viewpoint, there are a number of ways to deal with this problem. For example, in the *Mahāprajñā-pāramitā-śāstra* attributed to Nāgārjuna (ca. 150–250 C.E.), it is held that Ānanda, close disciple of the Buddha and entrusted by the monks after the Buddha's death to recite the full extent of the spoken teachings, chose not to recite the Mahāyāna teachings. He did so because he perceived that the monks would not understand the teachings of the Great Vehicle. For this reason, these teachings were safeguarded by the great Bodhisattvas in various secret places, such as the palace of the king of the *gandharvas* (musical spirits who feed on incense), and the palace of the king of the *nāgas* (serpent spirits). These teachings were later released when mankind was ready to receive them.[1]

Another point of view which could be taken is that the assemblies took place in spirit realms and are essentially ahistorical (visitors to Vulture Peak in India have remarked that it would be impossible to accommodate the thousands of beings recorded as having attended the preaching of the *Lotus Sūtra* there). In such a case, a sage with highly developed psychic abilities may be granted permission to attend the assembly in the spirit realm, later recording the proceedings according to his recollection and inspiration.

A third point of view is that these texts were composed by various Buddhist teachers, who expressed their insights and inspiration by writing in the traditional *sūtra* form.

Some historians of religion may speak of cultural diffusion, citing similarities between deities of neighboring cultures. They perhaps would emphasize the possibility of Aesculapius cults in the Gandhāra region, or Iranian and Mediterranean healing cults filtering into Central Asia as stimuli for the composition of *sūtras* on Buddhist healing deities.[2] Still, one must be cautious about such analyses, for, to Buddhist devotees, these deities are not mere intellectual abstractions or ideas traded across continents; they are potent forces who—though their origins may be mysterious and unexplained—through invocation can play a fundamental role in the inner life of those on the spiritual path.

The revelation of the existence of the Buddha of Healing could conceivably have been received by masters in various regions. However, it may be that worship of this Buddha was originally concentrated in one region, perhaps disseminated by one master or a circle of devotees. Let us now consider a possible time and place for the emergence of this cult, basing the discussion on archaeological and literary evidence.

Archaeological evidence would be important, for images of the Buddha of Healing found with great frequency in certain regions would indicate special popularity. Inscriptions on the images would aid considerably in providing some time parameters (though uninscribed images can be dated within the bounds of certain eras due to unmistakable characteristics of style and form). However, in searching through archaeological reports for records of images of the Buddha of Healing, there is the surprising discovery that no early Indian images of the Master of Healing remain in existence. Indeed, there seem to be no images of him from any of the Buddhist countries predating the initial transmission of the *Bhaiṣajya-guru-sūtra* to China in the early fourth century C.E. Although we must admit that such evidence is inconclusive of itself—since ancient images could have been destroyed, lost, or possibly were not created with distinctive iconographic features for this "new" Buddha—it bears an impressive weight when considered together with the indications of literary evidence.

By looking into the texts, it can be established that by the time of the initial transmission of large numbers of Buddhist texts to China, Bhaiṣajya-guru had already begun to take an important place in the Buddhist pantheon. He is mentioned in some fifteen texts translated into Chinese in the third, fourth, and fifth centuries. These citations range in significance from brief notes of the existence of a Buddha named "Master of Healing" (or a variation of that name) dwelling in a certain realm, to a chapter devoted to a Buddha known as "King of Healing" in Dharmarakṣa's translation (late third century) of the *Lotus Sūtra.*[3]

By noting the wide range of names given to the Buddha of Healing, a pattern emerges indicating a strong link to the earlier worship of the Bodhisattva King of Healing. The texts of the earlier transmissions to China especially emphasize the royal nature of this Buddha. For example, in the *Sūtra on the Names of the Buddhas* (*Buddhanāmasūtra,* T. XIV, 440), translated in the early sixth century by Bodhiruci, Buddhas of Healing are mentioned nine times, their names being:

King of Healing Buddha (five times)

King of Healing, the Buddha Who is King of the Sublime Sound

King of Healing Tree Buddha

Victorious Healing Tree Buddha

Supreme Healer Buddha.

In another version of that same text, translated three centuries later (T. 443), Buddhas containing the word *bhaiṣajya* (*yao*) in their names are mentioned four times, including:

King of Healing Tathāgata

Master of Healing, King of Lapis Lazuli Radiance Tathāgata

Master of Healing King Tathāgata (twice).

By the early T'ang period and later (from the mid-seventh century on), the Buddha of Healing in a wide range of texts is rarely mentioned by any names other than the following:

Master of Healing Tathāgata

Master of Healing, the Lapis Lazuli Radiance Tathāgata

Master of Healing, the King of Lapis Lazuli Radiance Tathāgata.

Though perhaps having significant connection to the earlier worship of the Bodhisattva King of Healing, the Buddha Master of Healing's name gradually became standardized to several close variants as his place in the pantheon became assured and his popularity grew. The standardization of his name, distinct from that of the Bodhisattva, probably occurred due to the dissemination of the special scriptures on the Master of Healing, the Lapis Lazuli Radiance Tathāgata. These texts—of which there are several variant editions extant—served to make the distinctive identity of the Buddha of Healing more properly recognizable.

The *Bhaiṣajya-guru-sūtra* was transmitted in several versions to China, the most popular translation being by the T'ang master Hsüan-tsang, who presumably brought the Sanskrit manuscript to China from his extensive journeys in India and Central Asia. According to tradition, however, the first translation of the *sūtra* was by Śrīmitra (active in Nanking in the first decades of the fourth century). Śrīmitra was from the Central Asian state of Kucha; it is said that he was a prince who renounced his royal ties to become a monk.[4] The *Healing Buddha Sūtra* is included in this version in a text known as the *Sūtra Spoken by the Buddha on the Abhiṣeka* [or, *Initiation*] *Which Eliminates Faults of the Past and Confers Freedom from Birth and Death,* T. 1331 (hereafter cited as *Abhiṣeka-sūtra*), constituting the twelfth and final chapter of the text. The *Abhiṣeka-sūtra* is primarily concerned with defense and protection—both spiritual and material—by invocation of various guardian spirits, and with the dispelling of various demons. There seem to be many intrusions of a Chinese nature in the first eleven chapters of the text, indicating that if the origin of the text is indeed Indian or Central Asian, it was adapted by the translator to fit the circumstances he found in the Eastern Chin period in China.

Study of the Chinese Buddhist manuscripts found at Tun-huang indicates that the *Abhiṣeka-sūtra* in general and the twelfth chapter (the Healing Buddha chapter) especially were popular in that Western oasis-outpost of China. No less than thirty-eight different copies of chapter twelve were recovered; some are fragments, others are complete. These manuscripts date to the sixth and seventh centuries. One sixth-century scroll (Giles No. 3535) bears a colophon indicating that it is number thirty in a series of copies of the *sūtra.* Another scroll (Giles No. 3559) bears two lines in Uighur, indicating interest on the part of Central Asians. See Giles, *Descriptive Catalog,* No. 3534–3570; and Louis de la Vallée Poussin, *Catalogue of the Tibetan Manuscripts from Tun-huang in the India Office Library, with an Appendix on the Chinese Manuscripts,* by Kazuo Enoki (London: 1967), mss. C67–C68.

Perusal of two principal *sūtra* catalogs yields some information of interest. The *Li-tai san-pao chi,* compiled in 597 C.E., lists an *Abhiṣeka-sūtra* translated by Śrīmitra.[5] However, the *Ch'u san-tsang chi chi,* written earlier in the sixth century, has no listing for the *sūtra* under Śrīmitra's name.[6] Under "Lost Canonical Texts" it does list eleven *sūtras* bearing the same titles as the first eleven chapters of the *Abhiṣeka-sūtra.* There it is noted that the twelfth chapter, still extant, is of doubtful authenticity. It is not listed as lost, but is discussed in a following section on scriptures of questionable authenticity.[7] In that latter section of the catalog, the text is noted under the title of *Abhiṣeka-sūtra.* Alternate titles given correspond exactly to the twelfth chapter of T. 1331: *Sūtra on the Master of Healing of Lapis Lazuli Radiance; Sūtra on the Abhiṣeka*

Which Eliminates Faults of the Past and Confers Freedom from Birth and Death. This text is attributed to the monk Hui-chien of the Liu Sung period, who is said to have composed it in 457 C.E. on the basis of another text. According to further comments in the catalog:

The latter part of the *sūtra* contains methods for prolonging life, and therefore it circulated widely in his age.[8]

The emphasis on the attainment of longevity in the teachings of the *sūtra* is surely an aspect that gladdens a Chinese heart, and it relates closely to emphases in various Taoist texts popular in that age and later.

In a preface to the Sui period (617 C.E.) translation of the *sūtra,* which is fundamentally the same as the version attributed to Śrīmitra (with some divergences), one of the principal members of the translation committee recorded his opinion about the Hui-chien text and the care taken by his committee in the retranslation. Apparently he was unaware of the Śrīmitra translation:

Formerly during the reign of Sung Hsiao-wu (454–465 C.E.) at the Deer Wilderness Monastery, the monk Hui-chien translated this text, and it was popular in his age. However, in comparing it to the Sanskrit text [it was seen that] this Sung monk did not fuse together the confused assortment of words and phrases. This caused numerous doubts to arise in readers.

I, Hui-chü, in my early studies of Indian texts constantly spread out leaves of the scriptures [for study]. I often thought of obtaining this *sūtra* in order to examine the errors [of the previous translation]. I first obtained the original text in 597. Still, due to the fear of circulating mistakes, I did not yet dare attempt this translation.

In 615 I obtained two more copies. I compared them and finally came up with the clearest and most definitive text. Subsequently, together with the monk Dharmagupta and the Sui translation masters, the monks Fa-hsing, Ming-tse, Ch'ang-shun, Hai-yü and others at the *sūtra* translation academy in the Shang-lin Garden, which is to the south of the Lo River in the Eastern Capital, we respectfully translated this scripture.

Deeply aware of the errors of the former rendering, we took them as a warning to prevent any mistakes in the present translation. For this reason, whenever a translation of a sentence was uttered, it would not be written down until it was considered in three deliberations. In the transmission of the subtle principles, we believe that no grave errors have been made.[9]

Paul Pelliot, in his brief study of the *sūtras,* wrote: "Les trois traductions de Śrīmitra, de Dharmagupta, et de Hsüan-tsang se suivent d'assez près."[10] Roy Andrew Miller, comparing the

Dharmagupta, Hsüan-tsang, and I-ching translations (the I-ching version, T. 451, will be discussed in section B of this chapter) holds that "all three translations ultimately go back to a single Indic original."[11] This is a reasonable supposition, for—especially with regard to the three transmissions prior to I-ching's greatly expanded version of the *sūtra*—the topics discussed are similar, with differences primarily being a matter of omission or addition of words, phrases, or in some cases, paragraphs.

Undoubtedly, there were several closely-related versions of the text circulating in Sanskrit. The only known extant manuscripts of the *sūtra* were found in the vault of a *stūpa* near Gilgit (Kashmir) in 1931, together with a number of other Buddhist texts. Five manuscripts of the text seem to have been found there: two fragments of a single leaf each, two nearly complete texts, and one complete text.

The complete text forms the nucleus of Nalinaksha Dutt's composite edition of the *sūtra,* which includes citations from the two nearly complete manuscripts. Dutt's edition corresponds roughly to Hsüan-tsang's Chinese translation. In preparing my English translation included here as Translation III, I have relied on the Chinese traditions and have translated the text emphasizing a Chinese Buddhist view of the scripture. Although study of Dutt's Sanskrit edition in conjunction with the Chinese proved valuable for clarification of a number of points, the problematic nature of his edition—as mentioned briefly by Lokesh Chandra and discussed at length by Gregory Schopen—must be noted.[12]

Still, Dutt's comments on the nature of the script and language of these texts are of great value:

> The language of the mss. is similar to that of the *Mahāvastu, Lalitavistara, Saddharma-puṇḍarīka,* or *Suvarṇa-prabhāsa.* . . . In a general way we may remark that the language of the early Mahāyāna texts is really a Prakrit of a peculiar type, using largely Prakrit words with Sanskrit inflections and Sanskrit words with Prakrit inflections, and in doing so the authors have conformed to the rules of either the Sanskrit or the Prakrit grammar. There are endless examples of irregularities, e.g., plural subjects having singular verbs and *vice versa,* same word referred to by pronouns of any gender, lack of sequence of tenses, indiscriminate euphonic combinations, arbitrary conjugations and declensions. It seems that the authors were well up in the Prakrit language and grammar and developed a linguistic medium containing a mixture of Prakrit and Sanskrit. *In view of the uniformity*

maintained even in their irregularities, it may be inferred that a language of the type used in the texts got currency at a certain period in the extreme north-west of India.[13]

By analysis of the script of the manuscripts ("mostly Upright Gupta"), Dutt dates them to the sixth or possibly seventh century. The name, "Śrīdeva Sāhi Surendra Vikramāditya Nanda," mentioned in a colophon at the end of one of the *Bhaiṣajya-guru-sūtra* manuscripts, is tentatively identified by Dutt as a prince of the Sāhis who probably ruled over the Dard country during the reign of King Bālāditya in Kashmir.[14] Dutt further observes:

> The mss. copies for Yuan Chwang [Hsüan-tsang] were therefore of the same time as our mss., and it is noteworthy that the Gupta scripts preserved by the Chinese for transcribing the Sanskrit *mantras* in their Chinese translations are similar to those found in the Gilgit mss.[15]

This observation is confirmed by the close correspondence of the Sanskrit text to Hsüan-tsang's Chinese renderings.

Other versions of the text have been found in Central Asian languages, these fragments of text corresponding closely to Hsüan-tsang's version. These include a fragment in Sogdian transcribed and discussed by E. Benveniste, and a Khotanese fragment discussed by E. Leumann.[16]

Further, in the only mention of the *Bhaiṣajya-guru-sūtra* in an extant text of known Indian authorship, Śāntideva includes a number of quotes from the *sūtra* (corresponding to Hsüan-tsang/Gilgit version) in his *Śikṣā-samuccaya (A Compendium of Discipline),* thus indicating that the *sūtra* achieved some popularity in India ca. the seventh century.[17] Though popular before the seventh century, it was by virtue of Hsüan-tsang's excellent translation that the *sūtra* was truly disseminated throughout East Asia. It appears to have been a period of popularity of the cult in Central Asia and the Indian borderlands as well.[18] Though one could theorize that the text was circulated in India during the preceding centuries, it could also be hypothesized that the text, around this time of its great popularity, was transmitted to India from Kashmir or Central Asia, thereby coming to Śāntideva's attention.

In addition to the versions already mentioned, there is also an extant Tibetan version of the *sūtra,* corresponding essentially to the Hsüan-tsang text. This text, found in the Tōhoku Tibetan

Canon, No. 504, was translated by Jinamitra, Dānaśīla, Ye-śes-sde, and others in the ninth century.[19]

There is also a Mongolian version of the Hsüan-tsang text. In a brief note found in his draft manuscripts, the late Professor F. D. Lessing indicated that the Mongolian text was translated from a Uighur version:

> [The Mongolian word] *otaci,* "physician" [is] a derivation from the Uighur word *ota,* "medicinal herb," which shows that they adopted this Buddha during their first Buddhist period in the thirteenth and fourteenth centuries, when translations of the texts were made largely from Uighur originals. When the second conversions took place in the sixteenth century, they chiefly patterned their terminology after that of their Tibetan masters.

In summary, it should be noted that extant fragments or entire manuscripts of the *sūtra* have been found in Gilgit and other Central Asian sites. In addition, complete versions of the text are extant in Chinese, Tibetan, and Mongolian Canons. The Sanskrit version itself is written in such a manner as to indicate Central Asian or northwest Indian authorship, and the absence of any early Indian images tends to confirm the impression that the origins of the cult are most likely Central Asian, rather than Indian. Further, none of the Chinese pilgrims mentions Bhaiṣajyaguru worship in the records of their travels in India.

Additionally, the Buddhist images of Gandhāra in the northwest of India (near the only source of lapis lazuli known to the ancient world), as well as Buddhist images of the Central Asian regions between India and China, are noted for their emphasis on the depiction of light or flames emanating from the form of the Buddha.[20] The Buddha of Healing is described in his special texts as radiating a lapis lazuli effulgence from his body, and the meditation text on the two Bodhisattvas of Healing especially emphasizes dramatic emanations of light from the bodies of various deities. Also, trinities can be found in Gandhāran art in which the divinities of the sun and moon flank a central figure. The most famous object on which this trinity is displayed is the metal reliquary of King Kaniṣka, which dates to the late second or early third century C.E., quite near the likely time of composition of the Healing Buddha *sūtra.*[21] The stress on cosmic harmony (here revolving around the divinized figure of the Kushan king) in this art is also vividly reflected in the symbolism of the Healing Buddha *sūtras* (to be discussed in chapter four). These aspects further support the impression that the earliest worship of the healing deities and the composition of their scriptures can be ascribed to a northwest Indian or Central Asian source.

The *sūtra* on the Buddha of Healing was already composed by the late third or early fourth century, when Śrīmitra was active (if we accept that either he or someone else of his age produced the first translation of the text into Chinese). Internal evidence (to be noted below) indicates that it was modeled, to a certain extent, on the *Lotus Sūtra* in its later form (dating to ca. mid-second century C.E.), and so we might estimate its composition as being perhaps within about fifty years of that date.

2. *Contents of the Sūtra: (The Hsüan-tsang Version)*

The contents of the *sūtra* can be divided into four categories:

a. Bhaiṣajya-guru's Twelve Vows (This includes the description of his Buddha-land, known as "Pure Lapis Lazuli," since such pure lands are considered to be established as a result of vows.)
b. Blessings Conveyed through Hearing, Concentrating On, and Reciting the Buddha's Name
c. Ritual Worship of Bhaiṣajya-guru
d. The Twelve *Yakṣa* Generals

a. *Bhaiṣajya-guru's Twelve Vows*

When the Master of Healing as a spiritual youth first set out upon the Bodhisattva Path, he made twelve vows to aid sentient beings. This moving act was a fundamental step in the course of his development, serving to spur him onward with a great sense of purpose. In *The Perfection of Insight in Eight Thousand Lines (Aṣṭasāhasrikā-prajñāpāramitā),* it is held that this desire to help others is a significant factor which motivates the young Bodhisattva in his zealous striving:

> [Śakra said:] . . . I am sure that this resolve to win full enlightenment will increase more and more in them, as they survey the ills which afflict

beings on the plane of birth-and-death. For through their great compassion they desire the welfare of the world with its Gods, men, and Asuras, desire to benefit it, are full of pity for it, they, who are endowed with this attitude of mind which is expressed in their resolution that "we have crossed over, we shall help beings to cross over! Freed, we shall free them! Recovered, we shall help them to recover! Gone to Nirvana, we shall lead them to Nirvana![22]

Bhaiṣajya-guru's twelve vows are summarized here:

1. May a radiant light blaze forth from my body after enlightenment, brightening countless realms, and may all beings have perfect physical form, identical to my own.
2. May my body be like pure and radiant lapis lazuli, with a radiance more brilliant than the sun and moon, illuminating all who travel in darkness, enabling them to tread upon their paths.
3. By my limitless insight and means, may I enable all beings to obtain the necessities of life.
4. May all beings be shown the path of enlightenment, and may adherents to the *śrāvaka* or *pratyekabuddha* paths become established in Mahāyāna practices.
5. May all beings be aided to follow the precepts of moral conduct. After hearing my name, those who have broken the precepts will be aided to regain their purity and prevented from sinking to a woesome path of existence.
6. May all who are deformed or handicapped in any way have their deformities removed upon hearing my name.
7. May all who are ill be cured upon hearing my name.
8. May women who, beset by woes, seek to become men be reborn as men in their next life.
9. May all who are caught in Māra's net, entangled in negative views, be caused to gain correct views and thus practice the Bodhisattva Way.
10. May all who are to be punished by the king be freed of their troubles.
11. May those who are desperately famished be given food. May they ultimately taste the sublime Teachings.
12. May all who are destitute of clothes obtain attractive garments and various adornments upon concentrating on my name.

Thus, two of his vows deal specifically with physical healing and medicines (6 and 7), while others deal with healing in the sense of alleviating suffering and making beings whole, physically and spiritually.

An important iconographic scroll, in the collection of the National Palace Museum in Taiwan, includes a section depicting the Celestial Assembly of the Buddha of Healing together with abbreviated forms of the twelve vows (much in the manner I have abbreviated them above), and brief scenes illustrating the vows.[23] This scroll dates to the 1170's and was painted at the court of the Ta Li kingdom in Yünnan by Chang Seng-wen, a Chinese artist. In addition to its unusual artistic value, the scroll is of special interest for this study because of several variant readings of the twelve vows, which have been inscribed in Chinese.

Four of the vows significantly differ from readings found in the standard Chinese translations. The third vow, according to Chapin's translation, states:

> . . . [Wisdom] will be widespread like an inexhaustible sea, quickening the withered and the dried up. Of the limitless crowd of beings, all will receive benefit. All shall be full to repletion, without a thought of hunger or thirst; they shall have good food and savory delicacies. All shall receive support and presents.[24]

The illustration shows the Buddha standing beside the roiling sea, handing a steaming bowl to a man and a woman. In this Ta Li version, the emphasis is more on wisdom, although the illustration of the Buddha providing the necessities of life accords with the Hsüan-tsang text.

The standard Chinese versions of the scripture render the fourth vow as a pledge to aid all beings to turn from inferior paths in order to practice the Mahāyāna. The Ta Li scroll reads:

> . . . When I come into the world and attain to Enlightenment, lofty and dignified as the moon among the stars, dissipating the clouds of birth and death, then there shall be nothing hidden, brightness shall shine in the world, travellers shall see the Way, those who are hot shall be cool and shall be freed from dust and dirt.[25]

The scroll depicts travellers crossing in both directions over a bridge in the night, the stars gleaming from above.

The fifth vow, though essentially similar to the standard Chinese version in its pledge to help all beings keep to the precepts of moral purity, adds to it the concept of *vīrya:* striving. The Ta Li text begins: ". . . When I come into the world, there shall arise a great tide of energy [*vīrya*] . . ."[26] The illustration here shows a monk seated in meditation, so pure that a deer fearlessly approaches him.

The most significant variation is the omission of the usual eighth vow: to aid all women to become men in their next incarnation. Here the scroll has:

> . . . For the sake of all simple and limited sentient beings, I shall proclaim the Marvelous Law. They shall be caused to gain passage [to the other shore, *nirvāṇa*], to escape [from the cycle of birth, old age, sickness, and death]. They shall enter the Gate of Wisdom. I shall cause all things to be clear to them, so that they shall no longer have doubts.[27]

It is apparent from remarks in the standard versions of the *Bhaiṣajya-guru-sūtra* that the text was composed in a region where women had low status, where life as a woman was accompanied by many sorrows. A vow to assist women to gain incarnation as men would be ludicrous and repellent, if this were not the case. It is likely that the *sūtra* may have been modified by a travelling monk eager to spread Buddhist teachings, who, finding himself in a region where women held high status, quickly realized that the eighth vow of Bhaiṣajya-guru would have a dampening effect on the eagerness of a substantial portion of the population to listen and learn.[28] In the illustration of this vow, a monk is lecturing to a group of men and women who apparently are studying as equals.

Hui-chien's translation of the *sūtra* (fifth century, South China), which was held by scholars of succeeding generations to be a translation of questionable reliability, may perhaps have been a similar adaptation of the text to the customs of a particular time and place.

In discussing further aspects of the Hsüan-tsang version of the *Bhaiṣajya-guru sūtra,* in the section on the vows, the Buddha is described by his name as the "Master of Healing, the Lapis Lazuli Radiance Tathāgata." His paradise realm in the Eastern regions is known as "Pure Lapis Lazuli." In his second vow, he states that his ". . . body will be like lapis lazuli within and without, bright with penetrating and flawless purity."

There is some question about the meaning of the Chinese term *liu-li* (or *pi-liu-li*), which I have translated as "lapis lazuli." There is no question that *liu-li* corresponds to the Sanskrit *vaiḍūrya*, one of the seven Buddhist gems, but the exact nature of this gem in its usage in Buddhist texts has been disputed.

Arthur Waley translated it as "crystal,"[29] though "rock crystal" in Sanskrit is properly *sphāṭika*. Yoshito Harada has sought to identify it as glass.[30] Edward Schafer, who has listed several possibilities in a number of publications, most recently translated *liu-li* as beryl in his book *Pacing the Void*.[31] Giuseppe Tucci has translated *vaiḍūrya* as lapis lazuli.[32]

Observation of depictions in art reveals that the substance known as *liu-li* is traditionally depicted as dark blue (as contrasted by the pale blue of beryl, or aquamarine). This can be seen, for example, in the numerous Tun-huang paintings of the Buddha of Healing, who holds a *vaiḍūrya* bowl. It is known from these paintings that the early T'ang Tun-huang painters considered glass or crystal to be a substance quite different from lapis lazuli, for in the Stein Collection of the British Museum there is a painting of a Bodhisattva who holds a transparent glass/crystal bowl.[33] In Nepalese and Tibetan paintings, the Buddha of Healing is traditionally depicted with skin colored the deep blue of lapis lazuli.

Consultation of T'ang period Buddhist dictionaries provides literary evidence which confirms the artistic tradition that in Buddhist texts *liu-li* refers to lapis lazuli. For example, Hui-lin (a Kashgarian monk active in Ch'ang-an from 788–810) discusses *liu-li* in his *I-ch'ieh-ching yin-i*. He states that it is a blue stone which is found on the south side of Mount Sumeru. It is radiant and has a penetrating lustre. (This last phrase may indicate translucence. I have found through practical experience in fashioning rough lapis lazuli into traditional gem-stone shapes that on occasion high quality material will prove to be semi-translucent upon final polishing.)

Hui-lin goes on to make the following important distinction: "This gem is a divine substance created by the *devas* [or, created in a celestial realm]. It is not the stone smelted by men; it is not the *liu-li* created by fire."[34] Thus, in Buddhist texts *liu-li* does not refer to the clear or colored glass (created by fire) which is also termed *liu-li* in native Chinese texts of Han-T'ang times.

Other T'ang commentators also hold that the stone is blue, and point to its Divine origins. For example Hsüan-ying states that it comes from a certain mountain, identified as the Distant Mountain, or as Mount Sumeru. It is, he suggests, perhaps related to the eggshell of the Divine *garuḍa* bird. Hsüan-ying indicates that it is broken apart by spirits in order to sell it to humans.[35]

The principal source of lapis lazuli known to the ancient world (Egypt and Mesopotamia as well as India, Central Asia, and China) is located in a mountain deposit, the Badakhshan deposit, in a highly inaccessible area of Afghanistan. The belief that *liu-li* is found on a sacred mountain so difficult of access that spirits must aid humans to obtain the gem is further indication that this gem is lapis lazuli.

The traditions surrounding lapis lazuli will be discussed further in chapter four, with specific relation to the iconography of the Bhaiṣajya-guru Assembly, and the nature of Buddhist healing. Akṣobhya Buddha, predating Bhaiṣajya-guru in the Buddhist pantheon, has his realm in the East and is colored blue like lapis lazuli. This has prompted some scholars to hold that the lapis of Bhaiṣajya-guru is a mere carry-over due to "displacing" Akṣobhya.[36] I believe that the lapis lazuli color is a key to more profound aspects of the Master of Healing's iconography. This is discussed in chapter four.

Joining Bhaiṣajya-guru in his Pure Lapis Lazuli realm are two Bodhisattvas who serve as leaders of the Bodhisattva Assembly and as Guardians of the Treasury of the Law. They are: All-Pervading Solar Radiance (Sūryavairocana or Sūryaprabha), and All-Pervading Lunar Radiance (Candravairocana or Candraprabha).[37] [Plate One] The realm itself, the Eastern Paradise, is described in words of splendor, glory, and majesty, having jewelled trees, gem-decorated lotus ponds, etc. It is said to be similar to the Western Paradise of Amitābha Buddha (which is described in detail in the *Sukhāvati-vyūha-sūtra*).

b. Blessings Conveyed through Hearing, Concentrating On, and Reciting the Buddha's Name

In many of his vows, the Buddha of Healing pledges to aid beings who hear his name. In the *Bhaiṣajya-guru sūtra,* Śākyamuni further describes nine instances in which sincere recitation or concentration upon Bhaiṣajya-guru's name has a potent saving force. Of these nine instances described, six deal with fairly common human faults. Some are described in their extreme manifestations, leading to drastic karmic repercussions, such as rebirth in a hell realm or as an animal. In these instances, by remembering the name of the Buddha of Healing (having heard it in the previous human incarnation), or by hearing it for the first time—concentrating on it and reciting it with utmost sincerity—such beings can gain release from their dismal circumstances. Reborn as humans, they will have the opportunity to become the opposite of what they were. It must be noted that even though the text often speaks of sinking to the woesome paths (rebirth in the realms of the hell denizens, the hungry ghosts, or the brutish animals) as a result of karmic repercussion for negative deeds, these realms are also states of mind which one can sink into in the present life. By calling on the Buddha of Healing and by striving for wholesome change, one can have a spiritual rebirth and gain freedom from the patterns of unrestrained greed, anger, and egocentric emotional response.

Some of these patterns are described: stingy persons will become generous donors of charity, sharing freely with others; those who break precepts due to conceit will become humble and truly practice the Teachings; those who are grudging, greedy, and self-righteous will attain the opposite; and those who cause dissent and schisms, who practice black magic to harm their enemies, will be caused to become kind, compassionate, and cooperative when they hear the name of the Master of Healing.

If there are any persons who have broken the precepts, if they call on the Buddha at the time of their death, the Buddha will prevent them from sinking to a woesome path. Also, for those who seek rebirth in Amitābha's Western Paradise, yet whose good karma is not developed enough to enable them to be reborn there, the Buddha of Healing will send eight Bodhisattvas at the time of their death, and the Bodhisattvas will guide them to the Western Paradise [Plate Two].

Four other examples of aid obtained through hearing the Buddha's name or calling it out do not refer to human faults. For example, in the case of a difficult childbirth, if the mother calls out to the Tathāgata, her pain will be removed and the child will be born without defect.

The Buddha will come to the aid of those threatened by drowning, fire, swords, prison, falling from a height, imminent attack by ferocious wild beasts, and he will also protect the devotee from invading armies and from thieves and robbers.

These latter instances, especially those in the paragraph above, are quite similar to the saving powers exercised by the Bodhisattva Avalokiteśvara, as described in chapter XXV of the *Lotus Sūtra.*[38] This is further indication of the likely influence of the *Lotus Sūtra* and the Amitābha/Avalokiteśvara cults on the composition of the *Bhaiṣajya-guru-sūtra.*

c. *Ritual Worship of Bhaiṣajya-guru*

The rituals associated with worship of the Buddha of Healing, including those which form an important part of the *Bhaiṣajya-guru-sūtra,* are discussed in chapter four.

d. *The Twelve Yakṣa Generals*

When Śākyamuni revealed the *sūtra* on the Buddha of Healing, there were twelve *yakṣa* generals in the assembly at that time. According to Indian tradition, *yakṣas* are fierce spirit-beings who often cause diseases through demonic possession. These fierce warrior generals, each having seven thousand *yakṣas* in his troops, all took refuge in the Three Jewels, aspiring to aid all sentient beings. They vowed especially to aid all who circulate the *Bhaiṣajya-guru-sūtra,* and all who accept and hold to the name of that Buddha of Healing. They and their troops pledged to guard and protect such persons, freeing them from pain and suffering, easing their path. They also recommended a simple ritual for invoking the Buddha of Healing, in order to cure disease.

In considering the general tenor of the benefits gained from hearing the Buddha of Healing's name, from invoking his spiritual force through calling out his name and from offering ritual worship (these rituals to be described in chapter four), it is seen that the Buddha of Healing is especially concerned with aiding beings to awaken to their past deeds and to seek to change their negative patterns. That is, he is especially concerned with prompting beings to a great awakening, a momentous turning-point at which the drifting life is cast aside for one of spiritual dedication. This is known, in Buddhist terms, as the arising of *bodhicitta,* the aspiration to attain enlightenment. Even when beings are brought back from deep coma by special rites and invocations (as in chapter four), an important aspect of this phenomenon is that during this period the "unconscious" one learns about the fruits and retribution of his karma. Upon return to consciousness, he retains the memory of his experience, and he dramatically changes the patterns of his life in accordance with his clarified vision of the workings of karma.

Similar to Vimalakīrti's concepts and to Śākyamuni's fundamental teachings, an illness when properly dealt with can serve as a major event that propels one onwards towards higher spiritual attainment. In the case of healings by Bhaiṣajya-guru, the sincere act of faith by the ill person results in healings granted. During the healing process, insight arises that causes the person to reform the patterns of his deeds, words, and thoughts, so that they accord with the quest for enlightenment.

Worship of the Buddha of Healing may have arisen due to the searching need for a potent being to whom prayers might be directed in times of fear-provoking illness (thus the many rituals for prolonging life). Yet, the scriptures emphasize the influence that the Buddha exerts in his healing activities: the influence of initiating the aspiration to attain enlightenment. This is a special aspect, which places the cult securely within Mahāyāna Buddhist traditions.

B. THE SEVEN BUDDHAS, MASTERS OF HEALING

The T'ang Emperor Chung-tsung, who lost the throne in 684 to his mother, Empress Wu, regained it upon her death in 705. He felt that his life had been saved during his years of banishment by the spiritual force of Bhaiṣajya-guru, to whom he had prayed and whose name he had constantly repeated. For this reason, he requested the learned and well-traveled monk I-ching to translate from Sanskrit a version of the *Bhaiṣajya-guru sūtra.* This version, the fourth extant transmission of the *sūtra* in China, is entitled the *Sūtra on the Merits of the Fundamental Vows of the Seven Buddhas, the Masters of Healing of Lapis Lazuli Radiance (Yao-shih liu-li-kuang ch'i-fo pen-yüan kung-te ching,* T. XIV, 451). As is apparent from the title, the scripture discusses various teachings regarding the seven Buddhas of Healing, and therefore is greatly expanded in length compared to the earlier transmissions. Emperor Chung-tsung assisted I-ching in the translation of this scripture by acting as the recording scribe.[39] This same *sūtra* later gained some popularity in Tibet, where it was translated by Jinamitra, Dānaśīla, Śīlendrabodhi, and Ye-śes-sde.[40]

I-ching's translation is divided into two *chüan* (literally "scrolls"), this logical division into two parts serving to make the greater length of this version of the *sūtra* more manageable. The first section consists of the usual introductory passages found in this type of Mahāyāna *sūtra,* and the complete listing of the vows of Bhaiṣajya-guru's six Buddha brothers, as well as descriptions of their Buddha-realms. The second half, for the most part, follows the Hsüan-tsang text closely, with the introduction of Bhaiṣajya-guru, discussion of his vows, etc. In addition, this section of the text has added to the *Bhaiṣajya-guru-sūtra* a series of protective *dhāraṇīs* given by the Seven Buddhas and by the Bodhisattva Vajradhara, a prominent interlocutor of this additional material.

In summarizing the text, it would not be appropriate to list all the vows, there being forty-four in all. However, a simple table listing the realms of the Seven Buddhas, distance eastward (beyond as many Buddha realms to the East as there are grains of sand in the Ganges River), names of the Buddhas (as given in the Chinese text), and the number of vows made by each will be of benefit in succinctly presenting certain aspects of the text.

If only by the number of his vows, it is apparent that Bhaiṣajya-guru remains the pre-eminent healing deity. Since his name occurs in the title of the *sūtra,* it appears that he is the senior member of the group.

As to the appearance of the Seven Buddhas, the rituals discussed in the earlier *sūtras* as well as this one all deal with multiples of seven: fasting for seven days, recitation of the *sūtra* forty-nine times, and worship of seven images with seven lamps placed before each image, each lamp having seven levels, and the lamps to be

REALM	DISTANCE Beyond as many Buddha realms to the East as there are grains of sand in the Ganges River	BUDDHA NAME	NUMBER OF VOWS
1. Radiant Victory	4x	Auspicious King	8
2. Marvelous Gem	5x	Majestic Light and Sound of the Moon-Jewel Insight	8
3. Perfect Incense Heap	6x	Radiant Gem of Golden Hue, Perfected in the Sublime Practices	4
4. Without Grief	7x	Without Grief, He Who is Most Excellent and Auspicious	4
5. Dharma Banner	8x	Thundering Sound of the Dharma Sea	4
6. Wholesome Abode in the Sea of Jewels	9x	Victorious Wisdom of the Dharma Sea, He Who Roams Freely by His Spiritual Powers	4
7. Pure Lapis Lazuli	10x	Lapis Lazuli Master of Healing	12

burned continuously for forty-nine days. More such "sevens" can be seen in the descriptions of rituals in chapter four.

Tucci believes, and I agree, that the emphasis on the numbers seven and forty-nine refers to the intermediate state between incarnations (Skt. *antarābhava;* Tib. *bar-do*), which in the *Abhidharmakośa* is said to be seven or forty-nine days in duration.[41] This aspect of the number symbolism is especially related to the ability of the Healing Buddhas to restore consciousness to those in comas who are on the verge of death, (as will be discussed in more detail in chapter four).

Seven is not an unusual number in Buddhism. Śākyamuni, upon birth, took seven steps and announced his intention to attain perfect enlightenment. Importantly, the healing meditation taught by Śākyamuni to his disciples consists of seven steps: the seven limbs of enlightenment.

In addition to the emphasis on seven Buddhas, rather than one, a fundamental difference between the I-ching text and the preceding transmissions of the *Bhaiṣajya-guru-sūtra* is the emphasis on the merits to be gained by reciting special *dhāraṇīs* (potent invocatory phrases), which were revealed by these Buddhas and by the Bodhisattva Vajradhara. The highlighting of *dhāraṇīs* in the text emphasizes the esoteric or tantric nature of the scripture. It is also a reasonable indication that this text is an expansion of the Hsüan-tsang version (rather than *vice versa*), since the esoteric schools grew in popularity several centuries after the introduction of fundamental Mahāyāna teachings.

1. T. XXV, 1509, p. 756B (As discussed in Étienne Lamotte's "Sur la formation du Mahāyāna," *Asiatica* [Leipzig: 1954], pp. 383-384.)
2. For such speculations, see for example Alexander Coburn Soper's discussions in *Literary Evidence for Early Buddhist Art in China*, pp. 174-178, 207-210.
3. T. IX, 263, chapter 10, pp. 99A-102B. For a list of references to the Buddha of Healing from the T'ang and prior periods in the *Taishō Shinshū Daizōkyō* edition of the Chinese Buddhist Canon, see my Appendix III.
4. For more on the life of Śrīmitra, see Erik Zürcher, *The Buddhist Conquest of China* (Leiden: 1972), pp. 103-104.
5. T. LIV, 2034, p. 69A.
6. T. LV, 2145, p. 10A.
7. T. LV, pp. 31A-B.
8. T. 2145, p. 39A.
9. From the "Preface to the *Sūtra on the Merits of the Fundamental Vows of the Master of Healing Tathāgata*," by Hui-chü, T. XIV, 449, p. 410A. A complete translation of the preface is included as Translation II of this work.
10. Paul Pelliot, "Le Bhaiṣajya-guru," *B.E.F.E.O.* 3 (1903), p. 34. [Romanization has been changed to the Wade-Giles system for consistency.]
11. Roy Andrew Miller, *"The Footprints of the Buddha": An Eighth Century Old Japanese Poetic Sequence* (New Haven: 1975), p. 27. In this work, Miller relates a series of poems carved on an image of the Buddha's footprints to the twelve vows of Bhaiṣajya-guru. The image is found at Yakushiji (Temple of the Buddha of Healing) in Nara, Japan.

12. Nalinaksha Dutt, *Gilgit Manuscripts*, vol. I (Srinagar, Kashmir: 1939). For photographic reproductions of the manuscripts, see Raghu Vira and Lokesh Chandra, *Gilgit Buddhist Manuscripts* (New Delhi: 1974). Lokesh Chandra briefly indicates on p. 1 that some problems exist in Dutt's edition; Gregory Schopen discusses some of these problems in detail in Appendix III of his article, "*Sukhāvatī* as a generalized religious goal," *Indo-Iranian Journal* 19 (1977), pp. 208-210. Mr. Schopen has been studying at length various mss. found at Gilgit, including the *Bhaiṣajya-guru sūtra*, for which he is preparing a new Sanskrit edition based on the Gilgit mss. and the Tibetan versions.

13. Nalinaksha Dutt, *Gilgit Manuscripts*, vol. I (Srinagar, Kashmir: 1939), pp. ii–iii. My emphasis of the last sentence.

14. Dutt, *Gilgit Manuscripts*, p. 42. The Sāhi princes were Turks of Tibetan origin who were strong supporters of Buddhism. For further discussion of the history of the Sāhis in Kashmir, see pp. 34–36.

15. Dutt, *Gilgit Manuscripts*, pp. 42–43. Hsüan-tsang is said to have dwelt at the king's palace in Kashmir for two years, where clerks employed by the ruler copied out Buddhist texts for him. (See Thomas Watters, *On Yuan Chwang's Travels in India* vol. I [London: 1904], pp. 258-259).

16. E. Benveniste, *Textes Sogdiens: Mission Pelliot en Asie Centrale*, vol. III (Paris: 1940), pp. 82–92; and E. Leumann, *Buddhistisch Literatur*, vol. I (Leipzig: 1920), pp. 104–110.

17. Cecil Bendall and W. H. D. Rouse, translators, *Śāntideva's Śikṣā-Samuccaya* (Delhi: 1971), pp. 14, 170–171.

18. Seventy manuscript scrolls of the Hsüan-tsang version—dating to the seventh and eighth centuries—have been recovered from Tun-huang. Giles #3572-3640 (British Museum); Indian Office Library mss. C51 and C52. There are undoubtedly further ancient manuscript copies of this *sūtra* in Leningrad, Paris, Peking, and other repositories of the Tun-huang scrolls, as well as in private collections. I have recently seen a manuscript scroll, most likely from Tun-huang, which includes the entire Hsüan-tsang version of the *sūtra*. This scroll, in the collection of Dr. Paul Singer, appears to date to perhaps mid-late eighth century and is written in the handwriting of a devotee, rather than that of a professional *sūtra* copyist.

19. *'Phags pa bcom ldan 'das sman gyi bla baiḍurya'i 'od kyi sṅon gyi smon lam gyi khyad par rgyas pa źes bya ba theg pa chen po'i mdo, Tōhoku Derge Canon,* vol. 87, #504; *Peking Tibetan Tripiṭaka,* vol. 6, #136; *Narthang Tripiṭaka,* vol. 89, #477.

20. See Alexander Coburn Soper, "Aspects of light symbolism in Gandhāran sculpture," *Artibus Asiae* XII (1949), pp. 252-283, 314–330; XIII (1950), pp. 63–85.

21. For illustrations of the reliquary, see John M. Rosenfield, *The Dynastic Arts of the Kushans* (Berkeley and Los Angeles: 1967), plates 60 and 60A. For translation and discussion of the inscription, see B. N. Mukherjee, "Shāh-jī-kī-ḍherī Casket Inscription," *British Museum Quarterly* 28 (1969), pp. 39–46; and further discussion in vol. 29 (1965) by V. V. Mirashi, pp. 109–110, and Mukherjee, pp. 110–111.

22. Edward Conze, trans., *The Perfection of Wisdom in Eight Thousand Lines* (Bolinas, California: 1973), p. 254. For further discussion on *praṇidhāna* (fundamental or original vows), see Har Dayal, *The Bodhisattva Doctrine in Buddhist Sanskrit Literature* (London: 1932), pp. 64–67.

23. See the book-length study of this scroll by Helen B. Chapin and Alexander C. Soper, *A Long Roll of Buddhist Images* (Ascona, Switzerland: 1972), Plates 28–31.

24. Chapin and Soper, *A Long Roll of Buddhist Images,* p. 124.

25. Chapin and Soper, *A Long Roll of Buddhist Images,* p. 124.

26. Chapin and Soper, *A Long Roll of Buddhist Images,* p. 123.

27. Chapin and Soper, *A Long Roll of Buddhist Images.* Translated from the text reproduced in Plate 30. Here, I differ somewhat from Chapin's phrasing.

28. Though I have not at this time been able to find any materials on the status of women in ancient Yünnan, Peter Goullart reminisces of his years among the tribal peoples of Likiang and Ta Li (ca. 1939–1949). He presents a vivid picture of the dominant role of women in business, trade, and the general management of material affairs of the region in more recent times. See Goullart's *Forgotten Kingdom* (London: 1957).

    The eighth vow found in the standard versions of the *Bhaiṣajya-guru-sūtra* is quite similar to one of the vows made by Amitābha Buddha when he first set out on the Bodhisattva Path (#34 in the Sanskrit version of the *Sukhāvatī-vyūha-sūtra,* #36 in the Chinese versions). This is one indication, among many, of the influence of Amitābha worship on the nascent Bhaiṣajya-guru cult. For a translation of this text, see F. Max Muller, trans., *The Larger Sukhāvati-vyūha-sūtra* included in E. B. Cowell, ed., *Buddhist Mahāyāna Texts* (New York: 1969, original edition 1894).

29. Arthur Waley, *A Catalogue of Paintings Recovered from Tun-huang by Sir Aurel Stein* (London: 1931), p. 67.

30. Yoshito Harada, "Ancient glass in the history of cultural exchange between east and west," *Acta Asiatica* 3 (1962), pp. 57–69.

31. Edward H. Schafer, *Pacing the Void: T'ang Approaches to the Stars* (Berkeley: 1978), pp. 255, 318. See also pp. 39–40.

32. Giuseppe Tucci, *Tibetan Painted Scrolls* (Rome: 1949), vol. I, p. 213.

33. As depicted in Denys Sutton, "The great game," *Apollo* 192 (1978), p. 85.

34. Hui-lin, *I-ch'ieh-ching yin-i,* T. LIV, 2128, p. 317B.

35. Hsüan-ying, *I-ch'ieh-ching yin-i,* reprinted by Academia Sinica, Institute of History and Philology (Taipei: 1963), Chapter 23, *chüan* 10, section #1073.

36. See, for example, Giuseppe Tucci, *Tibetan Painted Scrolls* (Rome: 1949), vol. II, p. 360.

37. Śrīmitra renders these as "Brilliance of the Sun" and "Purity of the Moon" (*jih-yao* [日曜] *yüeh-ching* [月淨]); Dharmagupta calls them "Sunlight" and "Moonlight" (*jih-kuang* [日光] *yüeh-kuang* [月光]), the names preferred in Japan; while I-ching uses the same characters as Hsüan-tsang (*jih-kuang pien-chao* [日光遍照] *yüeh-kuang pien-chao* [月光遍照]).

38. Tāra, consort of Avalokiteśvara, can save devotees from eight dangers, both external and internal. Though I have not found any special commentary on the "internal" aspects of the dangers to which the Buddha of Healing responds, many of them are found on Tāra's list (as given in Heather Karmay's *Early Sino-Tibetan Art* [Warminster, England: 1975], p. 104):

External Dangers	Internal Dangers
1. lion	1. pride
2. elephant	2. ignorance or stupidity
3. fire	3. anger
4. snake	4. jealousy
5. robbers and thieves	5. wrong views
6. prison	6. covetousness
7. water	7. desire
8. demons	8. doubt

For more on this, see Giuseppe Tucci, *Indo-Tibetica,* vol. III, part II (Rome: 1936), pp. 156–163.

39. Historical notes recorded in the *Fa-yün-chih-lüeh,* or *Record of the Vicissitudes of the Buddha-Dharma,* as translated by Jan Yün-hua (*A Chronicle of Buddhism in China,* 581–960 A.D., Santiniketan: 1966, pp. 48–49). For a complete English translation of I-ching's transmissin of this *sūtra,* see my *Translation IV.*

40. *'Phags pa de bshin gśegs pa bdun gyi sṅon gyi smon lam gyi khyad par rgyas pa źes bya ba theg pa chen po'i mdo, Tōhoku Derge Canon,* vol. 87, #503; *Peking Tibetan Tripiṭaka,* vol. 6, #135; *Narthang Tripiṭaka,* vol. 89, #476.

41. Tucci, *Tibetan Painted Scrolls,* vol. II, p. 361. See also Louis de La Vallée Poussin, trans., *L'Abhidharmakośa de Vasubandhu,* vol. III

(Paris: 1926), p. 49; and W. Y. Evans-Wentz, *The Tibetan Book of the Dead* (Oxford: 1927), p. 51.

According to Mkhas grub rje, Śākyamuni passed through a unique "intermediate state," setting the Wheel of the Law in motion (preaching his first sermon) forty-nine days after attaining enlightenment. See F. D. Lessing and Alex Wayman, trans., *Fundamentals of the Buddhist Tantras* (The Hague: 1968), p. 19.

Plate One

Plate Two

Plate Three

Plate Four

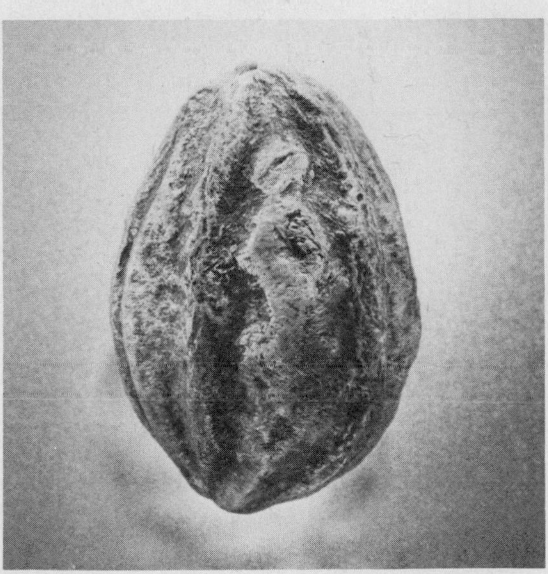

Plate Five

Plate Six

Plate Seven

Plate Eight

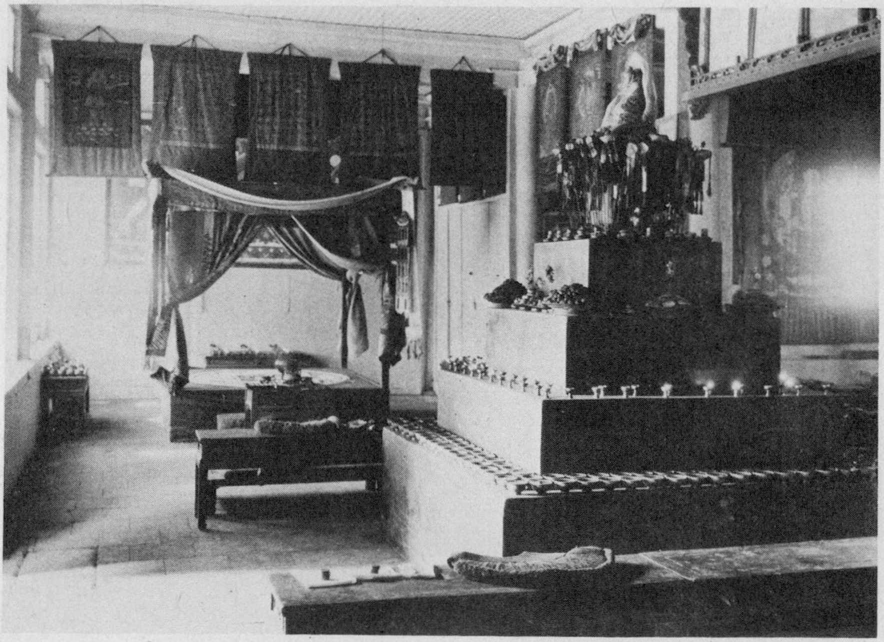

Plate Nine

Plate Ten

Plate Eleven

Plate Twelve

Plate Thirteen

Plate Fourteen

Plate Fifteen

Plate Sixteen

Illustrations

Cover. The Buddha of Healing, holding a medicine bowl in his left hand (in the gesture of profound meditation) and the healing myrobalan fruit in his right hand (in the gesture of bestowing blessings). Detail from a Tibetan blockprint.

Plate One. The Buddha of Healing with the two chief Bodhisattvas of his realm, All-Pervading Solar Radiance and All-Pervading Lunar Radiance. (From an early thirteenth-century Japanese compendium of esoteric Buddhist iconography, the *Kakuzen-shō,* as reproduced in *Taishō Shinshū Daizōkyō, Zuzō* vol. 4.)

Plate Two. The Buddha of Healing with the eight great Bodhisattvas, who will guide souls to a paradise realm after death. The Buddha has his right arm bent at the elbow, holding his hand palm outward, fingertips up in a variant of the gesture which banishes fear. (Also from a manuscript scroll of the *Kakuzen-shō.*)

Plate Three. East Pagoda, Temple of the Master of Healing (Yakushi-ji), Nara, Japan. Part of a complex of buildings created to reflect on earth the Buddha of Healing's spirit realm, Pure Lapis Lazuli. Constructed 730 C.E.

Plate Four. Interior of the Golden Hall, Yakushi-ji. Enormous bronze statues of the Buddha of Healing and his two Bodhisattva attendants (late seventh or early eighth century).

Plate Five. The dried fruit of the myrobalan (*harītaki*), the great healing herb.

Plate Six. Detail of Tibetan painted scroll of Bhaiṣajya-guru and his paradise realm. (Fifteenth-century Tibetan thangka.) Note the detail below the throne, which shows a *pūjā* scene. Los Angeles County Museum of Art, M.77.19.13. From the Nasli and Alice Heeramaneck Collection, Museum Associates Purchase.

Plate Seven. Tibetan blockprint representing the Bhaiṣajya-guru Assembly, with the Buddha brothers above, sixteen Bodhisattvas ranged around his aureole, and various *devas* and guardian spirits below.

Plate Eight. Detail of a painted version of the blockprint shown in Plate Seven. Here are seen the Guardians of the Four Directions and, directly above them, the Twelve *Yakṣa* Generals who pledged to aid the Buddha of Healing and all his devotees.

Plate Nine. Hall for the worship of Bhaiṣajya-guru (Hall IV) at Yung-ho-kung, the Lamaist temple in Peking. In the right center is seen the offering altar to the Buddha, while the "powder *maṇḍala*" is seen in the background.

Plate Ten. The altar in Hall IV, with offerings of bowls of water, lamps, cakes, banners, etc. Yung-ho-kung.

Plate Eleven. Model of the offering altar, showing freshly-painted details.

Plate Twelve. The great *maṇḍala* of the Buddha of Healing, formed of colored sands for the three days of healing ceremonies. The table in the background bears various offerings. Yung-ho-kung.

Plate Thirteen. Painted *maṇḍala* of the Buddha of Healing. Here the fifty-three deities are portrayed in symbolic form, each represented by its chief hand-held attribute (medicine bowl, book, sword, etc.).

Plate Fourteen. Detail of the central section of Plate Thirteen.

Plate Fifteen. The *maṇḍala* palace of the Buddha of Healing, here shown in three-dimensional form. Yung-ho-kung, Hall IV.

Plate Sixteen. Services in progress for the worship and invocation of the Buddha of Healing. Yung-ho-kung.

Note: Plates Seven through Sixteen are from the collection of the late Professor F. D. Lessing and are included here by courtesy of Professor Alex Wayman. These photographs are over forty years old and are somewhat deteriorated; excellent reproductions of them for the purpose of this book were made by Sheldan Collins. The myrobalan (Plate Five) is from the same collection; it was photographed by Sheldan Collins.

IV

Images, Meditations, and Ritual Worship

A. IMPORTANCE OF IMAGES IN THE WORSHIP OF BHAIṢAJYA-GURU

As art objects, Buddhist images have unique meaning, gracing a temple, household shrine, museum showcase, or collector's cabinet with a certain charm or strength of form, rhythm, and line. Still, images were (and continue to be) created for deeper purposes than the beauty of surface values. To the practitioner within the Buddhist tradition, images may be seen as profound reminders of spiritual forces. More importantly, they are used as conduits for the invocation of those forces, and in this role they are potent aids of incalculable value. Buddhist images find their intended context as supports for private meditative practice and as instruments for worship and ritual devotion.

Hui-kuo, the T'ang master of esoteric Buddhism, told his great disciple Kūkai:

> Since the Esoteric Buddhist teachings are so profound as to defy expression in writing, they are revealed through the medium of painting to those who are yet to be enlightened. The various postures and *mudrās* [depicted in *maṇḍalas*] are products of the great compassion of the Buddha; the sight of them may well enable one to attain Buddhahood. The secrets of the *sūtras* and commentaries are for the most part depicted in the paintings, and all the essentials of the Esoteric Buddhist doctrines are, in reality, set forth therein. Neither masters nor students can dispense with them. They are indeed [the experiences of] the root and source of the ocean-like assembly [of the Enlightened Ones, that is the world of enlightenment].[1]

Texts and images—both created as guides to enlightenment—have different ways of conveying the message. Texts speak to the mind, presenting principles and concepts for contemplation, study, and active mental digestion; while paintings and sculpture spark the imagination and set the psyche in vibration. The meanings of the art—conveyed especially through the formal language of symbols, colors, gestures, and attributes—cause hidden chords to resonate in the depths of our being.

Art and images play an unusually important role in the ritual worship of the Buddha of Healing. As evidenced by the vast extent of archaeological remains, temple treasures, and museum pieces that were originally dedicated to the Buddha of Healing, devotion to that Buddha often took material form in the creation of his image.

Some sought to recreate the Buddha's paradise on earth. For example, in the eighth century in Japan an extensive and impressive temple complex was built [Plates Three and Four]. This was called the Yakushiji, or "Temple of the Master of Healing." Through the use of soaring architectural structures placed in a formal manner, extensive painted decorations in the interiors of worship halls employing colors of jewel-like brilliance, sculptures majestic both in size and manner arranged hierarchically on raised altar platforms (thus benignly gazing down upon the worshipper); through the use of the various techniques known to artists, the devotee visiting such a temple is dazzled by splendor and uplifted by the majesty of the conceptions.

Much of the healing that Bhaiṣajya-guru has vowed to accomplish takes place within: the roots of many diseases with physical manifestations lie within the mind, and the spiritual afflictions, the *kleśas,* lie at the base of the entangled and crooked byways of the mind's clouded meanderings. Because of this, the role of art in focusing the mind, in changing and uplifting the consciousness by aesthetic and spiritual experience, has an importance difficult to overemphasize. By this experience attained in an atmosphere created by splendorous decorations of solemn grandeur, the world is transformed. The mind then is attuned with greater sensitivity to unseen currents, and thereby becomes far more receptive to the healing rays of the Buddha.

The spiritual forces which guide, guard, protect, and heal Buddhist devotees are, by their nature, invisible. Abiding in spirit realms, their deepest reality consists of principle rather than form. Still, these beings can be envisioned in formal ways which have been revealed to sages of yore. These experiences are recorded within the traditional structures of *sūtras*, ritual texts, and by the creation of images. What is by nature invisible and inconceivable is thus crystallized in a formal way, and is thus comprehensible to the human mind. The *Sūtra on the Contemplation of the Two Bodhisattvas, King of Healing and Supreme Healer* hints that the revelation of Divine form is dependent on the capacity of the perceiver when it describes King of Healing as ". . . twelve *yojanas* tall, though in response to sentient beings he may appear to be a hundred eighty or eight feet in height."[2]

There is a certain vastness about Divine beings which lies beyond the bounds of human comprehension. Images, then, crystallize this vastness in a readily comprehensible form, and serve as a focus for worship that can be grasped by the mind.

The deity may communicate to the devotee by means of revealing a form, a mental image to retain and cherish. But this communication can work in the opposite direction: by visualizing the image of the revealed form (based on the descriptions recorded by masters of the past), the devotee may enter into profound rapport with the deity. If a physical image is already prepared (painting or sculpture), it can be used as a conduit, a line of communication to the invisible realms. This is in part what is meant by the statement quoted above, that images ". . . are indeed the root and source of the ocean-like assembly."

In many rituals for the worship of Bhaiṣajya-guru, images and elaborate forms, such as the forty-nine seven-tiered lamps and the five-colored banners, are employed. These, as noted above, enable the devotees to have a focus for the mind, and, importantly, present them with forms comprehensible to the human mind, which resonate to the awesome force of the Divine spirits being worshipped and invoked. These concepts will be discussed further below, with specific relation to rituals for the worship of Bhaiṣajya-guru.

B. SYMBOLISM OF THE CELESTIAL ASSEMBLY OF THE BUDDHA OF HEALING

There are many levels of worship, ritual practice, and belief. There is the simple peasant, who presents a humble offering to the

Buddha and expects to receive in return whatever he has requested. To such a person, the Buddha of Healing may be one of a myriad of Divine beings, each a "specialist" to whom one turns for aid in specific types of problems. For the peasant, the members of the Bhaiṣajya-guru Assembly are seen as living beings, embodiments of profound spiritual forces who, due to their loving kindness and compassion, respond instantaneously to sincere pleas for aid. Their paradise is a realm where one may be reborn as a reward for devotion.

On another level, there is the searcher engaged in meditative praxis, engaged in profound spiritual work. The beliefs noted above may also be held by such a person, though on a higher octave of understanding. To such a person, the Buddha of Healing may exist in the interior life, irradiating meditations with a lapis lazuli splendor. This has a palpable healing effect on the inner pains or afflictions from which the practitioner must be "cured" in order to attain enlightenment.

To the meditator, images have potent impact. The images represent intangible concepts expressed through the language of symbols, and these symbols are brought to life by the Divine forces that are invoked. From this point of view, let us consider the symbolic aspects of the Celestial Assembly of the Buddha of Healing.

In viewing the Bhaiṣajya-guru Assembly, merely glancing without regard for detail, one's eyes are drawn to the center: to the Master of Healing who shimmers with intense deep-blue rays of lapis lazuli, accentuated here and there by the characteristic golden inclusions found in fine examples of this gem. Since lapis lazuli rays are part of the Master of Healing's full name, and since his realm, the locus of his spiritual force, is known as "Pure Lapis Lazuli," a brief discussion of this gem is of special relevance here.

Lapis lazuli, unlike the other important gemstones, is a rock rather than an mineral. It is opaque to semi-translucent, and its chief component is the blue mineral lazulite, with varying amounts of white calcite and inclusions of pyrite that appear to be flecks of gold imbedded in the stone. The finest specimens of lapis, intensely purple-blue with speckled waves and swirls of the shining gold-colored pyrite, resemble the night sky aglow with myriads of stars.[3]

The primary source for lapis in ancient and modern times has been the Badakhshan deposit in a mountainous region north of the Hindu Kush range in northeastern Afghanistan. There are also major deposits in Siberia and Chile, as well as minor deposits in Colorado and Burma. The ancient Mediterranean civilizations, for which lapis was among the most valued of gemstones, were aware only of the Badakhshan deposits, and regular expeditions were sent to these "lapis lazuli mountains" as early as the fourth millenium B.C.E.[4]

In ancient civilizations, it was generally believed that gemstones and the noble metals embody or reflect potent energies which may have a curative or strengthening influence on the wearer or may aid the wearer to be attuned to certain inner currents.[5]

The extensive use of lapis in the ancient world, despite the extreme difficulty in obtaining it (the mines are among the most inaccessible of all gem deposits in the world), indicates the potency with which the ancients believed the stone to be endowed. The frequent mention of lapis in Buddhist texts indicates the continuation of this belief.

Lapis was one of the favored gemstones of Buddhist authors of antiquity, the other identifiable gem of primary symbolic importance being diamond. Generally lapis lazuli was used to symbolize that which is pure or rare. In the first chapter of the *Lotus Sūtra,* the appearance of golden Buddhas is likened to the majestic appearance of wondrous, golden images within pure lapis lazuli (pyrite inclusions shaped like Buddhas?). Further, in the twentieth chapter of that same text, the teacher of the Law is compared to the purity of a lapis lazuli mirror, reflecting all images without distortion.

The extraordinary emphasis on lapis lazuli that is found in the *Bhaiṣajya-guru-sūtra* and in the meditation text on the Bodhisattvas of Healing indicates the special association of this stone with healing energies in Buddhism. This healing is seen in the context of the association of lapis with purity and mirror-like inner rectitude. The standard depiction in art of Śākyamuni's begging bowl (as well as that of other Buddhas) filled with *amṛta,* the Divine nectar of enlightenment, is carved from lapis lazuli and further indicates this association with healing substances.

Returning again to our view of the Bhaiṣajya-guru Assembly, we see the blue field of lapis lazuli, like the night sky awash with stars. To either side of the Buddha are his chief Bodhisattvas, called All-Pervading Solar Radiance and All-Pervading Lunar Radiance: the two luminaries. The association of the sun and moon with the Buddha of Healing finds its culmination in the formation of the Assembly, but it has its roots in a number of textual references, two examples of which are cited below.

In the *Vimalakīrti-nirdeśa-sūtra,* chapter thirteen, Śākyamuni relates the story of a Buddha, named King of Healing, who lived in the distant past. A young prince named Lunar Canopy became his fervent disciple. This prince was identified as a previous incarnation of Śākyamuni.

In the *Sūtra on the Contemplation of the Two Bodhisattvas, King of Healing and Supreme Healer,* the monk who initiated the two healers in a past life related by Śākyamuni was named Solar Womb. In observing the names of various participants in tales centered around the Buddhist healing deities, a recurring element is the reference to cosmic attributes: sun, moon, constellations, and so on.

Further, the Twelve *Yakṣa* Generals grouped below the Buddha and Bodhisattvas in the Assembly, though perhaps related to the twelve vows of Bhaiṣajya-guru, may also especially be related to the twelve astrological houses, and the twelve time-periods (two hours each) of the day, as was believed by the Chinese and Japanese.[6]

Thus, with the twelve astrological houses, the two luminaries, and the sky filled with stars, we have in the Celestial Assembly of the Buddha of Healing an image of time and space in harmony. This indeed is related to healing, for a healthy person feels in harmony with things, and he who is supremely healthy (that is, enlightened) enters into a profound harmony, which in some traditions is called "cosmic consciousness."

Looking once again to the center of the Assembly, at the Master of Healing, we see in his hands the symbols of his healing function: the lapis lazuli bowl of *amṛta* in his left hand and the myrobalan, the healing fruit, offered in his right [Plate Five].

The Buddha holds his left hand in *dhyāna mudrā,* the gesture of profound meditation, and thereby supports the bowl of *amṛta:* through meditation that Divine healing nectar is received. In

Japanese art, there are some well-known images of the standing Buddha of Healing, who holds a covered medicine jar in his left hand, while with his right hand he makes the *mudrā* signifying the banishment of fear. This "fear not" gesture is appropriate for Bhaiṣajya-guru, for his *sūtra* recalls his pledges to aid beings in various desperate straits, and those imperiled by the nine untimely deaths can be rescued by uttering his name.

More commonly, in the seated images, Bhaiṣajya-guru holds the myrobalan in his right hand, with his fingers pointed downward from his knee, palm out, signifying bestowal of blessings. The yellow myrobalan (Sanskrit, *harītaki;* Latin, *terminalia chebula*) was the healing fruit given by the two brothers, the Bodhisattvas of Healing, in their ancient act of devotion recorded in their *sūtra.*

Myrobalan is a healing substance well-known to practitioners of Indian medicine. Vāgbhaṭa, commenting on chapter six of the *Sutrāsthāna,* notes that there are three types of myrobalan fruit:

> *Terminalia chebula, phyllanthus emblica,* and *terminalia belerica* are the elixirs of long life. These three fruits eliminate eye diseases and benefit the eyes, and cure such diseases as wound discharge, skin troubles, bleeding of wounds, adipose disorders, pain in the passage of urine, as well as the overabundance of phlegm and blood.[7]

Among the three, *terminalia chebula* seems to be especially potent. Vāgbhaṭa describes its qualities in detail:

> The taste of *terminalia chebula* is astringent. It leaves a sweet taste upon digestion. It has a slightly dry taste. It has no salty taste. It is light. It is very heat producing, helps digest food, makes the mind attentive, and brings about a hearty old age in the finest sense. *Terminalia chebula* has the power to cleanse internally with great warmth. It grants long life and keenness of thought. The eye and the other senses become clear. It overcomes leprosy, discoloration of countenance and bodily appearance . . . [here follows a long list of diseases and ailments which it cures].[8]

It is notable that the myrobalan affects both the mind and body with its healing properties, indicating the comprehensive nature of Bhaiṣajya-guru's healing. The myrobalan is also used in early Mahāyāna texts as a symbol of "the creative power of thought, which in high levels of meditative praxis can materialize the unseen worlds in the manner of the myrobalan berry concretized upon the palm of the hand."[9] Thus, this sublime fruit is not just a medicine, but, in its materialization by the will of the Buddha upon his hand, it represents blessings from unseen realms, like the healing energy radiating upon devotees in their worship.

A variant of these well-established iconographic patterns appears in Chinese paintings of the ninth century and later (and is later incorporated into Japanese esoteric Buddhist art, as seen in the twelfth-century iconographic compendia, such as the *Zuzō-shō* and the *Besson Zakki*). Among the scroll paintings found at Tun-huang and now preserved in Paris at the Musée Guimet, there are several that are identified by inscription as depictions of Bhaiṣajya-guru. These paintings show the Buddha of Healing as a striding monk, holding the *khakkhara* staff in his right hand and a blue medicine bowl in his left hand. In this relatively late iconographic tradition of a healer bearing a caduceus-like staff striding with two attendants, some similarities to the Greco-Roman and Mediterranean cult of Asklepios can be seen. This late iconographic tradition may have arisen as a result of contact with the West.[10]

C. RITUAL WORSHIP; BHAIṢAJYA-GURU-SŪTRA AND RELATED TEXTS

Ritual worship is a fundamental feature of the traditions surrounding the Buddha of Healing, ranging from simple *pūjā* offerings of flowers, incense, and so on,[11] to highly complex ceremonies involving the construction of altars, images, banners, and lamps.

In the most popular version of the *Bhaiṣajya-guru-sūtra*, the Hsüan-tsang version, three special rituals are described which devotees may employ for worship. More fundamental than these, however, is the calling of the name of the Buddha: "O Lord, Master of Healing, the Lapis Lazuli Radiance Buddha." This name called out at any time or place invokes the Divine healing forces of that Buddha and his saving powers. According to the *sūtra*, the response will either be dramatically immediate, or it will manifest in the improved karmic circumstances of the next incarnation, depending on the nature of the karma incurred. No matter how deeply imbedded the roots of negative karma may be, a sincere plea to the Buddha of Healing will still result in substantial help.

The first rite described in the *sūtra* is recommended by Mañjuśrī, the Bodhisattva who, by tradition, especially reveres the sacred faculties of the written word. After pledging to Śākyamuni Buddha that he will diligently disseminate the name of the Buddha of Healing among all the good sons and daughters of pure faith, even whispering the name into their ears while they sleep, he said:

O Lord, now they should accept this *sūtra* and hold to it, read it, and recite it. They should furthermore lecture on it and explicate its points to others. They themselves should copy it or have others copy it, and worship and pay reverence to the *sūtra* with all sorts of fragrant flowers, perfumed unguents, powdered incense, burning incense, garlands, necklaces, banners, a canopy, drums and music, and they should perform *pūjā* with a five-colored cloth cover for it. They should sweep the site, sprinkle water to purify the area, and then set up a tall throne and securely place the *sūtra* on it. At that time the Four Great *Deva* Kings together with their retinue overflowing with countless hundreds of thousands in the *deva* assembly will all go to this place of *pūjā* and guard and protect it.[12]

This ritual also ensures that the Master of Healing will prevent untimely deaths from occurring at the place where the *pūjā* was held. The Buddha will cause all the demons who possess the vital spirits of the inhabitants of the region to release their hold and set them free. He will also prevent such a fate from falling upon any resident of that region in the future.

Following the description of this ritual and its benefits, a second method is suggested by Śākyamuni for the worship of the Buddha of Healing:

If there are any good sons or daughters of pure faith who wish to worship in *pūjā* that Lord Master of Healing, the Lapis Lazuli Radiance Tathāgata, first they should make an image of that Buddha's form, set up a pure throne, and securely place the image on it. They should scatter all sorts of flowers there, burn various incenses, and they should gloriously adorn the site with various banners and pennants. For seven days and seven nights they should accept and hold to the eightfold vows, eat pure food, bathe in fragrant and pure water, and wear new and clean clothing. They should give birth to the unstained single-minded state, with no thought of anger or harm. Towards all sentient beings there should arise the thoughts of blessings and benefits, peace, loving kindness, sympathetic

> joy, and equanimity. They should play musical instruments and sing praises while circumambulating to the right of the Buddha image. They furthermore should recall the merits of that Tathāgata's fundamental vows and study and recite this *sūtra*. They should think only of its principles and lecture on the *sūtra*, elucidating its main points.[13]

These acts, according to Śākyamuni, generate merit such that ". . . all those joyous things which are sought will come to pass."[14] Also, such negative things as nightmares, apparitions, and ominous portents can be dispelled by offering reverent *pūjā* in this manner to the Master of Healing.

Worship of this type is not unusual among the Mahāyāna devotional cults, and such *pūjās* (with resultant benefits) are described in *sūtras* of widespread popularity, such as the *Lotus Sūtra*. What is especially interesting is the recommendation to center devotions around an image.[15]

A third special method for ritual worship was explained by the Bodhisattva Saving Deliverance in relation to a highly important aspect of Bhaiṣajya-guru: his ability to save persons whose illnesses lead them to the brink of death. In such a circumstance, while the friends and relatives of the comatose person are engaged in prayer, that person—it is described—goes through his own experiences.

First his spirit-consciousness leaves his body and is led by the messengers of Yama before that King of the Law. He is questioned about his earthly deeds, and the two special spirits (the inborn spirits attached to all sentient beings) who record all good and bad deeds make their report to Yama.[16] The King of the Law, reviewing these accomplishments and mistakes, then passes judgment on the karma accrued by the person.

According to this text, it appears that this is a universal human experience. What is exceptional in this case is that if the friends and relatives pray to Bhaiṣajya-guru with proper sincerity (assisted by monks if possible), then the Buddha will respond, and there will be the possibility of bringing the person back to consciousness. This person will clearly remember what he has experienced, as if awakened from a vivid dream. Importantly, his life will be transformed, since—having personally observed the weighing of his karma on the impartial scales of justice, and being aware of the unusual nature of his "second chance"—he will no longer desire to create negative karma.

Here again we see the special Buddhist aspect in these healing and life-saving traditions: the act of healing involves also an inner transformation in which the person who is healed holds strengthened values, seeking to conquer his negativities, and, perhaps, strive for enlightenment.[17]

The special method of worship for this life-saving situation is explained by the Bodhisattva Saving Deliverance:

> If you desire to deliver a sick person from the pain of disease, for the sake of this person you should accept and hold to the eightfold vows for seven days and seven nights. You should collect together food, drink, and other property, and, in accordance with your means, provide a *pūjā* offering to the community of monks.
>
> You should worship with a *pūjā* offering that Lord Master of Healing, the Lapis Lazuli Radiance Tathāgata, six times during the day and night. Read and recite this *sūtra* forty-nine times. Light the forty-nine lamps and make seven images of the form of that Tathāgata. In front of each image arrange seven lamps. Make each lamp as large as a cartwheel, and for forty-nine days let their shining light ceaselessly burn. Make a five-colored variegated banner forty-nine hand-lengths in height. You should release forty-nine living creatures of varied species. Then the sick person will be able to obtain passage through this danger, and he will be removed from the grasp of evil demons.[18]

This rite for the invocation of the spiritual force of the Master of Healing may also be employed with efficacious results by kings beset by all manner of troubles, as well as officials and subjects seeking release from illnesses and difficulties. According to the Bodhisattva-mahāsattva Saving Deliverance, the creation of the "life-prolonging banners and lamps" also aids one to avoid the nine untimely deaths.

In addition to these three recommended methods for the ritual worship of the Buddha of Healing, the Twelve *Yakṣa* Generals, who are his aides, can be invoked according to their instruction:

> Those who seek release from the distress of illness should also read and recite this *sūtra.* Taking a five-colored rope, they should knot our names into it, untying the knots when their wishes are fulfilled.[19]

Highly complex rituals were later developed, stemming from the esoteric traditions. The introductory lines of the *Ritual for the*

Worship of the Master of Healing, the Lapis Lazuli Radiance Tathāgata Who Dispels Calamity and Eliminates Hardship (T. 922) conveys some of the solemn purpose of these rites:

> Having first purified my body, speech, and mind,
> I take refuge in the Buddha, the Teachings, and the Community.
> Reverently prostrating before the Illumined Ones
> And the sage assemblies of all the Ten Directions,
> I now seek to make known the essentials
> Of the esoteric method for dispelling calamity.
>
> This method, taught by the Blessed One,
> Is most excellent and supreme.
> By its practice one can swiftly escape the round of births and deaths,
> And rapidly ascend to the Great Enlightenment.
>
> In accord with [the needs and conditions of] the realms of sentient beings,
> The Lord explained how to eliminate calamity and hardship. . . .[20]

As representative of the vast bulk of Healing Buddha ritual texts translated by tantric masters in the mid-T'ang and succeeding dynasties, the *Ritual for the Worship of the Master of Healing Tathāgata* (T. 924A) may be cited.[21] Having uttered the Bhaiṣajyaguru *mantra,* Śākyamuni is quoted as saying:

> If you accept and hold to this *mantra,* you will be able to uproot in this life all the grievous faults incurred through the births and deaths of the past. You will never again pass through the three [woesome] paths of existence. You will eliminate the nine untimely deaths and be rid of all suffering. Subsequent incarnations in the realms of the Ten Directions will be in places which are peaceful and joyous. This is the way in which the sovereign and unobstructed Law responds.
>
> If there is a good son or daughter who accepts, holds to, reads, and recites this *mantra* day and night, that person should zealously bathe with perfumed water and don fresh and clean garments. He should maintain the various precepts as the Teachings have them.
>
> When he has recited the complete *mantra* 100,000 times, then he should purify a site, setting the ground in order in accordance with the proper method. Taking pure soil, he should pack it well and make it level, and with pure cow dung and sandal incense he should daub the entire circular *maṇḍala.* He should make the *maṇḍala* resplendent with various precious jewels.
>
> In the center of this *maṇḍala,* he should securely place an image of the Master of Healing Tathāgata. The Tathāgata grasps with his left hand a medicine vessel, which is also known as "the pearl beyond price." With his right hand he makes the gesture known as "Binding the Threefold World

[of Desire, Form, and Formlessness]."[22] Wearing the *kāṣāya* robes, he sits in the posture of meditation. Let him be placed on a lotus blossom platform.

Below the platform are the Twelve *Deva* Generals leading their 84,000 troops. It is necessary for them also to be on lotus platforms. Amidst the Tathāgata's sublime radiance, let there dwell the two Bodhisattvas Solar Radiance and Lunar Radiance. In this way the *maṇḍala* in the four directions is entirely surrounded and enwrapped by the five colors.

Approaching before the *maṇḍala*, place two vessels of scented water there, one made of conch shell and the other made of tile. In accordance with your wishes, you should make offerings and do service to the revered image. Making your recitations before this image for forty-nine days, if at dawn on the twenty-first day you place at the four corners of this *maṇḍala* of images the auspicious vases, and continue to do so in this manner for seven days and nights, reciting the *mantra* several hundreds, thousands, or tens of thousands of times, then you will boundlessly obtain the fruits and rewards of whatever your mind has sought. The only exception would be if you were not perfectly sincere: the Law responds in this manner. All sorts of benefits and blessings will accrue that cannot be fully described, and the overflow of their merit will extend through aeons too numerous to describe.[23]

In a later section of the text, devotees are also enjoined to copy and recite the *Sūtra of the Master of Healing;* to construct forty-nine bannered lamps seven stories high in the shape of cartwheels to be arranged before the image; and to make a five-colored rope, hanging one end upon one of the lamps and with forty-nine knots tying the other end to the devotee's body. After reciting the *sūtra* forty-nine times:

. . . Those persons will attain liberation from all their karmic hindrances. They will have long lives, not meeting with the suffering of untimely deaths, and they will obtain tranquility and stability. Illnesses caused by negative spirits will all be healed.[24]

A further ritual from the esoteric tradition consists of the evocation of Bhaiṣajya-guru through visualization, for the purpose of invoking the spirit force of that deity, in order to heal all diseases, inner and outer:

Now, having returned to the void, in this primal void there is the syllable *Baṃ*, which becomes a white lotus. Atop the lotus there is the syllable *Āḥ*, which becomes a lunar disc, and upon the lunar disc is one's own consciousness, which becomes the syllable *Hūṃ*, colored blue. This syllable radiates light. Having made offerings [to the Divine forces] and having bestowed benefits [to all sentient beings], this light again coalesces into the *Hūṃ* syllable previously described.

At this point one becomes [visualizes oneself as becoming] the Master of Healing, Bhaiṣajya-guru Tathāgata. The body is entirely blue, with one face and two arms. The right hand with palm facing outward is in the gesture of the bestowal of wishes, holding in the fingers the plant which eliminates the diseases and sufferings caused by the three poisons.[25] The left hand is in *dhyāna mudrā* signifying profound meditation, grasping an alms bowl filled with *amṛta* and medicinal substances. The face is handsome and is gloriously adorned with a shining radiance.

Wearing the *kāṣāya* robes, one is seated in the adamantine posture of meditation. Radiating boundless light, one is perfectly endowed with the body which is brilliant and dazzling. Upon the forehead there is the *Oṃ* syllable, colored white; within the throat there is the *Āḥ* syllable, colored red; and within the heart, there is the *Hūṃ* syllable, colored blue. These three syllables mark the three abodes, and they glow with light, inviting Bhaiṣajya-guru and other Buddhas to descend.[26]

This ritual also depends on an image, but it is a mental creation with which one endeavors to wholeheartedly identify. By entering into the prescribed form, revealed by sages of yore, and by practicing the various mental exercises indicated, one thereby invokes the deity and receives the potent healing benefits.

In concluding this section on ritual worship of the Master of Healing, it should be noted that a *mantra* associated with this Buddha is one of the thirteen principal *mantras* of the Shingon school of Japanese esoteric Buddhism. The *mantra* is: *Oṃ huru huru caṇḍāli mātaṅgi svāhā.* This is translated as "*Oṃ,* vibrate again and again; [there is the evil influence of] Mātaṅgī the Caṇḍālī *svāhā.*"[27] Mātaṅgī the Caṇḍālī was the temptress who bothered Ānanda, Śākyamuni's disciple. The intention of the *mantra* is to ward off all negative vibrations.

D. BUDDHA OF HEALING IN PRESENT DAY CHINESE BUDDHIST ART AND RITUAL

In more recent centuries, a special aspect of Chinese Buddhist practices has been the extensive worship of the Buddha of Healing. The most fundamental trinity of deities commonly depicted on the principal altar in the main worship hall of large monasteries,[28] as well as being found in most small local temples, consists of Śākyamuni in the center, with Amitābha seated to the West (Śākyamuni's right), and Bhaiṣajya-guru seated to the East, the direction of his paradise realm.

Bhaiṣajya-guru and Amitābha represent in this trinity the Divine forces watching over the living and the dead. Prayers for living persons, in this context, are directed to Bhaiṣajya-guru, while prayers for friends and relatives in the spirit realms are directed to Amitābha. Holmes Welch discussed the so-called "red services" performed for the living (as opposed to the "white services" performed for the deceased) in *The Practice of Chinese Buddhism:*

> Perhaps the most universal feature of the red services was the worship of the Buddha of Medicine, Bhaiṣajya-guru (*Yao-shih fo*), who presides in the East just as Amitābha presides in the West. When I have attended the birthday of a leading monk or layman, we circumambulated reciting "Homage to *Yao-shih fo* who annuls disasters and lengthens the life span," after which came a hymn to the incense (*hsiang-tsan*) and a vegetarian feast.[29]

This formula (*Na-mo hsiao-tsai yen-shou Yao-shih fo!*), one of the most common phrases chanted for the welfare of the living, is also recited when the monks file through the streets on their annual begging rounds (thus taking the opportunity to invoke benefits for all beings). It is also recited on the occasion of special rites requested for the benefit of aged parents.[30] It is sometimes displayed in temples: it can be seen, for example, written on the silk banners offered in front of the massive image of Bhaiṣajya-guru, in a new temple near Taroko Gorge, Taiwan (this temple was still being constructed when I visited it in 1972).

This conception of the Buddha of Healing as one who wards off disasters and grants longevity is found in all the versions of his *sūtra.* This was an important factor in his early popularity, as well as in his enduring importance in Chinese Buddhist practices.

In accordance with this special function of watching over the living, Bhaiṣajya-guru presides over the Hall of Longevity found in some large Chinese monasteries. In this hall, wooden tablets or slips of paper are marked with names, usually of aged parents. Monks then include those persons in their prayers to Bhaiṣajya-guru. After the person passes away, the tablet is removed and installed in the Hall of Rebirth, presided over by Amitābha.[31]

E. RITUAL WORSHIP AND IMAGES OF THE SEVEN BUDDHA BROTHERS: SŪTRA ON THE SEVEN HEALING BUDDHAS AND RELATED TEXTS

The rituals in I-ching's version of the *Bhaiṣajya-guru-sūtra* do not differ in form from those found in the earlier Hsüan-tsang text. The major difference, of course, is that the Seven Buddhas are worshipped rather than one, and images are made of the seven instead of only Bhaiṣajya-guru. Also, a number of *dhāraṇīs* are revealed as potent means of invoking protection and healing.

Five *dhāraṇīs* are given in the text. The first is uttered by the Buddha Radiant Gem of Golden Hue, Perfected in the Sublime Practices. The second, uttered by Śākyamuni (similar to the *dhāraṇī* in the modern Peking edition of the Hsüan-tsang text), is recited over food and drink. These blessed substances are then given to those who have contracted illnesses, the substances having been charged with a special healing potency.

Recitation of a *dhāraṇī* offered by the Seven Healing Buddhas (accompanied by the holding of moral precepts, fasting, and various ritual acts emphasizing purification and devotion) will gain for the devotee fulfillment of desires, protection by the Seven Buddhas, spiritual and physical purification, and rebirth in a Buddha land. Another formula for protection was offered by the Bodhisattva Vajradhara, Indra, Brahmā, and the Four *Deva* Kings. Further, the Seven Buddhas permitted Vajradhara to utter his own *dhāraṇī* which beings of the future can recite to draw that Bodhisattva's protection near. The proliferation of these mystic formulae emphasizes the esoteric, mysterious manner in which these Divine beings work to aid, protect, and heal devotees.

In considering the images of the Seven Buddhas made in accordance with this *sūtra* and related ritual texts, we find that they are most common in the Tibetan and Nepalese traditions (which were influenced to a greater extent by the later version of the *Bhaiṣajya-guru-sūtra,* than the Chinese and Japanese traditions). These images reveal that Bhaiṣajya-guru is traditionally considered to be the senior of the brothers, like the chief resident of a hospital together with his associates, eminent physicians all. This preeminent position is made clear by the size and placement of the Buddha among his brothers on paintings. Bhaiṣajya-guru is usually placed in the center of these distinctly hierarchical works, and he is often considerably larger than the other figures [Plate Seven]. Sometimes the six other Buddhas are arranged around him in a circle. In other depictions, where the entire grand Assembly is shown (arranged like waves emanating from the still, calm center occupied by Master of Healing), the Buddha brothers may be depicted at the top of the design, above Bhaiṣajya-guru.

Quite often eight Buddha brothers are depicted, rather than seven. This is at first puzzling, but the Tibetan penchant for inscribing names of deities below their depictions on *thangkas* (scroll paintings) simplifies the solution: it is generally Śākyamuni Buddha who is included among the eight, usually directly above the head of Bhaiṣajya-guru. Presumably, he is included because of his special role as Supreme Physician, bearer of the Divine teachings by which all may be cured of their afflictions. His inclusion allows the Healing Buddha group to correspond to the symmetrical, eight-fold division favored by Tibetan artists.

Professor Alex Wayman has allowed me to cite his draft translation of a native Tibetan *sādhana* text entitled *Bhaiṣajya-guru, the Seven Brothers.*[32] Since some material in this text is of special explicatory value for the present work, with his permission I have revised portions of the translation (that is, matched Tibetan names of the Buddhas with those in Sanskrit, rendered *mudrā* names into English, etc.) for inclusion and discussion here.

The passage in which the Seven Healing Buddhas manifest is of great interest. The devotee first invites them to appear:

> Lords of all sentient beings without exception,
> *Devas* conquering the impregnable host of Māra,
> Perfect knowers of all things without exception,
> Blessed Lords and your retinue, pray come here.[33]

Then, when the devotee has said a brief *mantra* seven times, the seven Buddhas manifest. They are described as:

1. Bhaiṣajya-guru (in the center), decorated with all ornaments.
2. Abhijñā-rāja, body colored red, right hand in the gesture of bestowal of blessings, left hand in the gesture of meditation.
3. Dharmakīrti-sāgaraghoṣa, body red, right hand in the *mudrā*

of bestowal of blessings, left hand in *dhyāna mudrā,* the gesture of meditation.

4. Aśokottamaśrī, body light red in color, both hands in *dhyāna mudrā.*
5. Suvarṇa-bhadra-vimala-ratna-prabhāsa, body red-yellow in color, right hand in the gesture of teaching the Law, left hand in the gesture of meditation.
6. Ratnaśikhin, body red-yellow in color, right hand in the gesture of teaching the Law, left hand in the gesture of meditation.
7. Suparikīrtita-nāmaśrī, body yellow in color, right hand in the gesture of teaching the Law, left hand in the gesture of meditation.[34]

In a later section of the ritual, the devotee recites:

> Guru Vajradhara and the rest, all the Buddhas and Bodhisattvas of the Ten Directions, pray remember me. I, of such-and-such a name, holding from now and until I attain the enlightened mind, request the Lord Master of Healing, King of Lapis Lazuli Radiance, as my tutelary deity; Preceptor, pray bestow upon me the necessary precepts.[35]

Repeating this request three times, and then repeating various precepts three times, the participating devotees are then told by the Preceptor leading the service: "On the heads of you, who in yourselves are ordinary, there is now the body of Bhagavan Bhaiṣajya-guru . . ."[36] His description is almost identical to the visualization previously quoted in Section C of this chapter.

To Bhaiṣajya-guru's right there is a white lunar disc and to his left there is a red-yellow solar disc, these symbolizing the two Bodhisattvas in his retinue. Upon the crown of the head of Bhaiṣajya-guru is the Guru Ngo-bo'i nor-bu rin-po-che dbang-gi rgyal-po (True Form of the Guru, Precious Jewel Who is the Powerful One Among Kings),[37] and upon his brow are the six remaining Buddhas of Healing, each atop the other's brow.

The devotee then says: "I pray that just as the fundamental vows have been pronounced for the Sugata Mtshan legs [Suparikīrtita-nāmaśrī], may the blessings of the Buddha [*adhiṣṭhāna*] be prepared instantly for myself and all sentient beings."[38] As he repeats this prayer, naming each Tathāgata in succession, that

Buddha melts into the light and is conceived as being absorbed into the body of the Buddha supporting him.

This meditative exercise reveals that the Seven Buddhas of Healing have a fundamental unifying link. Though Bhaiṣajya-guru's preeminence is shown by naming him first (as support for the others), the others freely merge with him, showing that, although each has his own identity, they may appear as a many-faceted gem, working as a team: the mystic brotherhood of spiritual healers.

F. THE BHAIṢAJYA-GURU MAṆḌALA: IMAGES AND RITUALS AT YUNG-HO-KUNG

Maṇḍalas, geometric designs of complex symbolic meaning, serve as a focal point in special rituals and meditations of the esoteric traditions. In the Tibetan Buddhist tradition, great *maṇḍalas* are constructed of colored sands and powders for the purpose of unusual services. In 1931, the late Professor Ferdinand D. Lessing observed a three-day long series of rites centered on Bhaiṣajya-guru at the famed Lamaist temple in Peking, the Yung-ho-kung.[39] Professor Alex Wayman has kindly given me access to Lessing's invaluable manuscripts on Bhaiṣajya-guru, which include descriptions of the *rajomaṇḍala* ("powder" *maṇḍala*), eyewitness notes on the central rituals related to this *maṇḍala,* and draft translations of various relevant Tibetan ritual texts.

The special ceremonies took place in the Bhaiṣajya-guru Hall of the Yung-ho-kung (Hall IV). In this hall, a room shimmering with rows of hanging scrolls of various deities, a ziggurat-like altar dominates [Plate Nine]. At the apex of the altar, a gilt-bronze image of the Master of Healing presides, wrapped according to Tibetan custom in a garment called *nab-sa.* To Bhaiṣajya-guru's right is the *rajomaṇḍala,* about which more will be said later.

On the altar [Plate Ten], there are a myriad of offering cups, bowls, and lamps, as well as banners set about the image. According to Lessing, "eight glorious offerings" are required for this altar, including: a mirror, bezoar (a concretion found in the stomach or intestines of certain animals, considered to be an antidote to poison), curdled milk, durva grass, the bilva fruit, a conch shell, and red lead or mercury (probably cinnabar).[40]

A model of the altar made in Peking during Lessing's stay there [Plate Eleven] indicates by its freshly painted designs that the ziggurat is a *maṇḍala*-like depiction of the Master of Healing's Buddha-land. Situated upon mountains rising from the cosmic seas, one of the outer walls and gates is seen, with chains of gems suspended from the mouths of dolphin-like *makaras.* On the next level are the "suburban" areas within the realm, with pavillions and lotus ponds. The third level shows the walls to the inner court of the *maṇḍala* palace, with auspicious vases on the parapets. Examination through a jeweler's loupe reveals the Guardian King Virūḍhaka, wielding his sword of the south and defending the gate to the inner court. Four Bodhisattvas are seen on the next level (four on each face of the surface of the structure totals sixteen; in some Tibetan depictions there are sixteen Bodhisattvas shown in the Bhaiṣajya-guru Assembly [Plate Seven]). Two Divine beings are shown below his throne; unfortunately they cannot be identified from the photograph [Plate Eleven]. Undoubtedly, there are two of these beings on each side, corresponding to the eightfold division traditional to many *maṇḍala* forms.

A closer look at the *rajomaṇḍala* [Plate Twelve] reveals that it is an extraordinary construction of various colored sands, rendered in a somewhat three-dimensional manner. According to Lessing's notes, a framed painting in his collection [Plates Thirteen and Fourteen] is identical to the Yung-ho-kung *rajomaṇḍala.* Since the plates used as illustration here are reproductions especially made from small and somewhat faded black-and-white photos (made in the 1930's), Lessing's detailed descriptions are invaluable for deciphering the symbolism.

Some brief discussion on *maṇḍalas* in general would be appropriate prior to noting the symbolism of the Bhaiṣajya-guru *maṇḍala.* According to the tantric master Saraha in his *Śrī-Buddhakapāla-tantrapañjika-jñānavatī:* "*Maṇḍa* means essence; *la* means seizing that—thus, 'seizing the essence' (*maṇḍala*)." Padmavajra wrote in the *Tantrārthāvatāravyākhyāna:* "*Maṇḍala* means 'enclosing of essence' (*maṇḍa-la*) because of having the 'essence' in the sense of 'enclosing' it."[41]

Thus, by symbolic means, the essence of the Buddha of Healing and his retinue of healing Buddhas, Bodhisattvas, and guardians is enclosed within the circles, squares, and divisions of the work of art. The *maṇḍala* seizes the essence of the spirit force; that is, it concentrates this force within the potent symbolic form, channeling the energy so that it may flow freely to the initiate who has symbolically entered the enclosure. This entrance will be discussed below, following the discussion of the identification of the figures comprising the retinue of Bhaiṣajya-guru.

In the center of the *maṇḍala* is a white circular area. Within this circle, the center of the inner palace, a lapis lazuli alms bowl with a myrobalan growing within rests upon a pink lotus. This symbolizes the Lord of the Palace, Bhaiṣajya-guru Tathāgata. Though barely discernible in the photograph, there are five, narrow, colored bands encircling this central area. From within, moving outwards, the colors are white, green, red, orange, and blue, indicating the walls made of precious gems which enclose the inner sanctum. These rings are clearly rendered as walls in the Yung-ho-kung *maṇḍala* [Plate Twelve]. Attached to the outside of the rings are sixteen golden balls, ringed by green, and giving the center section a wheel-like appearance. These golden balls appear like seeds of the lotus. Under high magnification, they can be seen on the photo of the Yung-ho-kung "powder" *maṇḍala* as pyramidal projections from the wall of the inner sanctum.

The lotus blossom itself consists of three concentric bands of petals. The innermost petals, eight in number, are colored a light red with tips of white. Seven of these contain lapis lazuli alms bowls upon white lotus blossoms, and within the bowls are branch-like medicinal herbs. These represent Bhaiṣajya-guru's six Buddha brothers and Śākyamuni Buddha. The eighth petal contains a symbol that is unidentifiable, due to its complexity and minuscule size in the photograph. [For the symbols of the Buddhas, Bodhisattvas, and guardians, note Plate Fourteen].

According to Professor Lessing's notes from the *Bcom ldan 'das sman bla dbe gdegs brgyad kyi sgrub dkhyil yongs rdsogs bsgrigs pa gśhan phan 'od źer,* folios 44–45, the eight petals hold the following deities:

Southeast	Śākyamuni
South	Suparikīrtita-nāmaśrī
Southwest	Svaraghoṣa-rāja

West	Suvarṇa-bhadra-vimala-ratna-prabhāsa
Northwest	Aśokottamaśrī
North	Dharmakīrti-sāgaraghoṣa
Northeast	Abhijñā-rāja
East	Tibetan, Yum-chen-mo

The initial seven are Buddhas, including Bhaiṣajya-guru's six brothers (here Ratnaśikhin has been replaced by Svaraghoṣa-rāja). The eighth could be considered a Buddha; she is the "Great Mother," the ineffable wisdom principle from which all Buddhas are born.[42]

The second circle of petals, colored deep red and tipped with green, bears sixteen symbols. According to Lessing's draft translation of an unidentified manuscript text, the sixteen symbols are matched to deities who all seem to be Bodhisattvas, as would be appropriate for this section of the *maṇḍala.* For some of these Bodhisattvas, no Sanskrit equivalent could be found for the Tibetan name.

Beginning with the eastern-most petal (pointing towards the "lower" gate) and moving in a clockwise direction, the Bodhisattvas are matched to the symbols:

EAST

1. Mañjuśrī; yellow, sword and book.
2. Avalokiteśvara; white, lotus.
3. Vajrapāṇi; blue-green, thunderbolt (*vajra*).
4. Sūrya-prabha; white, sun. [Though the text says white, the traditional color for this Bodhisattva is red.]

SOUTH

1. Candra-prabha; white, moon.
2. Mahāmati; yellow, eye.
3. Maitreya; yellow, [the text is unclear regarding the symbol, but the photo indicates a light-colored lotus. Maitreya is generally represented by a white lotus.]
4. Nāgavṛkṣa; [the text is unclear here also, though what is pictured is a book on a lotus.]

WEST

1. Pratibhānakūṭa; white, incense vessel.
2. Tibetan, Rnams-par gnon-po [possibly either Vikrāmin, Vikṣambhaṇa, or Viṣṭaṃbhanam]; blue-green, sword.

3. Darśanīya; white, book on lotus.
4. Tibetan, Mun-pa thams-cad nges-par 'joms-pa'i blos-gros; white, jewel-stick.

NORTH

1. Tibetan, Bsam-pa legs-par bsam-pa; white, vase of *amṛta.*
2. Merukūṭa; white, crescent on lotus.
3. Tibetan, Sang-sang-pa'i dbyangs; blue, thunderbolt.
4. Meruśikhara; white, vase of *amṛta.*[43]

Some of these Bodhisattvas are well-known, appearing in many texts and having important cults of their own. These include Mañjuśrī, Avalokiteśvara, Vajrapāṇi, and Maitreya. The two Bodhisattvas Sūrya-prabha and Candra-prabha are, of course, especially associated with Bhaiṣajya-guru as the principal Bodhisattvas of his realm, the land known as Pure Lapis Lazuli.

Others are less well-known. Mahāmati, the Bodhisattva Great Wisdom, is prominently featured in the *Laṅkāvatāra-sūtra.* Merukūṭa ("Summit of Mt. Meru") was a disciple aeons ago of the Buddha Victorious Through Great Penetrating Knowledge, as is discussed in Chapter Seven of the *Lotus Sūtra.* Sang-sang-pa'i dbyangs can be tentatively identified as Sarasvatī, a female Bodhisattva of Learning, to whom language students traditionally pray for much-needed eloquence. She is a counterpart and mystic consort of Mañjuśrī.

Others are still less well-known. The name Nāgavṛkṣa means literally "snake-tree" and is often used to refer to a general type of tree with golden bark. Perhaps this has healing significance. The Bodhisattva Nāgavṛkṣa may be related to the similarly named Nāgārjuna, who is pictured in a number of the great twelfth-century Japanese iconographic compendia of esoteric deities, including the *Zuzō-shō* (1135 version, as well as later copies), scroll number five. Here Nāgārjuna is shown dressed as a monk. His special *samaya* symbol by which he may be envisioned in meditation or depicted in art is a book, as is seen in Lessing's *maṇḍala.*[44] Pratibhānakūṭa, "Summit of Eloquence," appears in the opening passages of the *Vimalakīrti-nirdeśa-sūtra.* Rnams-par gnon-po means "Lion" or "Intrepid One." There are several Sanskrit names that might be equivalent to this Tibetan name, as has been noted above. Darśanīya can mean "Worthy of Being

Seen" or "Beautiful"; it is also the name of a plant known by Latin name as *asclepias gigantea.* This plant probably has healing qualities, since its Latin family name derives from Asklepios, the healing deity of the Greeks and Romans. (The *aesclepiadaceae* are primarily milkweeds.)

In the Western Quarter, there is a Bodhisattva identified only by his Tibetan name, Mun-pa thams-cad nges-par 'joms-pa'i blos-gros, which may be roughly translated as "Wisdom Which Surely Conquers All Obscurity." In the Northern Quarter, there is Bsam-pa legs-par bsam-pa, whose name refers to his "right thinking." The remaining Bodhisattva, who has not been found elsewhere in Buddhist literature, is also of the Northern Quarter, and is Meruśikhara, translated as "Crest of Mt. Meru."

In analyzing the pattern of names and locations of these Bodhisattvas, it is found that the names or known attributes of these beings fall primarily into three categories: wisdom and insight, healing, and compassion. As to their arrangement in the four quarters, I have been unable to discern any clear pattern of symbolic meaning.

Looking now at the outer ring, there are twenty-two white petals, tipped by blue, each lotus petal bearing a symbol. According to the *Bcom ldan 'das sman bla . . .* text, these symbols represent the guardians of the Ten Directions (*dikpālas*) and the Twelve *Yakṣa* Generals associated with Bhaiṣajya-guru.[45]

The unidentified *maṇḍala* text, according to Lessing's notes, states that the centermost symbol and the symbols in the two inner rings of petals are supported by moon discs, while the outer twenty-two symbols and the guardians of the four gates (to be discussed below) rest upon sun discs.[46] This is appropriate, for moon discs are associated with benefic deities, while fiery sun discs are associated with the fierce protectors.

The identification of the three rings of symbols as Buddhas, Bodhisattvas, and Protectors is confirmed by comparison with a blockprint of the *maṇḍala* of "The Fifty-onefold Healing Buddha," included in the book *Mystic Art of Ancient Tibet.*[47] This is the same *maṇḍala,* here having depictions of images rather than symbols. Though one *maṇḍala* has images of the deities and the other portrays them through symbolic means by representing the object that is conventionally held in the hand of the deity, it must be remembered that both, in fact, are portrayals of conventional symbol systems. What is actually being represented—Buddhas, Bodhisattvas, and other high forces in their spirit abode—supercedes the bounds of what humans can fully comprehend.

Returning to our description of the *maṇḍala,* the large lotus blossom bearing forty-seven deities (therefore called a "filled lotus," *viśva-padma*) is bounded by a narrow, blue band. Beyond that is a white band containing sixteen golden thunderbolts connected by a red line with gold superimposed. Lessing states: "In the (*maṇḍala*) palace itself, this ring of thunderbolts supports eight columns on which the cupola-shaped roof rests."[48] The eight columns are mentioned in the unidentified manuscript as supporting jeweled beams hoisted upon them.[49] In symbolic analyses of the construction of a *maṇḍala*-palace, these eight columns supporting the roof of the spiritual house represent the principles of the Noble Eightfold Path.

The entire circular figure within the palace is finally bounded by a thin red line. Outside the circle, the square with T-shaped breaks is divided into four quarters, each a different color. These T-shaped breaks in the square are the four gates to the palace, and the four guardian kings of the world (*lokapālas*) are depicted, one at each gate. They can be identified by the symbolic attributes shown, from the "lowest" gate clockwise as:

1. Dhṛtarāṣṭra, lute-playing Guardian of the East, the Quarter colored blue (lapis lazuli). He is the king of the *gandharvas,* the music-making spirits who feed on incense.
2. Virūḍhaka, who wields the sword of the South, the yellow Quarter. He is king of the *kumbhaṇḍa* demons.
3. Virūpākṣa is symbolized by the serpent, for he is king of the *nāgas.* He also is often depicted holding a miniature *stūpa,* a precious reliquary. Virūpākṣa is Guardian of the red, Western Quarter.
4. Vaiśravaṇa, Guardian of the green, Northern Quarter, is represented by a banner of victory. Often he is also shown holding a jewel-spitting mongoose. Vaiśravaṇa is king of the *yakṣas.*

The Guardians of the Four Quarters are associated with many assemblies of Buddhas and Bodhisattvas, and they are customarily invoked for the protection of various temples and monasteries, where (especially in China and Japan) they are often represented by massive statues at the gates to the temple compound.

They also have a special healing function in the Sino-Tibetan traditions. In that context, each of the *Lokapālas* is in charge of one of the four elements (*mahābhūta*): fire, water, air, and earth. These are the primary constituents of the universe, and also of man, who is a universe in microcosm. Since illness is an indication that the right proportion of the elements has been upset, harmony and balance are sought. The lama divides the courtyard of the home of the sick person into four quarters, raising a flag in each quarter for the Four Guardians. In the center, a flag is raised for the deities of the twenty-eight lunar mansions (*nakṣatras*), who are considered to be their daughters. On each of these flags is the famous *mantra Oṃ maṇi padme hūṃ.* Moved by the wind, the force of this *mantra* will call forth the healing aid of the *Lokapālas* and their daughters.[50]

The remaining components of Bhaiṣajya-guru's *maṇḍala*-palace —such as the elaborate structures over the gates, the walls of jewels, the protective rings of thunderbolts, and fire at the very edge of the *maṇḍala,* at the borders of this meditative universe— are no different from the customary depictions of *maṇḍalas* of this general type.[51] The actual three-dimensional structure of the palace of Bhaiṣajya-guru can be clearly seen in the remarkable photograph of a model palace in the Yung-ho-kung [Plate Fifteen]. In addition to the *maṇḍala* paintings, this miniature palace was also used in rituals in Hall IV of the temple [Plate Sixteen, note palace in glass case at right of photo].

Having briefly discussed the special offering altar and the Healing Buddha *maṇḍala,* we can proceed to discussion of their use in ritual worship. Three rites will be discussed here, based on Lessing's observations: the Thousandfold Myrobalan Offering (involving use of the altar), Initiation into the *Maṇḍala*-Palace, and the ritual Dissolution of the *Maṇḍala.* Since these rites can be of great length, taking several hours each to perform, only the essential aspects will be mentioned below.

1. Thousandfold Myrobalan Offering[52]

This rite is observed within the context of a series of offerings and prayers to the Seven Healing Buddhas. This series, in its most elaborate form, can take three days to perform in full. Whether the series is given in its elaborate or concise form, the offering of the myrobalans is considered an important aspect.

The rite commences with material offerings of cakes, flowers, incense, etc. These are transformed through the uttering of a mantra into "clouds of offerings" (*pūjāmegha*), which cover the skies. The officiant prays that these offerings be given:

> By the power of my meditation,
> By the power of the consecration bestowed by the Tathāgatas,
> By the power of the energies of the Dharmadhātu,
> For the benefit of all living beings . . .[53]

At this point in the liturgy, the myrobalan tree is described: green, beautiful, heart-gladdening and strength-bestowing, with branches, leaves and fruits; its fragrance spreads to infinite distances and its brightness illumines the earth and sky. The Buddhas of Healing and Śākyamuni, eight in all, are worshipped and requested to teach the truth to the devotees, and gratitude is expressed for their vows to aid all who worship them. Further, the devotees state:

> I and the others offer up this myrobalan to thee,
> the compassionate one, so that thou mayst take away
> all diseases from all sentient beings.[54]

Uttering *dhāraṇīs,* the supplicants further pray that all beings be liberated from their sufferings, that the Buddhas expel disease from all living things.

> May I and all the sentient beings in all imaginable regions, by the vow of confession made by the Tathāgata, be without disease and, quickly relieved from suffering, enjoy happiness.[55]

Additional prayers then follow, including:

> By the power of the drugs offered to the Conclave, by the far-reaching strength of the oblations, spells and medicines, may all sentient beings who are tormented by illness be liberated from pain and enjoy happiness. May all sentient beings who are deprived be refreshed by the medicine of commiseration and everywhere be relieved from the two obstacles

(*kleśāvaraṇa* and *jñeyāvaraṇa*) and speedily attain the stage of Bhaiṣajya-guru.[56]

Prayers such as those quoted above and various sacred formulae are repeated many times, some as many as a thousand, invoking the Divine healing rays and generating much compassionate energy. As these prayers are uttered, according to the text, light emanates in response from the bodies of the eight *Tathāgatas* and their retinue. These rays are absorbed by the consecrated water in the flask and the myrobalans that rest upon the "offering pyramid" [Plate Ten]. Thus, having received these transforming rays, they are considered medicines of great potency.

2. Abhiṣeka: Initiation into the Maṇḍala Palace

The *maṇḍala* is an important feature of a number of *abhiṣeka* (initiation/consecration/baptism) rites, some of which incorporate the Thousandfold Myrobalan Offerings within their structure. Lessing's notes on Bhaiṣajya-guru *abhiṣeka* ceremonies, though fragmentary, are voluminous, with notations of *mudrās, dhāraṇīs,* various offerings, and so on. In the interest of presenting what is essential for the purpose of understanding the nature and function of the Healing Buddha *maṇḍala,* I have here summarized various portions of Professor Lessing's notes on these aspects.[57]

What is common to these various rites and, indeed, what is essential is that, by recitation of sacred syllables and by conscious evocation and invocation of deities, the world is transformed. The *maṇḍala* becomes a center of sacred space, charged with vibrant energy, and the participants, merging with the Lords invoked, are spiritually transformed.

The rituals are extremely complex, with actions in this highly-charged atmosphere being carefully prescribed. Elements of the services include: prayers for the patron who has sponsored the services; consecration of ritual instruments and garments; offerings of rice, etc.; dispelling of demons; offerings to local spirits and starving ghosts (*pretas*), and their subsequent dispelling; invocation of the Guardians of the Ten Directions; purification by washing and by donning ritual garments; worship of the *maṇḍala,* entrance into it, and *abhiṣeka;* and various final offerings. All acts are accompanied by recitation of *dhāraṇīs* and *mantras.*

It is the *maṇḍala*-related practices that are of special interest in the context of this study, so the fundamental aspects of entrance into the *maṇḍala* and *abhiṣeka* will be described. Prior to entering the *maṇḍala,* the preceptor or hierophant overseeing the initiation prays for permission to enter, and he makes an offering in worship. Then, he visualizes himself seizing the thunderbolt in both hands and entering the *maṇḍala.* In the case of the *rajomaṇḍala,* the "powder" *maṇḍala,* the lama physically enters the curtained enclosure and then visualizes his entry into the *maṇḍala.* In some rituals the lama has merged with the vibrations of the Lord (Bhaiṣajya-guru) prior to this act, and in others the mystical union takes place upon entry into the palace. Then:

> A beam of light issues from the heart of the lama, who is identical with the Lord. It attracts all the Buddhas and Bodhisattvas of the ten regions of the universe as the conclave of deities, so to speak, of his own *maṇḍala,* so that they pour down like rain upon his body.[58]

The lama, having spiritually merged with the Buddha of Healing and thus having now properly entered his own *maṇḍala*-palace through the eastern gate, then opens that gate to admit his disciples, who take special pledges and vows prior to entrance.

The lama then consecrates his own person with sacred water from a flask; he swallows a few drops and feels the water penetrating into every part of his body, the surplus emerging through "Brahmā's crevice" (a suture in the crown of the head). This transforms itself into a mystic head ornament. His body—penetrated with bliss (*mahāsukha*)—becomes transformed and divine. This *abhiṣeka* is then conferred upon the disciples, to whom the lineage of spirit forces is transmitted.

The disciples are taught to evoke the Healing Buddhas by visualization; the forms and colors of these Lords are revealed at this point. The visualizations follow the general pattern of those previously quoted from the *Rin Lhan* and the *Yao-shih ju-lai hsien-kuan chien-lüeh i-kuei.* In some ceremonies, the disciples visualize the Lord of the *maṇḍala* (Bhaiṣajya-guru) in the space in front of them, and then they also visualize the Buddhas and Bodhisattvas of the Ten Directions, and the various guardians, etc.; and they take refuge in these Lords.

After the disciples pledge to never reveal the secrets of the mystic *maṇḍala*—what was communicated on an inner plane and the lama's oral teachings—the door of a miniature palace opens (invisible to the uninitiated), and the glory (*tejas*) of the Buddha descends upon those initiates who enter it.

3. Dissolution of the Maṇḍala

After the many rites associated with the Bhaiṣajya-guru *maṇḍala* are completed, one ceremonial act remains, and that is the ritual dissolution or destruction of the *maṇḍala.* According to his notes, Professor Lessing witnessed this on May 15, 1931, in Hall IV of the Yung-ho-kung.[59] The *maṇḍala* to be destroyed, of course, was the "powder" *maṇḍala,* the large "painting" especially prepared from colored sands for the ceremonies. Essentials of these rites are as follows:

1. While reciting certain formulae, the lamas remove from their sockets at the corners the magic daggers (Tib. *phur-bu*) that protect the *maṇḍala.* They are washed in milk.
2. Consecrated water is poured over the *maṇḍala,* describing a circle.
3. Then the center of the *maṇḍala* is cut in four directions with a magic dagger.[60] Dried myrobalan fruits (from the Thousandfold Myrobalan Offering) and pinches of the ground color are given to the participants as efficacious souvenirs of the ritual experience.
4. Finally, the *maṇḍala* is completely destroyed by sweeping the colors from the edges towards the center.
5. The lamas form a procession, carrying an offering table, banners, playing musical instruments (long horns, drums, cymbals), carrying a large water flask, and a bundle with varied contents. The large water flask has stood upon the offering altar during the several days of rites preceding this one, and the water within it has been transformed into Divine nectar (*amṛta*) by these manifold rites.
6. The procession halts at its destination, a well within a small court in the living quarters of the lamas. This well, it is believed, is connected to the ocean by subterranean channels. Having made an offering to the Lord of the place (the spirit who dwells in the courtyard), a text addressed to the serpent demons is read, and rice is thrown into the well at certain points. Offerings are arranged on the table (including cakes, milk, lamps, incense, and flowers).

7. A small painted *maṇḍala* of the Buddha of Healing, having been brought from Hall IV, is consecrated by washing it over the opening of the well with the sacred *amṛta*. Then, the ground colors —having been collected in a small bag—are thrown into the well and the consecrated nectar/water is poured over them, to propitiate the serpent demons (*nāgas*).

That concludes the ceremonies centering around the use of the *maṇḍala* of the Buddha of Healing.

G. CONCLUSION

Images and art are especially important for the worship and invocation of the Buddha of Healing. This can be viewed from the aspect of aesthetic experience and its role in intensifying spiritual experience, uplifting the consciousness to aid in the healing process. Also, images are used as tools for the invocation of the deity in meditation, prayer, and ritual worship. Descriptions of the *rajomaṇḍala* of Bhaiṣajya-guru constructed at the Yung-ho-kung and the associated rituals convey some of the complex symbology and solemn reverence associated with the use of such images, while the translated visualization texts point to the essentially personal aspect of such practices. To become healed, one must do more than construct an image (either physically or mentally): the image must come alive with the spirit force of the Buddha and merge with the viewer. When one's own body becomes the Tathāgata's body, and when one's own mind merges with the Divine Mind, then the most profound healing can take place.

1. Yoshito S. Hakeda, trans., *Kūkai: Major Works* (New York: 1972), pp. 145-146. Phrases in brackets added by translator.
2. Part Two, *Translation I*, p. 124.
3. Lapis has a hardness of 5 to 6 on Mohs' scale. The gem material is in the form of a granular aggregate, with a specific gravity ranging from 2.50 to 3.0 (depending on the amount of pyrite inclusions). See Gemological Institute of America, *Colored Stones*, vol. I (Los Angeles:

1975), chapter sixteen, p. 7. Much of my technical information regarding lapis lazuli and its mine sites is derived from this massive loose-leaf compendium.

4. In addition to Babylonian amulets and cylinder seals made of lapis, numerous Egyptian beads from the predynastic period have been found. See Cyril Aldred, *Jewels of the Pharoahs* (New York: 1971), pp. 33–34.

5. There are several books, unfortunately of varying scholarly reliability, which treat these aspects, including: G. F. Kunz, *The Curious Lore of Precious Stones* (New York: 1971, original edition 1913), dealing with Asia and the Ancient Near East as well as with the European traditions; B. Bhattaccharyya, *Gem Therapy* (Calcutta: 1958), on traditional Hindu healing techniques which employ gems (by the noted author of *The Indian Buddhist Iconography*); W. T. Fernie, *The Occult and Curative Powers of Precious Stones* (Blauvelt, New York: 1973, original edition 1907), chiefly relying on Latin and Greek sources, and the later European traditions.

6. See M. W. de Visser's charts relating the Twelve *Yakṣas* to zodiacal signs in *Ancient Buddhism in Japan,* vol. II (Leiden: 1935), pp. 551–553. Japanese iconographic drawings reflecting T'ang Chinese traditions often depict the Twelve *Yakṣas* with a different animal astrological symbol in the headdress of each general.

7. Alex Wayman, "Notes on the three myrobalans," *Phi Theta Annual* 5 (1954–5), p. 67.

8. Wayman, "Notes on the three myrobalans," pp. 64–65.

9. Alex Wayman and Hideko Wayman, trans., *The Lion's Roar of Queen Śrīmālā* (New York: 1974), p. 52.

10. For more on Asklepios, see C. Kerenyi, *Asklepios* (New York: 1959), and W. A. Jayne, *The Healing Gods of Ancient Civilizations* (New York: 1962, reprint of 1925 edition). For the Tun-huang paintings, see Nicole Nicolas-Vandier, *et al.*, *Bannières et Peintures de Touen-houang Conservées au Musée Guimet,* 2 vols. (Paris: 1974–1976).

11. See Plate Six, where the artist of a Tibetan *thanka* has depicted a *pūjā* offering performed by monks, apparently for the benefit of a wealthy donor and his family. This scene is depicted directly below the throne of Bhaiṣajya-guru with his two Bodhisattva attendants.

12. Part Two, *Translation III,* p. 161. By the inclusion of this ritual we can see that the composers of the *sūtra* were influenced by the burgeoning Mahāyāna cult of the book, in which the physical scripture was worshipped as a locus of the Buddha's strength, protection, and blessings. This "cult of the book" is especially evident in the *Lotus Sūtra* and other works of that tradition. For more information on this aspect of early Mahāyāna practices, see Gregory Schopen,

"The phrase *'sa pṛthivīpradeśaś caityabhūto bhavet'* in the *Vajracchedikā:* notes on the cult of the book in Mahāyāna," *Indo-Iranian Journal* 17 (1975), pp. 147-182.

13. Part Two, *Translation III*, p. 162.
14. Part Two, *Translation III*, p. 162.
15. *Sūtras* specifically advocating the manifold blessings derived from the creation of images and their worship were among the earliest texts translated into Chinese. For example, there is the *Sūtra Spoken by the Buddha on the Creation of Buddha-Images (Fo-shuo tso fo-hsing-hsiang ching)*, T. XVI, 692, believed to be transmitted to China in the late Han, second century C.E.
16. These two spirits are mentioned in various other Buddhist texts, for example, the *Hua-yen ching*, T. IX, 278, p. 680C. Often they are called the Youths of Good and Bad. For a study of them, especially in the context of their association with the Bodhisattva Kṣitigarbha, see Michel Soymié, "Notes d'iconographie chinoise: Les acolytes de Ti-tsang," *Arts Asiatiques* 14 (1966), pp. 45-78; and 16 (1967), pp. 141-170.
17. Of course, self-transformation is not exclusively Buddhist. Compare this traditional Buddhist account of the dying process, the judgment of karma, and return to consciousness to the strikingly similar contemporary accounts of personal experiences as told by persons of widely dissimilar backgrounds who have shared the experience of "clinical death" and subsequent revival. See Raymond A. Moody, Jr., *Life After Life* (New York: 1976).
18. Part Two, *Translation III*, p. 166.
19. Part Two, *Translation III*, p. 169.
20. Anonymous, *Yao-shih liu-li-kuang ju-lai hsiao-tsai ch'u-nan nien-sung i-kuei*, T. XIX, 922, p. 20B.
21. Amoghavajra, trans., *Yao-shih ju-lai nien-sung i-kuei*, T. XIX, 924A, pp. 29B-30B. See also T. XIX, 922-928, pp. 20B-67B. Most of these texts suggest similar rituals, and they repeat variants on the Bhaiṣajya-guru *mantra: "Namo bhagavate bhaiṣajya-guru-vaiḍūrya-prabhā-*guru *mantra: "Namo bhagavate bhaiṣajya-guru-vaiḍūrya-prabhā-rājāya tathāgatāyārhate samyak-saṃbuddhāya tad yathā. Oṃ bhaiṣajye bhaiṣajye bhaiṣajya-samudgate svāhā."* See also my Translation III, p. 160.
22. According to Dale Saunders, this *mudrā* "is so called because this gesture, by binding sentient beings, prevents them from falling into fear or calamities." Cf. his *Mudrā* (New York: 1960), p. 220.
23. T. XIX, 924A, pp. 29B-C.
24. T. XIX, pp. 29C-30A.
25. The three poisons are lust, anger, and delusion. The commentary to

the text identifies the plant as the *a-ru-ru* (myrobalan), calling it the "king among medicines."

26. Sun Ching-feng, ed. and trans., *Yao-shih ju-lai hsien-kuan chien-lüeh i-kuei (Concise Rituals for Meditation on the Master of Healing Tathāgata)* (Shanghai: 1940), pp. 2A–B. This appears to be a Chinese translation of a native Tibetan *sādhana.*
27. Anonymous, *Shingon Buddhist Service Book* (Kōyasan, Japan: 1975), p. 29. Also discussed in Yoritomi Motohiro, *Jōyō Shingon no Kaisetsu* (Tokyo: 1975), pp. 358–359. John Blofeld remembers having learned this *mantra* during his early studies of Shingon in Hong Kong. The Sino-Japanese pronunciation of the Sanskrit, according to his memory, is "Ong kalo kalo sendari matongi sawaka." He states that "it has proved to be peculiarly effective in allaying fear or hysteria in others." See his *Mantras: Sacred Words of Power* (New York: 1977), p. 12.
28. Johannes Prip-Møller, *Chinese Buddhist Monasteries* (Hong Kong: 1968), p. 36.
29. Holmes Welch, *The Practice of Chinese Buddhism, 1900–1950* (Cambridge, Mass.: 1967), pp. 195–197.
30. Welch, *The Practice of Chinese Buddhism,* p. 197.
31. Welch, *The Practice of Chinese Buddhism,* p. 203.
32. From *Rin Lhan,* vol. *Ga,* folios 121a–2 to 127a–6. The draft translation was made from the copy of this text in the library of the University of California at Berkeley.
33. Alex Wayman, draft translation, *Bhaiṣajya-guru, the Seven Brothers,* p. 3.
34. The Sanskrit names were derived by matching them to the corresponding Tibetan names written on the blockprint series of the "Three Hundred Icons" published by Lokesh Chandra (New Delhi: n.d.). It becomes obvious through comparison that the *mudrās* described in the *sādhana* text do not fully correspond to those depicted in the blockprints; in fact, there is some variation of these gestures in various art renderings. Also, there is some variation in colors. L. A. Waddell, in *The Buddhism of Tibet, or Lamaism* (Cambridge: 1967, second edition), p. 354 lists the Seven Healing Buddhas identical in all respects to the *sādhana* text description, except here Suvarṇa-bhadra-vimala-ratna-prabhāsa is colored yellowish-white, rather than red-yellow.
35. Wayman, draft translation, *Bhaiṣajya-guru, the Seven Brothers,* p. 5.
36. Wayman, draft translation, *Bhaiṣajya-guru, the Seven Brothers,* p. 5.
37. I have been unable to identify this being; Professor Wayman has suggested to me that this person may be the guru under whom Bhaiṣajya-guru made his original Bodhisattva vows.

38. Wayman, draft translation, *Bhaiṣajya-guru, the Seven Brothers,* p. 6.
39. For further information about the Yung-ho-kung, including studies of the deities in the entrance courts and Halls I and II, see F. D. Lessing's *Yung-ho-kung* (Stockholm: 1942).
40. F. D. Lessing draft manuscripts, Bhaiṣajya-guru IV. 47a–b. Lessing lists seven of the eight offerings. However, based on Mkhas grub rje's statement regarding offering materials for different types of rites: ". . . for appeasing rites (*śāntika*) and their superior *siddhi,* barley and milk are required." (F. D. Lessing and Alex Wayman, trans., *The Fundamentals of the Buddhist Tantras* [The Hague: 1968], p. 177): barley is most likely the eighth offering material. With regard to the rites centered around the Bhaiṣajya-guru altar, Alex Wayman briefly notes: "Perhaps the most important of all special rites in the category of 'appeasing' is the cult of Bhaiṣajya-guru." (Alex Wayman, *The Buddhist Tantras* [New York: 1973], p. 77).
41. Quoted in F. D. Lessing and Alex Wayman, trans., *Mkhas grub rje's Fundamentals of the Buddhist Tantras,* (The Hague: 1968), p. 270, fn. 1.
42. Lessing notes (according to an unnamed manuscript text) that "The dwelling place of Yum-chen-mo is the *prajñā-pāramitā.*" Lessing draft manuscripts, Bhaiṣajya-guru: Description of *Maṇḍala* (B), p. 5. Giuseppe Tucci also identifies Yum-chen-mo with the female deity Prajñā-pāramitā, who is usually portrayed as a Bodhisattva, in *Tibetan Painted Scrolls,* vol. II (Rome: 1949), p. 700, fn. 620.
43. Lessing draft manuscripts, Bhaiṣajya-guru: Description of *Maṇḍala* (B), p. 6.
44. I wish to thank Professor Alexander C. Soper of the Institute of Fine Arts, New York University, for giving me the opportunity to study the reproduction scrolls of this series in his collection.
45. Lessing draft manuscripts, Bhaiṣajya-guru: Descriptions of *Maṇḍala* (B), p. 2.
46. Lessing draft manuscripts, Bhaiṣajya-guru: Descriptions of *Maṇḍala* (B), p. 4.
47. B. C. Olschak and Thubten Wangyal, *Mystic Art of Ancient Tibet* (New York: 1973), p. 38. Here again, the images are so small as to preclude anything more than tentative identifications.
48. Lessing draft manuscripts, Bhaiṣajya-guru: Descriptions of *Maṇḍala* (A), p. 2.
49. Lessing draft manuscripts, Bhaiṣajya-guru: Descriptions of *Maṇḍala* (2nd ed.), p. 3.
50. For more on the Four Guardians and their healing functions, see Lessing's *Yung-ho-kung,* pp. 38–51.
51. For further discussion of *maṇḍala* symbolism, see Alex Wayman's

chapter "Symbolism of the *Maṇḍala*-Palace," in his *The Buddhist Tantras*, pp. 82–109. Here, quoting from commentarial sources, the complex symbolism underlying the construction of the *maṇḍala*-palace is revealed. Also, see Giuseppe Tucci's *Tibetan Painted Scrolls*, vol. I, pp. 318–320; and Tucci's *The Theory and Practice of the Maṇḍala* (London: 1969).

52. Lessing's notes are based on observation of the ceremony at Yung-ho-kung and his reading of the corresponding Tibetan text, *A-ru-ra stom-mchod kyi 'don bsgrigs* [*Order in Which to Read the Thousandfold Myrobalan Offering*]. His notes are found in two sections of his draft manuscripts: "Bhaiṣajya-guru Cult: Various Texts Analyzed and Annotated" (25 pp.) and "Bhaiṣajya-guru Cult: Thousandfold Myrobalan Oblations—Analysis and Notes (4 pp.).

53. *A-ru-ra stom mchod kyi 'don bsgrigs*, fol. 1, as quoted in Lessing draft manuscripts, Bhaiṣajya-guru Cult: Thousandfold Myrobalan Oblation—Analysis and Notes, p. 1.

54. Lessing draft manuscripts, Bhaiṣajya-guru Cult: Thousandfold Myrobalan Oblation, fol. 2b, p. 3.

55. Lessing draft manuscripts, Bhaiṣajya-guru Cult: Thousandfold Myrobalan Oblation, fol. 2b, p. 3.

56. Lessing draft manuscripts, Bhaiṣajya-guru Cult: Thousandfold Myrobalan Oblation, fol. 2b–3b, p. 4.

57. Including his Bhaiṣajya-guru Cult: *Mdun bskyed abhiṣeka* (2 pp.); Bhaiṣajya-guru Ritual: Summary of Observations (2 pp.); Bhaiṣajya-guru Cult: Consecration Text A (2 pp.); Bhaiṣajya-guru Cult: Various Texts Analyzed and Annotated (25 pp.); and Bhaiṣajya-guru Cult: *Abhiṣeka* Text C, Observations and Analysis (7 pp.).

58. Lessing draft manuscripts, Bhaiṣajya-guru Cult: *Abhiṣeka* Text C, Observations and Analysis, p. 5.

59. As described in Lessing draft manuscripts, Bhaiṣajya-guru: Destruction of the *Maṇḍala* (3 pp.).

60. Lessing draft manuscripts, Bhaiṣajya-guru: Destruction of the *Maṇḍala*, p. 2. Lessing was not permitted to observe this.

PART TWO

TRANSLATIONS FROM THE CHINESE BUDDHIST CANON

TRANSLATION I

Sūtra Spoken by the Buddha on the Contemplation of the Two Bodhisattvas, King of Healing and Supreme Healer

(Fo-shuo kuan Yao-wang Yao-shang erh-p'u-sa ching)

From the Chinese version by the Central Asian Tripiṭaka Master Kālayaśas (ca. 424), T. XX, 1161.

INTRODUCTION: HIGHLIGHTING THE TWO BODHISATTVAS

Thus have I heard; once the Buddha dwelt at the monastic abode of the Blue Lotus Pond in the Markaṭa (Monkey) Grove of the state of Vaiśālī. Together with him was an assembly of 1,250 eminent monks, including the Venerable Mahākāśyapa, the Venerable Śāriputra, the Venerable Mahāmaudgalyāyana, the Venerable Mahākātyāyana, and other learned disciples. Also there were 10,000 Bodhisattva-mahāsattvas,[1] including the Bodhisattva Wonderful Arm, the Bodhisattva Skillful Voice, the Bodhisattva Tranquil Voice, the Bodhisattva Jewel Virtue, the Bodhisattva Wise Virtue, the Bodhisattva Gentle Glory (Mañjuśrī), the Bodhisattva Loving Kindness (Maitreya), and other supreme leaders like them. Further, 10 million Bodhisattva-mahāsattvas came from the ten directions,[2] including the Bodhisattva Sage Leader, the Bodhisattva Talented Leader, the Bodhisattva Observer of the Cries of the World (Avalokiteśvara), and Bodhisattva Gainer of Great Strength (Mahāsthāmaprāpta), the Bodhisattva King of Healing, the Bodhisattva Supreme Healer, the Bodhisattva Universally Worthy (Samantabhadra), the Bodhisattva Sage Protector, the

Bodhisattva Brahmādeva, the Bodhisattva Pure Banner, and others. Further, five hundred Licchāvis of Vaiśālī,[3] including the elder[4] Lunar Canopy, his son Jewel Heap, and others all gathered there.

At that time the Lord entered into the *samādhi* (profound concentration, meditative trance) of Universal Light. All the pores of his body emitted multi-hued rays, illuminating the Markaṭa Grove with the colors of the seven precious substances.[5] The light rising above the grove became a jeweled canopy, and various phenomena, rare to the realms of the Ten Directions, appeared within the canopy.

Then Jewel Heap, the elder's son, rose from his seat, faced Ānanda's place, and addressed him: "O Virtuous One, today the Lord has entered into *samādhi,* and his entire body has blazed with light. Surely he will speak on the sublime doctrine. I sincerely wish, O Virtuous One, to know when he shall do so."

Ānanda replied, "Son of the elder, the Buddha has entered into *samādhi,* and I dare not ask him."

When he said these words, the Buddha's eyes radiated light which illumined the foreheads of the two Bodhisattvas King of Healing and Supreme Healer. Above their foreheads, all the limitless Buddhas of the Ten Directions dazzlingly manifested like a diamond mountain, and all these Lords also emitted light from their eyes which universally illumined the foreheads of all the Bodhisattvas [in the assembly]. Above the foreheads of the Bodhisattvas, all the Bodhisattva-mahāsattvas of the realms of the Ten Directions who had attained the *śūraṃgama samādhi* brilliantly appeared, resembling a lapis lazuli mountain.[6]

At the manifestation of this form, a jeweled lotus blossom arose in the Markaṭa Pond. It was the color of a white gem, but this color was a white so rare that there is nothing to which it can be compared.

Various manifested Buddhas[7] were seated on the lotus blossom, their bodies subtle and sublime. They, too, entered into *samādhi.* Each radiated light from his eyes which illumined the foreheads of the two Bodhisattvas King of Healing and Supreme Healer, and further illumined the foreheads of all the Bodhisattvas.

At that time, the Lord withdrew from *samādhi.* With a subtle smile of radiant harmony, the Buddha exhaled through his mouth five-colored rays, which completely illumined his full-moon-like face. Then, there were manifold changing manifestations of light from the features of the Buddha's face, which appeared a million times more glorious than his ordinary appearance.

THE NAMES OF THE TWO BODHISATTVAS AND THEIR SACRED FORMULAE

The elder's son, Jewel Heap, observed the awesome features of the Buddha and said in praise, "This is rare indeed." Then he rose from his seat, adjusted his clothing, and—baring his right arm [as a mark of respect]—he circumambulated the Buddha seven times. He knelt, clasped his palms together, and reverently gazed upwards at the Honored One. With unwavering gaze, he addressed the Buddha and said: "O Lord, today you have emitted a great radiance which has shined upon all the Buddhas and Bodhisattvas of the Ten Directions. They now have all gathered together like a cloud. I seek a few answers in the ocean of the Buddha-Law, and I sincerely wish, O Lord, that you will explain them for my sake."

The Buddha told Jewel Heap, "You may question me freely."

Then Jewel Heap addressed the Buddha and said: "O Lord, today you have emitted rays from both eyes, and these rays rest upon the foreheads of the two Bodhisattvas King of Healing and Supreme Healer, like a diamond mountain. All the Buddhas and Bodhisattvas of the Ten Directions dazzlingly manifest as this mountain of light. The radiance of the awesome virtue of these two Bodhisattvas is like the brilliant manifestation of the permutations of the *cintāmaṇi* gem.[8]

"Their excellence exceeds that of the other Bodhisattvas a millionfold. After your *parinirvāṇa,* when the genuine Teachings have perished, if there are any beings who hear the names of these two Bodhisattvas, they will obtain whatever blessings they seek. If a good son or daughter [of the Buddhist family] seeks to cut off the fetters of negative karma, how should he contemplate the radiant bodies of King of Healing and Supreme Healer?"

The Buddha told Jewel Heap: "Listen carefully, and with excellent thoughts be mindful of what I say. I will analyze and explain it for you."

When he spoke these words, the sons of the 500 elders rose simultaneously and made obeisances to the Buddha. Each offered blue lotus blossoms to the Buddha, wishing for the joy [of the teachings] and desiring to hear [his words].

At that time the entire great assembly including the Bodhisattvas praised Jewel Heap in unison, chanting: "Excellent, excellent, Jewel Heap. On behalf of those blinded beings of the future age, you are able to ask about the method of *abhiṣeka* by the sublime medicine of the sweet dew bestowed by the Tathāgata."[9]

Having spoken these words, they all became silent. The Buddha told Jewel Heap: "Beings in the future may hear the names of the two Bodhisattvas King of Healing and Supreme Healer by achieving five prerequisites. What are the five? (1) One's mind should unceasingly radiate loving kindness. One should perfect the Buddha's moral precepts, never breaking the principles of majestic conduct. (2) One should see to the filial care of one's parents, and should practice the ten wholesome precepts of life in the world.[10] (3) One's body and mind should be peaceful and quiescent, with thoughts bound to that which is free of disorder. (4) One should listen to the *vaipulya sūtras* (the "expanded," Mahāyāna texts) without harboring suspicions or doubts, neither drowning [in emotions] nor backsliding [in spiritual progress]. (5) One should believe in the eternity of the Buddha, and the mind should unceasingly flow like a running stream towards ultimate truth."

The Buddha told Jewel Heap: "If there are any living beings who are complete in these five qualities, in incarnation after incarnation they will always hear the names of these two Bodhisattvas, and they will also hear the names of the various Buddhas and Bodhisattvas of the Ten Directions. When they hear the *vaipulya sūtras*, they will harbor neither doubt nor suspicion. Due to the awesome spiritual force transmitted through hearing the names of these two Bodhisattvas, in incarnation after incarnation for 500 *asaṃkhyeya*[11] aeons, they will never sink to a woesome path of existence."

When the Buddha said these words, the Bodhisattva King of Healing, receiving [through inspiration] the Buddha's awesome spiritual force, uttered a *dhāraṇī,*[12] saying:

> A-mu-chia mo-ho-mu-chia tso-li mo-ho-tso-li t'o-ch'ih mo-ho-t'o-ch'ih ch'ang-ch'iu-li mo-ho-ch'ang-ch'iu-li wu-mo-chih mo-ho-wu-mo-chih t'o-ch'ih-t'o-ch'ih mo-ho-t'o-ch'ih t'ou-ti-t'ou-ti mo-ho-t'ou-ti a-t'ou-a-t'ou mo-ho-a-t'ou shu-che-chia mo-ho-shu-che-chia t'o-she-mei mo-ho-t'o-she-mei to-t'ou-to-t'ou mo-ho-to-t'ou chia-liu-ni-chia t'o-she-lo-so-ha a-chu-ch'iu-a-chu-ch'iu mo-teng-ch'i po-teng che-ti'i che-shu-chia-t'i fo-t'o che-li chia-liu-ni-chia so-ha.

After the Bodhisattva-mahāsattva King of Healing uttered this *dhāraṇī,* he addressed the Buddha and said: "O Lord, the 80 million Buddhas of the past have disseminated sacred formulae like this one. Now the present Buddha—Śākyamuni—and the 1,000 Buddhas to come in this [present] aeon known as Bhadra (Auspicious)[13] also will utter this *dhāraṇī.* After the Buddha's *parinirvāṇa,* if there are any monks or nuns, laymen or laywomen who recite it and who hold to it, they shall be purified of all their veils of karma, veils of karmic retributions, and defilements. Such a person will speedily obtain their removal and extinction, and in the present life he will cultivate various *samādhis.* In the midst of his thoughts, he will see the Buddha's form. To the end of his life, he will neither forget nor lose the aspiration to attain Perfect Enlightenment. Such a person will never encounter in the present life *yakṣas* [who sometimes cause disease through demonic possession], feverish *pretas* [ghosts with enormous stomachs and throats the size of a needle, thus having an insatiable appetite], *rākṣasas* [a type of demon], *kumbhāṇḍas* [demons shaped like gourds, who devour the vitality of men], *kṛtyas* [corpse-raising demons], *piśacas* [a sort of goblin], and all other evil spirits who feed on man's vitality and are able to harm him. When the life of such a person reaches its end, the Buddhas of the Ten Directions all will come to welcome him. In accordance with his choice, he will be reborn into a pure land of another region."

At that time the Lord praised the Bodhisattva King of Healing, saying, "Excellent, excellent, good son. I am profoundly happy that you have uttered this *dhāraṇī*, which has also been uttered by all the Buddhas of the past, present, and future."

Then, the Bodhisattva Supreme Healer also came before the Buddha and uttered a *dhāraṇī*, saying:

> Nan-na-mou cheng-t'un-ching liu-ching-ch'iu-liu-ching ch'iu chia-liu-ni-chia li-mou-li-mou-chia-liu-ni-chia pi-t'i-pi-t'i chia-liu-ni-chia a-pi-t'i-t'o-a-pien-t'o-a-pien-t'o chia-liu-ni-chia shan-che-lo so-ha.

After the Bodhisattva Supreme Healer uttered this *dhāraṇī*, he addressed the Buddha: "O Lord, I now have uttered before you this consecrating *dhāraṇī* that subdues the sea of afflictions. This *dhāraṇī* is what has been disseminated by the Buddhas of the past, present, and future. If there are any monks, nuns, laymen, or lay-women who listen to this *dhāraṇī*, recite it, and hold to it, they will gain the ten meritorious blessings. What are these ten?

1. Due to the awesome spiritual force of this *dhāraṇī*, they can obtain purification from diseases, [even those stemming from] the retribution for killing a living being.
2. The bad reputation gained by breaking the precepts can be completely eliminated.
3. A human or non-human being cannot take advantage of them.
4. Everything that is recited, read, or reflected upon will be retained without forgetting, just as Ānanda is able to do.[14]
5. They will be revered by Indra, Brahmā, the Lokapālas, and all the *devas*.
6. They will be profoundly respected by kings and great ministers.
7. The masters of the ninety-five types of heretical doctrines will be unable to oppress them.
8. Their minds will roam in *dhyāna* and *samādhi* from this unhappy world to a joyous one.
9. They will be held in the protective thoughts of the Buddhas and Bodhisattvas of the Ten Directions.
10. When they reach the end of their span of life, they will purify and eliminate their karmic obstructions. The Bud-

dhas of the Ten Directions will emit golden-hued rays, and Buddhas will all come to receive and welcome them, speaking to them about the sublime teachings. In accordance with their choice, they will be reborn in [one of the] pure Buddha lands."

After the Bodhisattva Supreme Healer uttered this *dhāraṇī,* he clasped his palms together, reverently prostrated himself with his head at the Buddha's feet, and withdrew to one side.

The Lord then praised the Bodhisattva Supreme Healer, saying, "Excellent, excellent, my good son. I am pleased that you have uttered this *dhāraṇī,* which also has been uttered by the past, present, and future Buddhas of the Ten Directions. I am truly delighted with you."

When the two Bodhisattvas had uttered these formulae, each took off a necklace of precious gems, offering them in worship to the Buddha. The necklace which the Bodhisattva King of Healing offered rested on the Buddha's left shoulder like Mt. Sumeru, while the Bodhisattva Supreme Healer's necklace took a similar form on the Buddha's right shoulder. Upon the crest of the two mountains there was a palace of the Brahmā King and there were hundreds of thousands of millions of Brahmādeva kings reverently clasping their palms together in attendance.[15]

Within the palace there was a jeweled lotus blossom, which entirely covered the 3000 myriads of worlds like the *maṇi* gem. Those beings atop the palace walls suddenly descended in unison, appearing like [the opening of] a thousand petals of a golden flower. Going within the palace walls, Buddhas from the Ten Directions were seated on golden blossoms. The name of the Buddha from the East was Radiant Lamp of Mt. Sumeru. The name of the Buddha of the Southeast was Glorious Adornment of the Precious Treasury. The Buddha of the South was Chien-tang Maṇi Light.[16] The Buddha of the Southwest was the Sovereign King of the Golden Sea. The Buddha of the West was the King of the Radiance of Great Compassion. The Buddha of the Northwest was named Rare Lotus of the Abundant Alms-Bowl. The Buddha of the North was the King Gloriously Adorned with a Lotus Blossom Beard. The Buddha of the Northeast was named Sovereign King of Adamantine Strength. The Buddha of the Zenith was named the King as Rare as the Moon, and the Buddha of the Nadir was named King of the Rays of Sun and Moon.

From their separate mouths, these Buddhas of the Ten Directions spoke as one: "Praiseworthy indeed are the words of the Bodhisattvas King of Healing and Supreme Healer. The formulae which you have uttered have been disseminated by all the Buddhas of the Ten Directions and Three Ages. When we ourselves were about to enter onto the Bodhisattva Path [in the distant past], we heard these *dhāraṇīs,* and from the depths of our hearts we responded with joy. Due to the causes of this joyous response and our wholesome roots, we obtained release from the faults incurred in 596 million aeons of dwelling in *saṃsāra,* and now we have obtained perfection as Buddhas. In hearing the names of the Buddhas of the Ten Directions, you have obtained elimination of the faults of a million aeons of dwelling in *saṃsāra.* How much more so [will you gain] if you accept and uphold, read and recite these names, and worship them, offering *pūjā.*"

PROPHECY OF THE FUTURE ACHIEVEMENTS OF THE TWO BODHISATTVAS

When the Buddhas of the Ten Directions had spoken thus, they entered into meditative trance, became silent, and were seated. Then, Śākyamuni Buddha told the great assembly: "You now have seen the two Bodhisattvas King of Healing and Supreme Healer worship me by offering jeweled necklaces and clasping their palms together before me, have you not?"

At this time Maitreya, as leader of the great assembly, addressed the Buddha and said, "O Lord, it is indeed so. I have seen it."

The Buddha told Maitreya: "Invincible One, this Bodhisattva King of Healing has long cultivated the pure path, and when he has fulfilled his various vows, he will—in a future age which can be ascertained—become a Buddha named Pure Eye Tathāgata, Arhat, Omniscient One, Perfect in Knowledge and Conduct, Well Gone, Knower of the World, Supreme Master, Tamer of Passions, Teacher of *Devas* and Men, Buddha, Lord. His realm will be named Radiance of Constant Peace and Joy, and his aeon shall be known as Fully Victorious.

"When that Buddha emerges in the world, his land will be adamantine, its white gem-like hue extending to its diamond borders. White jewel flowers will spontaneously rain forth from the sky, completely covering his realm for fifty *yojanas*[17] around.

"The beings of his land will be immune from disease, both physical and mental. The heavens will bestow upon them sweet dew [*amṛta,* the Divine nectar]. However, they will not consider it food; instead they will purely ingest the taste of the unsurpassed Mahāyāna Teachings.

"That Buddha's lifespan will be 500 billion *asaṃkhyeya* aeons. His genuine teachings will abide in the world for four million *asaṃkhyeya* aeons, while the replica doctrine[18] will abide in the world for a billion *asaṃkhyeya* aeons. All who are born in his realm shall dwell within the *dhāraṇī* gates, and whatever they reflect on and concentrate on will not be forgotten."

After the Bodhisattva King of Healing received this prophecy, he arose from his seat, leapt bodily into space, and performed eighteen transformations. Flowers from above were scattered upon the Buddha, and these scattered flowers became arranged in the sky like a grove of golden-blossomed trees.

The Lord then told Maitreya: "This Bodhisattva Supreme Healer will become a Buddha next after King of Healing. He will be called Pure Matrix[19] Tathāgata, Arhat, Omniscient One, Perfect in Knowledge and Conduct, Well Gone, Knower of the World, Supreme Master, Tamer of Passions, Teacher of *Devas* and Men, Buddha, Lord. When Pure Matrix Tathāgata appears in the world, this white-jeweled land will take on a golden hue, and golden flowers and golden rays will completely fill the realm. All the beings in his land will be completely endowed with forbearance of the unoriginated natures.[20]

"The lifespan of Pure Matrix Tathāgata will be sixty-two small aeons, his genuine teachings will abide in the world for 120 small aeons, and the replica teachings will abide for 560 aeons."

When the Bodhisattva Supreme Healer heard and received this prophecy, he entered into *samādhi* and transformed his body into a flower. Like a grove of yellow-blossomed *campaka* trees resplendent with the seven gems, he transformed himself into a cloud of flowers. By means of this cloud of flowers, he paid worship to the Buddha.

From this cloud of flowers golden rays were emitted, and from the midst of these golden rays there emerged a lapis lazuli cloud. From the midst of this lapis lazuli cloud a hymn was chanted:

> O Omniscient Lord,
> Pure Lion of the Śākyas,
> There is none like you in all the Ten Directions.
> The radiance of your wisdom illumines all.
> Out of the all-encompassing sympathy for sentient beings
> You emerged in the world.
> Bowing head and face, I worship you now,
> You, whose great compassion depends not
> On whether creatures accept, do not accept,
> Or are unsure of your Teachings.[21]

When the recitation of this verse was concluded, the Bodhisattva Supreme Healer returned to his original seat.

CONTEMPLATION OF KING OF HEALING

Then, the Buddha told the great assembly: "After my *parinirvāṇa,* if there are any beings who [wish to] fix their thoughts on the sole contemplation of the Bodhisattva King of Healing, they should practice the following five meditations:

1. The meditation of stabilizing thought by counting breaths.
2. The meditation of pacifying and settling the mind.
3. The meditation of the non-exhalation of breath.
4. The meditation of reflection on Absolute Form.
5. The meditation of serene abode in *samādhi.*"

The Buddha told Maitreya: "If any good son or daughter cultivates these five meditations, that person will, in an instant, have a vision of the Bodhisattva King of Healing. This Bodhisattva is twelve *yojanas* tall, though in response to [the limited perception of] sentient beings he may appear to be either a hundred eighty or eight feet in height. His body is purplish gold in hue, and the thirty-two primary marks and eighty secondary marks are excellent in every detail, exactly like those of the Buddha. There are fourteen *maṇi* gems within the tuft of hair on his forehead [the *ūrṇā*], each gem having fourteen facets. Within each of these facets, there are fourteen flowers which adorn his heavenly crown. The Buddhas of the Ten Directions and the various Bodhisattvas are within this heavenly crown, all reflected manifestations, like inlaid jewels. From the mark of the tuft of hair between his eyebrows, there streams out a ray of light the color of white glass,[22] enwrapping his body seven times like a scarf of white jewels.

"A radiant light flows out from the pores of his body. [These beams of light], like fully 84,000 *maṇi* gems, each one turning to the right like a wheel, appear like a wall made of the seven gems or an abundant mass of *pāla* flowers. Upon each flower there is a manifestation Buddha, each having the correct (standard) body sixteen feet tall, just like Śākyamuni.[23] Each Tathāgata has five hundred Bodhisattvas as attendants.

"The two arms of this Bodhisattva King of Healing [glitter] like the hues of a hundred jewels, and the seven precious gems rain forth from the tips of the ten fingers of his hands. If there are any beings who contemplate this Bodhisattva's ten fingertips, then the 404 diseases will spontaneously disappear [in them], and none of the bodily afflictions will arise.

"Diamonds rain down from his two feet, each gem becoming a cloud terrace. On each of these cloud terraces there is a manifestation Bodhisattva with countless *devas* in attendance. At this time the manifestation Bodhisattvas will expound upon the Four Noble Truths, suffering and emptiness, impermanence and egolessness. They also will speak on the profound Bodhisattva practices.

"When this meditation is complete, it is called the 'Initial Contemplation on the Meritorious Form and Appearance of the Bodhisattva King of Healing.'

"The second contemplation consists of the gradual expansion of the mind for the attainment of a vision of the complete form of the Bodhisattva King of Healing. At this time the mind of the Bodhisattva King of Healing is like the *cintāmaṇi* gem, which sends forth ten million rays of light from its pure blossoming. These rays of light encircle his body a hundred times and appear like ten million jeweled mountains. Each of these mountains has ten million jeweled caves, and in each cave there are a million manifestation Buddhas. The marks on their bodies are excellent, and they are all gloriously adorned. From their separate mouths, these manifestation Buddhas will speak as one in praise of the causes and conditions of the fundamental deeds[24] of the Bodhisattva King of Healing. When this form manifests in the midst of one's reflections, the Buddhas of the Ten Directions are seen, who will speak to various wayfarers in accordance with what is suitable [for their development.]

"Then each pore of the Bodhisattva King of Healing will emit rays like ten million *maṇi* gems which illumine all wayfarers. When the wayfarers see this, they will gain purification of their six sense organs [eye, ear, nose, tongue, body, and mind]. When they search them out, they will see all the realms in the Ten Directions and the fifty million billions of Buddhas and the various Bodhisattvas, who will speak to the wayfarers of the sublime medicine, the sweet dew which removes faults. Having swallowed this medicine, the wayfarers will gain [entrance] to the gate of the fifty billion revolving *dhāraṇīs.* This accomplishment is attained through the force of the Bodhisattva King of Healing's fundamental vows. It is due to the conditioned thoughts [of sentient beings] that the Bodhisattva King of Healing gloriously adorns himself.

"The Buddhas of the Ten Directions and the Bodhisattvas will then go before the wayfarers and speak to them about the profound six perfections.[25] Then the wayfarers, due to seeing all the Buddhas, will gain [entrance to] the gate of the *samādhi* sea of the trillion contemplating Buddhas."

The Buddha told Maitreya: "After my *parinirvāṇa,* if there is a *deva* or a *nāga,* a monk or a nun, a layman or a laywoman—if any of them desire to envision the Bodhisattva King of Healing or desire to reflect upon the Bodhisattva King of Healing, that person should cultivate two types of pure conduct. First is the development of the aspiration to attain enlightenment. [Also,] the principles of the majestic conduct of the complete Bodhisattva vows should never be broken. Due to this attainment of the perfection of the Bodhisattva precepts, all the Bodhisattvas of the Ten Directions will accompany this person. When they assemble before him all at once, the Bodhisattva King of Healing shall be their leader. Then, for the sake of the wayfarer, the Bodhisattva King of Healing will expound on the gate of the trillion revolving *dhāraṇīs.* Due to hearing these *dhāraṇīs,* the wayfarer shall be exempted from the faults accrued in ninety million aeons of *saṃsāra.* In response to this, he will then obtain the forbearance of the unoriginated natures.

"Now, secondly, those of the common people bound by their afflictions and passions, who seek to see the Bodhisattva King of Healing after my *parinirvāṇa,* should cultivate four things:

1. They should cultivate thoughts of compassion, neither killing nor offending by committing the ten negatives. Constantly holding [the principles of] the Great Vehicle in their thoughts, they should never let them stray from their minds, and they should fervently cultivate striving zeal, as if to save themselves from fires burning upon their heads.

2. They should provide their guru and parents with the four requisites for life [food, clothing, shelter, medicine], and with lamps fueled by butter, oil, or the oil of the jasmine blossom. Further, they should provide illumination for their guru and parents by means of fires of bamboo and wood. Further, they should provide light by means of lamps fueled by butter, oil and jasmine blossom oil to worship the Three Jewels of the Buddha, the Teaching, and the Order, as well as all who expound the Dharma.

3. They should engage in profound cultivation of *dhyāna* and *samādhi,* taking delight in isolation [for the sake of meditation]. They should constantly joyously dwell below trees in cemeteries. Dwelling in solitude and tranquility, they should strive to cultivate the twelve profound *dhūtas.*[26]

4. They should reject the concepts of body, life, and riches and should not give rise to any fondness [or attachments, desires].

"Practicing this teaching, in the midst of their thoughts, they shall have a vision of the Bodhisattva King of Healing, and he will speak to them on the Teachings. Or, they may see the Bodhisattva King of Healing in a dream, and he will confer his medicine of the

Teachings. After such a person awakes and returns to his usual consciousness, he will be able to remember the manifold affairs of countless hundreds and thousands of past lives, and his mind will be joyous and gladdened.

"He should enter into *stūpas,* contemplate the images there, and prostrate in worship. Before those images, he will obtain a vision of the Buddha in the *samādhi* sea, and he shall see the boundless assembly of Bodhisattvas. He will sincerely envision the Bodhisattva King of Healing, who will speak to him on the Teachings."

The Buddha told Ānanda: "After my *parinirvāna,* if there are any in the four-fold assembly who are able to contemplate the Bodhisattva King of Healing in this way, or who are able to uphold the name of the Bodhisattva King of Healing, it will eliminate the faults of an aeon or even eighty thousand aeons of dwelling in *saṃsāra.* If there are any who are able to call this Bodhisattva King of Healing by his name and whole-heartedly worship him, these persons shall not meet with woeful opposition, and, in the end, they will not have untimely deaths.[27]

"After my *parinirvāṇa,* if there are any beings who are able to contemplate in this manner, it shall be known as the 'correct contemplation.' If they contemplate in different ways, such contemplations are to be known as 'incorrect contemplations.' "

CONTEMPLATION OF SUPREME HEALER

The Buddha told Maitreya: "After my *parinirvāṇa,* if there are any among the fourfold assembly who ask how to contemplate the pure body of the Bodhisattva Supreme Healer, those persons should cultivate seven things. What are these seven?

1. They should take constant delight in holding to the [Bodhisattva] precepts. In this way, to the end of their lives, they will grow close to neither the *śrāvakas* nor the *pratyekabuddhas.*[28]

2. They should constantly cultivate the excellent methods for dwelling within the world and the excellent methods for escaping the world.

3. Their hearts, like the earth, should not give rise to arrogance

and pride. They should develop universal compassion towards all beings.

4. Their hearts should be passionless, incorruptible as diamonds.

5. They should abide in the undifferentiated truth, and never forsake majestic conduct.

6. They should always cultivate discernment, and they should diligently cultivate the calming of the mind.

7. They should not be alarmed when they attain the mind of the great liberating perfection of insight."

The Buddha told Maitreya: "Those good sons or daughters who are complete in these things will speedily obtain a vision of the Bodhisattva Supreme Healer. This Bodhisattva Supreme Healer is sixteen *yojanas* tall. He is purple-gold in hue, and his body emits a radiance like the golden color of the *jambu* (rose-apple) and sandalwood trees. Within this circle of light [his radiant aura], there are 16 millions of manifestation Buddhas, all having a standard height of eight feet, seated in the posture of meditation upon jeweled lotus blossoms. Each manifestation Buddha has sixteen Bodhisattvas in attendance, who each grasp a white blossom.

"This light about his body whirls to the right. Within the radiance that permeates his body are the realms of the Ten Directions, with all the Buddhas, Bodhisattvas, and pure lands manifested there. The *uṣṇīṣa* upon the crown of his head has a *maṇi* gem, like the *śakrābhilagna.*[29] The four sides of the *uṣṇīṣa* glow with golden rays, and in each ray there are four precious blossoms with all the colors of a hundred jewels. On each blossom, there is a manifestation Buddha and there are Bodhisattvas. Some appear, while others are concealed: their number cannot be known.

"This Bodhisattva Supreme Healer has all of the thirty-two primary and eighty secondary marks [of the great man], excellent in every detail. In each of these primary marks there is a five-colored ray, and in each of the secondary marks there are a hundred thousand rays. The mark of the curl of hairs between the eyebrows [the *ūrṇā*] is golden-hued, like that of the *jambu* and sandalwood trees.

"He wears a necklace consisting of a hundred thousand white pearls, and each of these pearls emits white gem-like rays. He is gloriously adorned with golden hairs like crystal pennants, which hold genuine golden images and precious things, rare and marvelous in the world. Glorious adornments all manifest in their midst.

"If there are any in the four-fold assembly who hear the name of this Bodhisattva Supreme Healer, and hold to the name of the Bodhisattva Supreme Healer, and call out the name of the Bodhisattva Supreme Healer, and contemplate the form of this Bodhisattva Supreme Healer, then this Bodhisattva Supreme Healer shall emit a shining light from his body to gather up and receive that person. The radiance of this Bodhisattva may become an image of Iśvaradeva, of Brahmādeva, Māradeva, or of Śakra. It may become images of the Four *Deva* Kings, an *asura,* a *gandharva,* a *kiṃnara,* a *mahorāga,* a *garuḍa,* or a human being or non-human. It may become an image of a serpent, an emperor, a great minister, an elder, a learned layman, a monk, a brahman, a sage, a grandfather or grandmother, a father or mother, or even a brother, sister, beloved wife and children, or relative. It may become an image of an adept physician or an excellent friend.

"At this point, the wayfarer will see in his dreams the various images previously described which accordingly appear to utter to him the *dhāraṇīs* spoken by King of Healing and Supreme Healer. He will then obtain—as has been previously discussed—the elimination of the faults of an aeon. After he awakens, he will still remember these experiences and hold to them, and to the end of his days, he will never forget or lose them. Binding his thoughts in *samādhi,* in this settled state, he will obtain a vision of the pure and sublime form of the Bodhisattva Supreme Healer. [In this vision] the Bodhisattva then will speak to the wayfarer in praise of the names of the Fifty-three Buddhas of the Past. The way in which he recites the names of the Buddhas of the Past is as follows:

1. Universal Light
2. Universal Brilliance
3. Universal Tranquility
4. Incense of *Tamala* Leaves and Sandalwood
5. Sandalwood Light
6. *Maṇi* Banner
7. Joyous Treasury of the Heap of *Maṇi* Jewels

8. Supreme in the Great Striving, Whom All the World Takes Joy in Seeing
9. Shining Lamp of the *Maṇi* Banner
10. Torch of Wisdom Who Illumines the Ten Directions
11. Radiance of the Virtue as Vast as the Sea
12. Universally Radiated Golden Light of Adamantine Firm Strength
13. Great Strength in Striving and Courage
14. Light of Great Compassion
15. King of Merciful Force
16. Treasury of Mercy
17. Gloriously Adorned Excellence of the Sandalwood Cave
18. Worthy and Excellent Leader
19. Excellent Mind
20. King Who is Adorned by Vast Glory
21. Light of the Golden Flower
22. Sovereign King of the Precious Canopy Which Illumines Space
23. Light of the Precious Flower of the Void
24. King Who is Gloriously Adorned with Lapis Lazuli
25. Light of the Universally Manifested Form
26. Light of Unshakable Insight
27. King Who Causes All Demons to Submit
28. Radiance of Adept Talent
29. Victorious Insight and Wisdom
30. Sagely Light of Loving Kindness
31. Light Which Makes the World Serene
32. King of the Sublime and Honored Insight, and Excellent Quiescent Lunar Sound
33. Honored King of the Supreme Insight of the *Nāgas*
34. Light of the Sun and Moon
35. Light of the Gems of the Sun and Moon
36. King of the Victorious Banner of Wisdom
37. King of the Sovereign Force of the Lion's Roar
38. Victory of the Sublime Sound
39. Banner of Eternal Light
40. Lamp That Observes the World
41. Awesome Lamp of Wisdom King
42. Victory of the Dharma King
43. Light of Mt. Sumeru
44. Light of the Jasmine Blossom
45. King as Extraordinary as the Udumbara Blossom (which blooms only once every 3,000 years)

46. King Who Has the Force of Great Wisdom
47. Light of Imperturbable Joy
48. King of Limitless Sound
49. Adept Light
50. Light of the Golden Sea
51. Sovereign and Universal King of the Wisdom of Mountains and Seas
52. Great Universal Light
53. Buddha Who is King of the Eternal Completion of All Things

"When the Bodhisattva Supreme Healer recites the names of the Fifty-three Buddhas of the Past, he will become silent and remain in his place. Then, the wayfarer will obtain a vision in *samādhi* of the Seven Lord Buddhas of the Past.

"Vipaśyin Buddha will praise him, saying: 'Excellent, excellent, good son! The Fifty-three Buddhas whom you have mentioned dwelt on the earth in the far-distant past. They brought all beings to maturity and achieved *parinirvāṇa.* If there are any good sons or daughters, indeed, if there are any beings at all who hear the names of the Fifty-three Buddhas, these beings will not fall onto a woesome path of existence for ten trillion *asaṃkhyeyas* of aeons.

'If, furthermore, there is a person who is able to praise these Fifty-three Buddhas, in whatever place he is reborn, he will constantly meet with the various Buddhas of the Ten Directions.

'Further, if there is a person who is able to revere and worship the Fifty-three Buddhas with perfect sincerity, he will be able to eliminate the four grave offenses,[30] the five rebellious acts,[31] slander, disobedience, and so on: all these faults will become completely purified due to the fundamental vows made by the Buddhas [when they first stepped out upon the Bodhisattva path]. Thus, in recalling the Buddhas, he will obtain the elimination of these various faults as has been described above.'

"Śikhin Buddha, Viśvabhu Buddha, Krakucchanda Buddha, Kanakamuni Buddha, and Kāśyapa Buddha all will praise the names of the Fifty-three Buddhas. Further, they will praise those good sons and daughters who are able to hear the names, and who are able to revere and worship them, thus eliminating the obstructions created by faults, as has been explained above."

At this point, Śākyamuni Buddha told the great assembly: "Once, when I lived in an aeon in the unfathomable past, in the period of the degeneration and extinction of the teachings of the Buddha Sublime Light, I left my home to study the Way. I heard the names of these Fifty-three Buddhas, and after hearing them I clasped my palms together and joy arose in my heart. Afterwards, I taught others and enabled them to hear and uphold [the names]. When other persons heard, they in turn taught still more, amounting in the end to 3,000 persons. These 3,000 persons from their separate mouths spoke as one in praise of all the Buddhas' names and whole-heartedly revered and worshipped them. Because of the force of the merits gained through revering and worshipping the Buddhas, they obtained release from the faults of countless millions of aeons of dwelling in *saṃsāra.* The initial 1,000 persons began with Buddha Flower Ray as head, down to the Buddha Viśvabhu. In the aeon 'Glorious Adornment,' they obtained perfection as the 1,000 Buddhas of the Past. The middle 1,000 Buddhas began with Krakucchanda Buddha as head, down to Rucika Tathāgata. In the *Bhadra kalpa,* the 'Auspicious' aeon, one by one, in order, they will attain enlightenment. Of the final 1,000 Buddhas, Solar Ray Tathāgata will be the head down to Merudhvaja. They will become Buddhas in the 'Stellar' aeon."

The Buddha told Jewel Heap: "All the present Buddhas in the Ten Directions, those Tathāgatas of excellent virtues, each have also achieved Buddhahood in the Ten Directions because they heard the name of the Fifty-three Buddhas.

"If there are any sentient beings who desire to obtain release from the faults of the four grave prohibitions, if they desire to obtain confession and repentance of the five rebellious acts and the ten negative things, if they desire release from the extremely grave fault of baseless slander of the teachings, they should zealously recite the formulae of the two Bodhisattvas, King of Healing and Supreme Healer, which were previously described. Also, they should reverently worship the Buddhas of the Ten Directions mentioned previously. Further, they should reverently worship the Seven Buddhas of the Past, they should reverently worship the Fifty-three Buddhas, the Thousand Buddhas of the *Bhadra kalpa,* and the Thirty-five Buddhas. Finally, they should universally worship all the countless Buddhas of the Ten Directions. Six times during the day and night, with heart and mind clear and keen like a flowing river, they should practice the teachings of confession and repentance. Afterwards, they should fix their thoughts on the pure forms of the two Bodhisattvas, King of Healing and Supreme Healer.

"Now, you should know that one who concentrates on these two Bodhisattvas King of Healing and Supreme Healer has already in limitless past aeons sown wholesome seeds in the places of various Buddhas. Due to the glorious adornment of the force of these fundamental wholesome seeds, such a person can, in a moment's flash, obtain a vision of the countless Buddhas of the East. At this time, all the Buddhas of the East will enter together into the *samādhi* of 'The Universal Manifestation of Form.' The Buddhas of the South, North, the Four Intermediate Directions, the Zenith and the Nadir also will all similarly enter together into the *samādhi* of 'The Universal Manifestation of Form.' They all will manifest their forms before the wayfarer in order to speak to him about the extremely profound six perfections.

"When the wayfarer has seen all the Buddhas at this time, joy will well up in his heart. Before all the Buddhas, he will then attain to the *samādhi* sea of the profound contemplation on the Buddha, and he will view countless Buddhas. Unanimously all these Lords will confer a prophecy on the wayfarer, saying these words: 'Because you now have recalled these two Bodhisattvas, in a future age you will become a Buddha.'

"When the wayfarer hears this prophecy, his body and mind will be glad and joyous, and he will then attain to a *samādhi* known as 'Beyond Adornment.'[32]

"Due to the force of this *samādhi,* his spiritual progress will be increased twofold. When he sees the innumerable Buddhas of the Ten Directions universally, some of them—for the sake of the wayfarer—will speak on the perfection of giving. Some will speak to this wayfarer on the perfection of morality, some will speak to him on the perfection of forbearance, some will speak to him on the perfection of striving, some will speak to the wayfarer on the perfection of meditation, some will speak to the wayfarer on the perfection of insight, some will speak to the wayfarer on the perfection of expedient means, some will speak to the wayfarer on the perfection of vows, some will speak to the wayfarer on the perfection of strength [of purpose], some will speak to the wayfarer on the perfection of wisdom. Some will speak to the wayfarer on:

compassion, loving kindness, sympathetic joy, and equanimity; the four stations of mindfulness;[33] the four right efforts;[34] the four steps towards supranormal powers;[35] the five spiritual faculties; their five powers;[36] the seven limbs of enlightenment;[37] the eightfold noble path;[38] the noble truth of suffering; the noble truth of the origination [of suffering]; the noble truth of the extinction [of suffering]; the noble truth of the path; the six points of reverent harmony [in a monastery or convent];[39] the six thoughts on which to dwell;[40] and in this way they will analyze and describe the gates to the boundless Law.

"Next, due to the force of this *samādhi* known as 'Beyond Adornment,' they will analyze and explain for the wayfarer the profound teaching of twelvefold dependent origination.[41]

"Due to the awesome spiritual force of the two Bodhisattvas, King of Healing and Supreme Healer, he then will have a vision of the limitless Buddhas of the East, and the various Bodhisattvas. Their forms are purple-gold in hue and their features are excellent beyond compare. He will also see all the Buddhas of the South, West, North, and East, the Four Intermediate Directions, the Zenith, and the Nadir, and the form and features of each of these Buddhas will be excellent. Broadly described, it is similar to the *samādhi* sea attained by contemplation on the Buddha.

"A wayfarer who calls out the names of these two Bodhisattvas King of Healing and Supreme Healer, who recollects the names of these two Bodhisattvas, who holds to the names of these two Bodhisattvas, who contemplates the forms of these two Bodhisattvas, or who recites the spiritual formulae uttered by these two Bodhisattvas will cast away his attachment to form and in a future age he will attain the purification of the six sense organs. Persevering, he will attain birth into the great Bodhisattva family. His face and appearance will be extremely majestic like Sovereign Śakra, with none of the features of one who is able to commit negative acts. Having great physical strength, he will be like [the hero of Divine power] Nārāyana, to whose awe all beings submit. Wherever he is reborn, he will constantly meet various Buddhas and Bodhisattvas and hear the profound teachings. Having heard the teachings, he will exclaim with delight and will attain the gate to the limitless sublime *samādhis* and *dhāraṇis*."

The Buddha told Ānanda: "If there is any being who merely

hears the names of these two Bodhisattvas, he will obtain blessings which are limitless and inexhaustible. How much more complete would these blessings be if he cultivated the practices which I have described!"

PAST LIFE OF THE TWO BODHISATTVAS

When Ānanda had heard the Lord Buddha, he praised the deep wisdom and boundless virtuous practices of these two Bodhisattvas. He rose from his seat, circumambulated the Buddha seven times, knelt, clasped his palms together, and addressed the Buddha: "O Lord, what path and practices were cultivated, and what [seeds of] merit were planted in a past age by those two Bodhisattvas King of Healing and Supreme Healer? Today, resembling pure banners to this assembly, they have been praised by you, and they also have been praised and exalted by the great assembly. Today, you have emitted rays from your two eyes, which appeared like the *maṇi* gem upon their foreheads. This sublime and auspicious sign has never been seen before. I sincerely wish, O Lord, that you would explain to me the [karmic] causes and conditions engendered in a [key] past life of the two Bodhisattvas."

Then the Lord replied to Ānanda: "Listen carefully, and with excellent thoughts be mindful of what I have to tell you, for I will explain and describe to you the causes and conditions engendered by the past lives of these two Bodhisattvas."

The Buddha told Ānanda: "When they dwelt in the past, boundless and limitless *asaṃkhyeya* aeons ago, indeed so many times that number that it cannot be reckoned in speech, there was a Buddha whose name was Illuminating Ray of Lapis Lazuli Tathāgata, Arhat, Omniscient One, Perfect in Knowledge and Conduct, Well-Gone, Knower of the World, Supreme Master, Tamer of Passions, Teacher of *Devas* and Men, Buddha, and Lord. His aeon was known as Genuine Tranquility, and his state was called 'Land Where the Banner of Victory is Suspended.'

"All beings born in that Buddha-land had life-spans of eight great aeons, while that Lord Buddha manifested in the world for sixteen great aeons. Afterwards, the Buddha entered into *nirvāṇa* in the Lotus Blossom Lecture Hall. The genuine Teachings remained in the world for a full eight great aeons following the Buddha's *nirvāṇa,* and the replica teachings existed in the world for eight great aeons following the disappearance of the genuine teachings.

"In this period of the replica teachings, there were a thousand monks who expressed the aspiration to attain enlightenment and sought [to maintain] the Bodhisattva precepts. These monks, for the sake of all sentient beings, traveled about teaching and transforming them.

"At that time in this assembly, there was a monk of intelligence and insight named Solar Womb. He traveled successively through hamlets, villages, and cities. In places ranging from monks' quarters to halls and pavillions, from abodes of hermitage to halls of debate, he extensively praised the meritorious acts of the past lives of the Bodhisattvas to the various members of the great assembly. He also spoke of the supreme purity, equanimity, and great wisdom of the Tathāgata.

"At that time, there was a wealthy donor in the assembly whose name was Star Light. Hearing the description of the equanimity and great wisdom of the Great Vehicle, joy welled up in his heart. He arose from his seat, grasped a *harītakī* fruit (myrobalan) and various assorted medicinal herbs, and he went towards Solar Womb, saying: 'O Virtuous One, I have heard you, benevolent one, speak of the medicine of sweet dew [the teachings of the Tathāgata]. It is as you have said: he who takes this medicine will neither grow old nor die.'

"Having said this, he bowed his head and face and prostrated in worship at the feet of the monk. Then he took the healing herbs which he held and offered them to the monk, saying: 'O Benevolent One, I now offer these healing herbs to you and to the Order of Great Virtue.'

"Then Solar Womb, uttering the *dhāraṇī* spoken on behalf of a donor, accepted the *harītakī*. The wealthy donor, having heard the Teachings and further having heard the *dhāraṇī,* was overjoyed. He universally worshipped the boundless Buddhas of the Ten Directions, and before Solar Womb, he expressed vast aspirations and vows, saying: 'O Benevolent One, I have heard you speak of the healing medicine of the Buddha's wisdom. As you have said, it is true, not false. Now, grasping an excellent healing herb from the Himalayas, I have offered it to you and to all in the Order. By means of this vow of meritorious virtue, in my future births and rebirths, I will not seek the blessings and rewards of incarnation as a human or *deva* in the Three-fold World. With utmost sincerity, I will turn towards the perfect and complete enlightenment. Today, I have sincerely expressed the aspiration to attain the Supreme Enlightenment, and in a future age I will surely become a Buddha. This vow is not empty: I will inevitably attain—as you, revered sir, have described—the Buddha wisdom.

" 'When I obtain the pure force of enlightenment, even though I have not yet become a Buddha, if there are any sentient beings who hear my name, they will be cured of the sufferings from the three types of diseases which afflict all sentient beings. The first comprises the 404 diseases afflicting the bodies of all sentient beings. By merely calling on my name, they will be completely cured. Secondly, I vow throughout eternity to reject the sufferings caused by false views, stupid doubts, and the woesome path. When I become a Buddha and am born in my Buddha-land, all the sentient beings there will awaken to the liberating universal Mahāyāna teachings, and further, no variant paths will exist there. Thirdly, in Jambudvīpa and in other regions, the three woesome paths are known. Those who hear my name will never again, throughout eternity, be incarnated in one of these three woesome paths. As long as they sink into woesome paths, I will withhold from achieving my ultimate attainment of perfect and complete enlightenment.

" 'If there are any sentient beings who worship, fix their minds upon, and contemplate my form and features, I vow to remove the three fetters from these beings.[42]

" 'When the body of a Buddha is seen in a vision, it appears to have the penetrating luminosity of pure lapis lazuli. If there are any sentient beings who see the pure body of a Buddha, I vow that these beings will experience the non-differentiating wisdom. They will neither withdraw from nor lose this state of mind for eternity.'

"After expressing these vows, he prostrated himself in worship with his knees, elbows, and forehead touching the ground and universally worshipped all the limitless Buddhas of the Ten Directions. Having worshipped the Buddhas, he grasped a blossom made of pearls which he scattered upon Solar Womb, whom he addressed, saying: 'O revered sir, it is due to you that I have heard the supremely pure Buddha wisdom. I have heard this in front of you, revered sir. Having heard the Buddha wisdom, I have expressed a deep aspiration to attain enlightenment, and the vows which I have made are not empty: I will surely achieve Buddhahood. Now, I will cause the marvelous pearl blossom which I scattered to become a flowering canopy above you, O revered sir.'

"When he had made this speech, the precious pearls which he scattered became arranged in space like a jeweled lotus blossom, and then they changed into a flowery canopy. This canopy was endowed with a golden radiance and was altogether complete. All in the great assembly who saw this event unanimously praised the great wealthy donor Star Light, saying: 'Excellent, excellent, great wealthy donor. You are able within this great assembly to have made the profound expression of vast aspirations and vows and to manifest this subtle and marvelous auspicious sign. We have observed this auspicious sign today, and we have no doubt that you will inevitably achieve Buddhahood.'

"The wealthy donor Star Light had a younger brother named Shining Lightning. When Shining Lightning saw his elder brother aspire to attain enlightenment, he accordingly was pleased in body and mind. He said to his elder brother: 'In my home at present, there is a large amount of ghee and various excellent medicines. I vow, as you hear me, that I shall donate all these without limiting my charity solely to the Order.'

"His brother replied: 'I have heard you, and you should proceed in accordance with your wish.'

"Then the wealthy donor Shining Lightning said to his elder brother: 'I would also like to follow you further. I wish to express the aspiration to attain the profoundly perfect and complete enlightenment.'

"His elder brother replied: 'If you wish to express this aspiration, you now should worship the Buddhas of the Ten Directions. It would be proper to express the aspiration for the profound and supreme enlightenment in front of the great reverend, the monk Solar Womb.'

"The younger brother said to his elder: 'I now, [as signified] by [the offering of] this ghee and excellent medicines, by charity to all beings, and further by [the manifestation of] a marvelous flower above the Buddhas of the Ten Directions, turn to these vows of merit, these vows which are no different from the aspirations and vows expressed by my elder brother. If my vows have been sincere and not false, then let the marvelous lotus flowers that I have scattered form a blossoming tree in the sky.'

"Then the great assembly saw the lotus blossoms scattered by the wealthy donor Shining Lightning become arranged in the sky. Each flower looked like a *bodhi* tree. Although arranged in the sky, they were altogether endowed with blossoms and fruits.

"The members of the great assembly from their separate mouths spoke as one in praise of the wealthy donor Shining Lightning, saying at that point: 'The auspicious response to your vows today is identical to that received by your elder brother. In a future age you inevitably will achieve Buddhahood. Of this we have no doubt.' "

The Buddha told Ānanda: "You now should know that when this great wealthy donor [Star Light] gave the *harītakī* and the excellent healing herbs from the Himalayas to all the monks, after the assembly of monks swallowed these things, they heard the sublime Teachings. Due to the force of the medicines they were rid of two types of diseases. The first type was the ascendancy or depression of the four elements [the inharmonious balance of the four elements in the body, thus causing the 404 diseases], while the second was the defilement of anger. Due to these medicines, all in the great congregation then expressed the aspiration to attain perfect and complete enlightenment, and they chanted these words: 'In a future age, we will all achieve Buddhahood.'

"Then, each in the great assembly praised the others, saying: 'Because of this great being's gift of the two types of medicines, we today have expressed the aspiration to attain the Supreme and Sovereign Teachings. We will become kings of 3000 myriads of world-realms. In gratitude, we should give him a name. Due to his actions, we shall name him 'King of Healing.' "

The Buddha told Ānanda: "You now should know that when this Bodhisattva King of Healing heard the great assembly confer this name, he revered and worshipped them and said the following: 'Monks of the Assembly of Great Virtue, you have conferred upon me the name "King of Healing." I now should take refuge in this name and establish its reality. If my giving accords with the Buddha Way and I inevitably attain perfection, I vow that with my two hands I shall rain down all varieties of medicines, cleansing all beings and freeing them from all diseases. If there are any sentient beings who hear my name, worship me, and contemplate my form and features, I will cause these beings to swallow the medicine of the profound and sublime *dhāraṇī* of the Unobstructed Teachings. I will cause these beings, in their present incarnations, to be rid of all negativity and to fulfill all their aspirations. When I achieve Buddhahood, I vow that all sentient beings will be complete in the practices of the Great Vehicle.'

"When he had spoken these words, from the midst of space there rained down a canopy made of the seven precious things, which covered King of Healing. From within the radiance of the canopy, this verse was said:

'O great being, by your sublime and excellent vows,
You have given the medicines which aid all beings.
In the future you will become a Buddha,
And your name shall be Pure Eye.
Rescuing great numbers of *devas* and men,
Your compassionate heart will have no bounds, no limits.
With your eye of wisdom, you shall illumine all things.
Indeed, in the future you will become a Buddha.'

"When King of Healing heard this verse, joy welled up in his whole being and he entered into *samādhi.* This *samādhi* was called 'Beyond Adornment.' Due to the force of the *samādhi,* he saw Buddhas beyond numbering. He gained purification of various karmic fetters and was rid of them, and he obtained release from the faults amassed during 900 billion *asaṃkhyeya* aeons of *saṃsāra.*

"Then, those in the assembly who had named him said: 'Now, this is the Bodhisattva-mahāsattva King of Healing.'"

The Buddha told Ānanda: "You now should know that when the younger brother gave medicines to all men, he was praised by all in the world because of his act. He gave these medicines not only to all in the Order, but also to all beings. Those who swallowed these medicines gained a superior vitality and marvelously supreme health. They also heard of the healing medicine of the supreme and marvelous Great Vehicle Teachings.

"Due to his actions, all in the world named him 'Supreme Healer.' When this Bodhisattva heard these persons praise him and confer upon him the auspicious name of 'Supreme Healer,' he said: 'Due to the expression of my aspirations and vows, today in this world all the members of this great assembly have conferred upon me the name "Supreme Healer." I vow that when I, in a future age, achieve the ten types of pure force,[43] I will give to all beings the medicine of the Supreme Teachings. I vow that all beings who hear my name will rapidly obtain release from the plenteous fires of their afflictions. If there are any sentient beings who worship me, who call out my name, and who contemplate my form and features, I will cause these beings to obtain a dose of the Supreme Medicine, the sweet dew of the supreme and marvelous undying liberation.'

"When the great assembly heard these words, each person took off a necklace of precious stones and together they offered them to the Bodhisattva Supreme Healer. These necklace offerings settled in the sky, appearing like a seven-jeweled pavillion. Within the pavillion there was a light of pure yellow-golden hue, and a sound like the pure voice of Brahmā resonated, reciting this verse:

'Excellent, O victorious Great Being
You have illustriously expressed vast aspirations and vows,
And you inevitably shall ferry all sentient beings
Across the bitter waters.
There is no doubt in my heart:
In a future age you will become a Buddha.
Your name shall be "Pure Matrix."
Saving and protecting all in the world,
You will remove all beings from the sea of suffering.' "

CONCLUSION: SUMMARY OF MERITS, NAMING THE SŪTRA, SPIRITUAL ATTAINMENTS

The Buddha told Ānanda: "You now should listen carefully. Be attentive to my words and do not forget or lose them. These two

Bodhisattvas, King of Healing and Supreme Healer, are the consecrated Dharma-sons of all the Lord Buddhas of the past, present, and future. If there are any sentient beings who hear the names of these two Bodhisattvas, they will be eternally ferried over the sea of suffering, and they will not sink into *saṃsāra.* They will constantly meet with Buddhas and Bodhisattvas. How much more will they be endowed [with blessings] if they cultivate the practices that I have explained.

"If there is a good son or daughter who hears the spiritual formulae uttered by the two Bodhisattvas, and if such a one contemplates the forms and features of the two Bodhisattvas, that person will obtain a vision of King of Healing and Supreme Healer in the present incarnation and will also see the thousand Buddhas of the present aeon. In future ages, he will see Buddhas beyond numbering, and each of these Lords will speak to him about the Teachings. He will be born in Buddha-lands, and his mind will be solid and firm. To the end he will never turn back from his aspiration to attain perfect and complete enlightenment."

At this point, Ānanda arose from his seat, worshipped the Buddha, and circumambulated him seven times. He addressed the Buddha and said: "O Lord, what should we call this *sūtra?* [By what names] should we receive and uphold it?"

The Buddha told Ānanda: "Listen carefully, listen carefully, and with excellent thoughts be mindful of what I have to say. The essence of this teaching is called 'Elimination of Faults and Fetters.' It is also called 'The Spiritual Formula for the Confession and Repentance of Negative Acts.' Also, it is known as 'The Sublime Medicine, the Sweet Dew which Cures Afflictions and Illness.' Also, it is called 'The Contemplation on the Pure Forms of King of Healing and Supreme Healer.' "

The Buddha told Ānanda: "The essence of these teachings has extraordinary, excellent, and sublime names such as these. After my *parinirvāṇa,* if there are any monks or nuns who hear this *sūtra* and with utmost sincerity take joy in it for even a moment, they will be purified of the four gravely negative acts. If there are any laymen or laywomen who hear this *sūtra* and with utmost sincerity take joy in it for even a moment, if they have transgressed against the five moral precepts or if they have broken the eightfold vows, they will obtain purification. If there are kings of states, great ministers, *kṣatriyas,* learned laymen, *vaiśyas* (merchants), *śūdras* (peasants), brahmans, or any others who hear this *sūtra,* if with utmost sincerity they should take joy in it for even a moment, they will obtain purification from the five rebellious acts and the ten negatives."

The Buddha further told Ānanda: "The causes and conditions of the fundamental acts of King of Healing and Supreme Healer are an excellent medicine for the diseases of the people of Jambudvīpa."

After the Lord had spoken these words, he became silent and, remaining where he was seated, he entered into *samādhi.* Then, the son of the elder Jewel Heap, the Venerable Ānanda, and the countless members of the great assembly who had heard the words of the Buddha all were greatly pleased and joyous. Because of this joy, the five thousand elders in the assembly all attained the forbearance of the unoriginated natures. On the other side of the assembly, the ten thousand Bodhisattvas dwelled in the *śūraṃgama samādhi.* The disciple Śāriputra and the 500 monks were no longer subject to the defilements, and they all became arhats. Boundless numbers of *devas, nāgas,* and others of the eight classes of spirit beings all expressed the intention to attain the Supreme and Genuine Way.

Then all the monks, nuns, and all in the great assembly who heard the discourse of the Buddha were pleased and joyous. Having received these teachings and put them into practice, they made obeisances and withdrew.

Thus ends the *sūtra* spoken by the Buddha on the contemplation of the two Bodhisattvas King of Healing and Supreme Healer.

1. A Bodhisattva is a being advanced on the path to Buddhahood who seeks enlightenment in order to aid all others. A possible translation of the word is "one who has enlightenment (*bodhi*) as his essence." (Cf. Christopher George, *The Caṇḍamahāroṣaṇa Tantra* [New Haven: 1974], p. 44, fn. 1). Mahāsattva, "great being," is an epithet for Bodhisattva. Where commonly identifiable, the Sanskrit forms of their names are given in parentheses.
2. Ten directions: the cardinal directions (north, south, east, west); intermediate directions (northwest, etc.); and the zenith and nadir.

3. The Licchāvis were *kṣatriyas* (warriors) who founded the city-state centered around Vaiśālī.
4. The text has *ch'ang-che,* which is used variously to translate two Sanskrit words: *gṛhapati,* "householder"; and *śreṣṭhin,* "a person of rank or authority, a rich man." I here translate it as "elder," though in the later section of the *sūtra* where the past life of the Bodhisattvas is discussed, it seems more appropriately translated as "rich man" or "wealthy donor."
5. Seven precious substances: gold, silver, lapis lazuli, quartz crystal, agate, ruby or rose-hued pearl, and carnelian. This list varies in different traditions.
6. Lamotte translates *śūraṃgama samādhi* as "la concentration de la marche héroïque," explaining that one who keeps it goes everywhere as a hero (*śūra*) without meeting resistance. Alternately, it bears its name because it is traversed by heroes such as Buddhas and Bodhisattvas. Cf. E. Lamotte, "La Concentration de la marche héroïque" (*Śuraṃgamasamādhisūtra*), *Mélanges Chinois et Bouddhiques* XIII (Brussels: 1965), p. 1. The *sūtra* itself indicates that Bodhisattvas of the tenth stage (the most advanced stage of development) attain this *samādhi.* Cf. R. E. Emmerick, *The Khotanese Śūraṃgama samādhisūtra* (London: 1970), p. XV.
7. *Hua-fo* is the equivalent of the Sanskrit, *nirmāṇa buddha,* the incarnate manifestation of a Buddha. Buddhas and Bodhisattvas of advanced spiritual development have the ability to manifest at will throughout the realms of the universe.
8. The marvelous wish-granting jewel.
9. *Abhiṣeka* is an esoteric method of initiation or consecration in which sacred water is sprinkled upon the forehead. "Sweet dew" is the literal translation of the Chinese rendering for *amṛta,* the Divine nectar.
10. The ten wholesome precepts involve abstention from the ten negative acts. These are wayward acts of body, speech, and mind, including: killing, stealing, adultery; lies, slander, harsh language, frivolous talk; and covetousness, malice, and wayward views.
11. A number so great as to be essentially beyond calculation.
12. A *dhāraṇī* (lit. wholly grasping) is a potent phrase or set of phrases used especially for invocation of spiritual forces. It also represents the concentrated vocalization of a spiritual principle or spiritual being. Thus, the bestowal of a *dhāraṇī* can indicate the transmission in esoteric form of the concentrated essence of a spiritual teaching.
13. These 1,000 Buddhas are discussed in the *Bhadra-kalpa-sūtra,* translated into Chinese by Dharmarakṣa in the early fourth century (T. XIV, 425).
14. Ānanda, close disciple of Śākyamuni, was able to recite from memory

long after the *parinirvāṇa* all the oral teachings of the Buddha which he had heard.

15. Brahmā is the creator and lord of the universe; there is a Brahmā king for each of the manifold universes.
16. Though literally translated as "Sandalwood-gem Radiance," the pronunciation is close to *cintāmaṇi* and probably refers to that wish-granting gem.
17. A *yojana* measures several miles.
18. Also translated as "counterfeit." The three ages of the Teachings are the age of the genuine teachings, the age of the replica or counterfeit teachings (which are not entirely complete, remaining primarily in form rather than essence), and the age of the dissolution of the teachings, when the profound meanings are lost. At this point, after the teachings have vanished, a new Buddha will incarnate to point out once again the path to liberation.
19. The principal meanings of the Sanskrit "*garbha*" are "womb, interior, embryo." I here use "matrix," a dictionary synonym for "womb," in the sense of "that which gives origin or form to a thing; essence."
20. *Anutpattikadharmakṣānti.* Thus they are not upset by the stream of dream-like entities (*dharmas*). This could also be translated more freely as the forbearance stemming from the recognition that things (*dharmas*) are not born. Edward Conze, based on his readings in the *prajñā-pāramitā* literature, translates *anutpattikadharmakṣānti* as "the patient acceptance of dharmas which fail to be produced." (Cf. his *Materials for a Dictionary of the Prajñā-Pāramitā Literature,* [Tokyo: 1967], pp. 31-32). For more on this term, see Alex and Hideko Wayman, *The Lion's Roar of Queen Śrīmālā* (N.Y.: 1974), p. 75, fn. 39. See also D. T. Suzuki's explanations in his *Studies in the Laṅkāvatāra Sūtra* (London: 1930), pp. 125-6, 380-1.
21. The last (Chinese) line of this verse is freely rendered according to the meaning given in Ting Fu-pao, *Fo hsüeh ta-tz'u-tien* (Taipei: reprint 1977), vol. I, p. 309A-B.
22. There seems to be a *lacuna* in the text here, so this rendering is tentative. *Liu-li* is translated as glass, as is sometimes seen in Chinese texts, rather than the usual lapis lazuli of Buddhist texts, since the color is noted as white.
23. That is, twice the stature of an ordinary man.
24. "Causes and conditions of the fundamental deeds"—the karma generated by those past life deeds, both the obvious manifestations and the more subtle aspects.
25. The Six Perfections (or *pāramitās*) of the Bodhisattva path include the perfection of: giving, morality, forbearance, striving, meditation, and insight.

26. The ascetic practices that yield non-attachment to clothing, food, and dwelling. The word *dhūta* refers to "shaking off" worldly attachments, and the practices by which this is done include: (1) living in a forest, (2) taking whatever seat is offered, (3) living on alms, (4) using the same seat for meditating and eating, (5) wearing coarse garments, (6) eating only at regulated times (not after noon), (7) wearing clothes made of discarded rags, (8) having three robes and no more, (9) dwelling in or near a cemetery, (10) living under a tree, (11) living in the open air, and (12) sleeping in a seated position.

27. "Untimely deaths"—violent or sudden deaths by "unnatural cause." See Translation III, pp. 167–168, for more on the nine untimely deaths.

28. A *śrāvaka* is a disciple of the Buddha, an "auditor," who seeks to gain enlightenment for himself alone by listening to the Buddha's teachings. A *pratyekabuddha* attains enlightenment by his own effort, for his own sake.

29. A type of gem or glowing pearl; perhaps originally an auspicious ornament worn by Indra. Hui-lin suggests that this headdress ornament is lapis lazuli. Cf. his *I-ch'ieh-ching yin-i,* T. LIV, 2128, p. 317C.

30. Killing, stealing, adultery, falsehood.

31. Patricide, matricide, killing an arhat, causing a Buddha to shed blood, destroying the harmony of the *Saṃgha.*

32. Literally translated as "merely has no glorious adornments," implying transcendence to an unconditioned state.

33. Mindfulness of (1) body as impure, (2) sensation or consciousness as suffering, (3) mind as impermanent, and (4) all things as having no nature of their own.

34. (1) To prevent negatives from arising, (2) to put an end to existing negatives, (3) to initiate things which are wholesome, and (4) to strengthen wholesome things already in existence.

35. Described by Har Dayal in *The Bodhisattva Doctrine in Sanskrit Buddhist Literature* (London: 1931), p. 106, as follows:

"A bodhisattva develops (or cultivates) the first *ṛddhi-pada* by uniting a strong Desire or Will (*chanda*) to the moulding forces of concentration and effort.

"He develops the second *ṛddhi-pada* by uniting Thought (*citta*) to the moulding forces of concentration and effort.

"He develops the third *ṛddhi-pada* by uniting Energy (*vīrya*) to the moulding forces of concentration and effort.

"He develops the fourth *ṛddhi-pada* by uniting Investigation (*mimaṃsa*) to the moulding forces of concentration and effort."

36. The faculties are: faith, striving, mindfulness, *samādhi,* insight. The five powers are the developed aspects of the five spiritual faculties.

37. Mindfulness, investigation of *dharmas*, striving, joy, tranquility, *samādhi*, and equanimity.
38. Right views, right aspirations, right speech, right action, right livelihood, right effort, right mindfulness, and right meditation.
39. Harmony of action in worship, harmony of speech in chanting, harmony of thought in faith, harmony of morals in observing the precepts, harmony of views in the Teachings, and economic harmony in community of goods.
40. The six things to keep in mind are: the Buddha, the Dharma, the Saṃgha, morality, generosity, and deities.
41. The cycle of *saṃsara* in twelve phases: nescience, motivations, perceptions, name-and-form, six sense bases, contact, feelings, craving, indulgence, gestation, birth, and old age and death.
42. The three fetters, barriers, or hindrances, are: the "poisons" of lust, anger, and delusion; deeds done; and the karmic retributions of those deeds.
43. These give complete knowledge "as it really is" of: (1) what can be as what can be, and what cannot be as what cannot be; (2) the karmic results of past, future, and present actions and undertakings of actions; (3) the various elements of the world; (4) the various dispositions of other beings and persons; (5) the higher and lower faculties of other beings and persons; (6) the Way that leads everywhere; (7) the various meditative states, as well as their defilement, their purification, and the condition in which they are well established in their purity; (8) [one's own] past lives; (9) with the heavenly eye, one knows the decease and rebirth of beings as it really is; and (10) through extinction of the outflows, one dwells in the attainment of that emancipation of heart and mind. See Edward Conze, "List of Buddhist terms," *The Tibet Journal* I (1975), pp. 47–48.

TRANSLATION II

Preface to the Sūtra on the Merits of the Fundamental Vows of the Master of Healing Tathāgata

(Yao-shih ju-lai pen-yüan kung-te ching hsü)

By the monk Hui-chü, 617 C.E. (Sui), T. XIV, 449.

The *Sūtra on the Fundamental Vows of the Master of Healing Tathāgata* is an essential method for bringing about blessings and putting an end to calamities. Due to the force of his loving kindness and compassion, Mañjuśrī requested [Śākyamuni] to speak on the honored name [of the Healing Buddha]. This [Master of Healing] Tathāgata by his altruistic mind abundantly spreads meritorious karma. The twelve great vows display the far-reaching qualities of his motivations and actions, while the seven gems that gloriously adorn him reveal the purity of the fruits [of his motivations and actions] and their virtues.

Those who recall, concentrate on, and call out the Buddha's name will be freed from all suffering. Those who make requests of the Buddha and worship him with *pūjā* offerings will have all their wishes fulfilled. This even extends to the case of a sick person whom one seeks to save. Though that person ought to die, he will live again. A king can drive off woes and turn calamities into blessings. Faith in this Buddha will annul a hundred uncanny spirit charms. It is the sublime method which eliminates the nine untimely deaths.

Formerly, during the reign of Sung Hsiao-wu (454–465) at the Deer Wilderness Monastery, the monk Hui-chien translated this text, and it was popular in his age. However, in comparing it to the Sanskrit text, [it was seen that] this Sung monk did not fuse together the confused assortment of words and phrases. This caused numerous doubts to arise in readers.

I, Hui-chü, in my early studies of Indian texts constantly spread out leaves of the scriptures [for study]. I often thought of obtaining this *sūtra* in order to examine the errors [of the previous translation]. I first obtained the original text in 597. Still, due to the fear of circulating mistakes, I did not yet dare attempt this translation.

In 615 I obtained two more copies. I compared them and finally came up with the clearest and most definitive text. Subsequently, together with the monk Dharmagupta and the Sui translation masters, the monks Fa-hsing, Ming-tse, Ch'ang-shun, Hai-yü and others at the *sūtra* translation academy in the Shang-lin Park, which is to the south of the Lo River in the Eastern Capital, this scripture was respectfully translated.

Deeply aware of the errors of the former rendering, we took them as a warning to prevent any mistakes in the present translation. For this reason, whenever a translation of a sentence was uttered, it would not be written down until it was considered in three deliberations. In the transmission of the subtle principles, we believe that no grave errors have been made.

This year, on the eighth day of the twelfth lunar month [January 21, 617 C.E.], the translation and revision editing were completed, and this translation was made into one scroll, as in the previous version.

We wish that the deep principles of the *sūtra* will be understood by everybody and that the name of this Buddha will be heard in all places. We wish that the Twelve *Yakṣas* may think of the grace of the Buddha and protect the nation; may the seven thousand troops [of each of the Twelve *Yakṣa* Generals], receiving the force of this *sūtra,* benefit the populace. May the Imperial Throne be eternal. May the people all be peaceful and joyous. Thereby, may this preface be bequeathed to future generations.

Sūtra Spoken by the Buddha on the Fundamental Vows of the Master of Healing Tathāgata. New translation of the *Master of Healing Sūtra* [completed on the] twelfth year of *Ta-yeh,* twelfth lunar month, eighth day, [by] *Śrāmaṇa* Hui-chü and six others at the Shang-lin Park south of the Lo River in the Eastern Capital. This edition is the most definitive. We wish that no doubts be caused in those who read and recite this text. If any mistakes are found, they should not be treated lightly.

TRANSLATION III

Sūtra on the Merits of the Fundamental Vows of the Master of Healing, The Lapis Lazuli Radiance Tathāgata

(Yao-shih liu-li-kuang ju-lai pen-yüan kung-te ching)

From the Chinese version of the Tripiṭaka Master Hsüan-tsang (T'ang, 650 C.E.). T. XIV, 450.

Oṃ. Homage to the Omniscient One. Homage to the Lord Master of Healing, the Lapis Lazuli Radiance King Tathāgata.[1]

Thus have I heard; once, when the Lord was traveling through the various states to teach and transform the inhabitants, he arrived at Vaiśālī. There he dwelt at the base of a tree from which music resounded. Together with him was a great assembly of monks, totaling 8,000. Thirty-six thousand Bodhisattva-mahāsattvas were there, and the king of the state, his great ministers, brahmins, learned laymen, *devas, nāgas, yakṣas,* and beings human and non-human also were in attendance. This immeasurably large assembly respectfully gathered around the Buddha, and he then expounded his teaching to them.

The Dharma Prince Mañjuśrī, receiving through inspiration the Buddha's sublime spiritual force, arose from his seat, bared his shoulder on one side, and knelt with his right knee on the ground. Bowing down towards the Lord and clasping his hands together, Mañjuśrī addressed him and said: "O Lord, I sincerely wish that you expound upon the forms and varieties of all the Buddhas' names and on the rare merits of their fundamental great vows [made when they first set out on the Bodhisattva Path]. All who hear this will be caused to be purified of their karmic fetters, so that they may confer benefits and joy to all the sentient beings in the age of the replica teachings [when form rather than content remains of spiritual teachings]."

The Lord then praised the youth Mañjuśrī, and he said: "Excellent, excellent, Mañjuśrī. You have implored me with your great compassion to expound on all the Buddhas' names and the merits of their fundamental vows, in order to tear off the karmic fetters which bind sentient beings and to benefit, enrich, and bring peace and joy to all sentient beings in the period of the replica teachings. You should listen now with utmost care and consider well what I shall tell you."

Mañjuśrī said, "I sincerely wish that you will speak. We all will listen with great joy to your explanations."

THE BUDDHA OF HEALING: HIS TWELVE VOWS AND HIS EASTERN PARADISE

The Buddha told Mañjuśrī: "If you go eastward beyond as many Buddha fields as there are ten times the number of grains of sand in the Ganges River, you will find a realm known as 'Pure Lapis Lazuli.' The Buddha there is known as Master of Healing, the Lapis Lazuli Radiance Tathāgata, Arhat,[2] Perfectly Enlightened One, Perfect in Mind and Deed, Well-Gone, He Who Knows the World, Unsurpassed Being, Tamer of the Passions, Teacher of *Devas* and Men, Buddha, and Lord. Mañjuśrī, when that Buddha Lord Master of Healing, the Lapis Lazuli Radiance Tathāgata first set out on the Bodhisattva Path, he made twelve vows to enable all sentient beings to obtain that which they seek.

"*First Great Vow:* 'I vow that when I attain the unexcelled complete enlightenment in a future age, a radiant light will blaze forth from my body. It will brilliantly illumine limitless, countless, boundless realms. This body will be excellently adorned with the thirty-two marks of the great man and the eighty secondary marks.[3] I will cause all sentient beings to wholly resemble me.'

"*Second Great Vow:* 'I vow that when I attain enlightenment in a future age, my body will be like lapis lazuli within and without, bright with penetrating and flawless purity. The radiance will be of great merit and will be imposing, indeed. My body will be an excellent and tranquil dwelling, adorned with [an aureole like] a glowing net surpassing the sun and moon in its radiance. I will show the dawn to those beings who are completely concealed in darkness, so that they may act in accordance with their desired paths.'

"*Third Great Vow:* 'I vow that when I attain enlightenment in a future age, with infinite and boundless insight and means, I shall cause all beings to obtain all that they need. They shall never lack [the necessities of life].'

"*Fourth Great Vow:* 'I vow that when I attain enlightenment in a future age, if there are sentient beings who tread upon heretical paths, I will cause them all to peacefully abide within the path of enlightenment. If there are those who are adherents of the *śrāvaka* or *pratyekabuddha* vehicles, they will all become securely established in the Great Vehicle (Mahāyāna).'

"*Fifth Great Vow:* 'I vow that when I attain enlightenment in a future age, if there are limitless and boundless sentient beings who cultivate and practice the pure conduct of my teaching, I will cause them all to be able to follow perfectly the rules of conduct and be complete in the three cumulative precepts.[4] Those who slander and offend will, after hearing my name, be able once again to attain purity, and they will not sink to a woeful existence.'

"*Sixth Great Vow:* 'I vow that when I attain enlightenment in a future age, if there are sentient beings whose bodies are inferior, whose sense organs are impaired, who are ugly, stupid, deaf, blind, mute, bent and lame, hunchbacked, leprous, convulsive, insane, or who have all sorts of diseases and sufferings—such beings when they hear my name shall obtain proper appearances and practical intelligence. All their senses will become perfect and they shall have neither sickness nor suffering.'

"*Seventh Great Vow:* 'I vow that when I attain enlightenment in a future age, if there are any sentient beings who are ill and oppressed, who have nowhere to go and nothing to return to, who have neither doctor nor medicine, neither relatives nor immediate family, who are destitute and whose sufferings are acute—as soon as my name passes through their ears, they will be cured of all their diseases and they will be peaceful and joyous in body and mind. They will have plentiful families and property, and they will personally experience the supreme enlightenment.'

"*Eighth Great Vow:* 'I vow that when I attain enlightenment in a future age, if there are any women who suffer from any of the hundred woes that befall women, who are wearied at the end of their lives and wish to abandon their female form—when these women hear my name, they all will obtain transformation in rebirth from female into male physical forms. They all will personally experience the supreme enlightenment.'[5]

"*Ninth Great Vow:* 'I vow that when I attain to enlightenment in a future age, I will cause all sentient beings to escape from Māra's net. They will be freed from the fetters of all deviant paths. If there are those who have sunk into various negative views as dense as a jungle, I will embrace them and establish them in correct views. I will gradually cause them to cultivate and study all the Bodhisattva practices, and they will soon personally experience the supreme enlightenment.'

"*Tenth Great Vow:* 'I vow that when I attain enlightenment in a future age, if—according to that which is recorded in the king's laws—there are any sentient beings who are bound and whipped, tied up and thrown into prison, or who will be subjected to capital punishment; and to whom boundlessly catastrophic difficulties occur that are humiliating, grievous, and distressing, their bodies and minds suffering these bitternesses—if such persons hear my name, due to the awesome spiritual force of my auspicious virtues, they will be freed from all sorrows and sufferings.

"*Eleventh Great Vow:* 'I vow that when I attain enlightenment in a future age, if there are any sentient beings who are tormented by hunger and thirst and who create bad karma in their [desperate] search for sustenance—if they hear my name and firmly retain it in their minds and hold to it, then I will provide them first with incomparably marvelous food and drink to fully satisfy their bodies. Afterwards, through providing them with the taste of the Teaching, they will ultimately become peaceful and joyous and well established in it.'

"*Twelfth Great Vow:* 'I vow that when I attain enlightenment in a future age, if there are any sentient beings who are poor and, having no clothing, are annoyed and irritated through the day and night by flies and mosquitos, heat and cold—if they hear my name and firmly retain it in their minds and hold to it, in accordance with their wishes, they will obtain all sorts of superior and marvelous clothing. They will also obtain every precious adornment, garlands, powder incense, music, and [the enjoyment of] various performing arts. I shall cause them to have in abundance whatever their hearts desire.'

"Mañjuśrī, these are the twelve subtle, sublime, and superior vows expressed by that Lord Master of Healing, the Lapis Lazuli Radiance Tathāgata when he set out onto the Bodhisattva Path. As to the merits and glorious adornments of his Buddha-land, if I tried to speak of them for an aeon, or even for longer than an aeon, I would not be able to describe them in full. The Lord Master of Healing's Buddha-land has been singularly pure up to the present, and there is no temptation there,[6] no woeful paths of existence, and no cries of suffering. The ground is made of lapis lazuli, and roads are marked with gold. The walls and gates, palaces and pavillions, balconies and windows, draperies and curtains are all made of the seven precious substances.[7] It is similar to the Joyous Realm of the West; its merits and adornments are no different.

"In this land, there are two Bodhisattva-mahāsattvas. One is named All-Pervading Solar Radiance and the other is named All-Pervading Lunar Radiance. They are the leaders of the limitless, numberless host of Bodhisattvas there. They are fully able to uphold the treasury of the genuine teachings of the Lord Master of Healing, the Lapis Lazuli Radiance Tathāgata.

"For these reasons, Mañjuśrī, all the good sons and daughters [of the Buddhist family] having faithful hearts should aspire to be reborn in that Buddha's realm."

THE BUDDHA AIDS THOSE WHOSE KARMA HAS LED THEM TO DISTRESS

The Lord then told the youth Mañjuśrī: "Mañjuśrī, there are beings who do not distinguish between good and bad, who only cherish greed and stinginess. They know nothing of spreading charity and of the fruits and rewards of giving. Stupid and dense, they have no insight and lack the roots of faith. Amassing wealth and jewels, they industriously guard and protect [their hoard]. When they see a beggar coming, they become displeased, and if they fail to protect themselves and are forced to give in charity, they generate such deep and painful resentment that it seems as if they are cutting a piece off their own bodies.

"Furthermore, there are sentient beings who are boundlessly stingy and avaricious. They amass riches, and since they do not even spend it on themselves, how could they possibly be able to give to their parents, wives, children, or to their maidservants, laborers, or to beggars.

"At the end of their present lives, these sentient beings will be reborn as starving ghosts or animals. Because in a former incarnation as a human being, such a being briefly heard the name "Master of Healing, the Lapis Lazuli Radiance Tathāgata," in this woesome path of existence he will suddenly remember that Tathāgata's name. When he recalls the Tathāgata's name, he will disappear from that place and once again be born among humans. Obtaining knowledge of his past lives and dreading [return to] the woesome paths, he will no longer take joy in worldly pleasures. He will come to like to practice benevolent charity, he will praise those who delight in giving, and he will not be greedily attached to his possessions. One after the other, using his head, eyes, hands, feet, blood, flesh and torso, he will be able to distribute charity to all who come seeking it. How much more will he be able to distribute his other property.

"Next, Mañjuśrī, there may be sentient beings who have broken the precepts of moral purity (*śīla*) even though they have accepted the various points of the teachings of the Tathāgata. There may be those who, even if they have not broken the precepts, have broken regulations of the Order. There may be those who, even though they have followed the precepts and rules in a manner which is not improper, have defamed right views. Also, there may be those who, even though they have not defamed right views, have abandoned the practice of studying. Thus, they fail to comprehend the profound principles of the *sūtras* taught by the Buddha. There may be those who, though learned, have become conceited, and because their minds are clouded by conceit, they think they are right and all others are wrong. They come to detest and hate the genuine Teachings, becoming companions and associates of Māra. In this way, these stupid persons themselves practice heretical views. They repeatedly send vast millions of sentient beings plunging into the pitfalls of danger. These persons will sink to the Naraka hell realms, or to the paths of animal or ghostly rebirth, endlessly remaining in *saṃsāra.*

"If they should hear the name of this Master of Healing, the Lapis Lazuli Radiance Tathāgata, it will cause them to abandon their negative practices and cultivate and practice the wholesome Teachings. They will not sink to the pits of woeful existence. But if there are some who are unable to reject negative practices, who are unable to cultivate and practice the wholesome teachings, then they will [continue to] sink to the woesome paths. Due to the awesome force of the fundamental vows made by this Tathāgata, such beings will be caused to arise from their present state to hear the Buddha's name for a fleeting moment. Then, following the end of that life, they will be reborn as humans. They will obtain correct views, and—making effort—they will control the desires of the mind. Furthermore, they will be enabled to reject the path of the householder by taking refuge in the teaching of the homeless Tathāgata. They will accept and hold to the points of the teachings and will have nothing to do with that which is offensive and breaks the precepts. Holding to correct views, they will become learned and understand the deep meanings of the *sūtras.* Divorced from pride, they will no longer slander the genuine Teachings. They will not become Māra's companions. Gradually, they will cultivate and practice the various aspects of the Bodhisattva Path, and they will soon attain to that Path's fulfillment.

"Next, Mañjuśrī, there may be sentient beings who are grudging and greedy, envious and jealous, who praise themselves while slandering others. These beings will sink to the three woesome paths. For limitless thousands of years they will suffer all sorts of miseries. When they have suffered these miseries, at the end of their lives they will be reborn into the world of men, as oxen or horses, camels or donkeys. Constantly whipped, annoyed and irritated by hunger and thirst, they will always be burdened with heavy loads on their backs as they follow the roads and thoroughfares.

"If they obtain human rebirth, it will be as a menial in someone's home, as a male or female servant who constantly receives orders to do manual labor for others. Such a one will never be free.

"In the former life as a human, if such a one ever heard the name of the Lord Master of Healing, the Lapis Lazuli Radiance Tathāgata, due to this good cause, he will be led to recollect it, and he will take refuge in the Buddha with utmost sincerity. By means of the Buddha's spiritual power, he will be liberated from all his sufferings. He will gain perceptive and sharp senses, he will become insightful and learned. He will ever seek for the sublime teachings, constantly meeting wholesome [spiritual] friends. He will sever his ties to Māra for eternity, piercing through the veils of ignorance. The river of afflictions will dry up, and he will be liberated from the sorrows and sufferings of birth, old age, sickness, and death.

"Next, Mañjuśrī, if there are any sentient beings who take delight in schisms, who quarrel and cause irritations between themselves and others; and if by means of deeds, words, and thoughts they create, increase, and prolong all sorts of negative karma; if they constantly further matters which are not beneficial; if they plot revengeful injury; if they summon the spirits of the mountains, forests, and tomb mounds; if they kill living creatures in order to obtain their blood and flesh as sacrificial offerings to the *yakṣa* and *rākṣasa* demons and others; if they write down the names of the cursed, make images of them, by means of evil sorcery curse and harm them, and practice evil magic to raise ghouls, thus putting an end to the life of the enemy and destroying his body—if any of these sentient beings hear the name of this Master of Healing, the Lapis Lazuli Radiance Tathāgata, they will become unable to do injury by all those evil ways. In all the turnings of their minds, there will arise thoughts of loving kindness. They will think of benefits for others, of peace and joy, and they will have no thoughts of torment or hate. Each will be delighted with whatever he receives, and he will be satisfied. These beings will not encroach upon or maltreat others, but will seek to benefit each other.

"Next, Mañjuśrī, there may be some among the four classes of monks, nuns, laymen, and laywomen, among the good sons and daughters of pure faith, who are able to accept and maintain the eightfold vows, observing all the aspects of them for a year or three months.[8] By means of these wholesome roots, they expect to be granted rebirth in the Realm of Utmost Joy of Amitāyus Buddha in the western regions. However, though they have heard the genuine Teachings, they are not yet established in them. If they hear the name of the Lord Master of Healing, the Lapis Lazuli Radiance Tathāgata, then when they reach the end of their lives, eight great Bodhisattvas will ascend through space using their spiritual powers, and they will come to point out the route [to the Western Paradise].[9] In that [Western] realm, they will be spontaneously reborn in multi-colored jeweled flowers.

"If there are those who—even though they have been born in this celestial realm and have established wholesome roots in their previous lives—still have not exhausted [their karma], because they have been born in this celestial realm they will never again be born into any of the woesome paths. When their stay in the celestial realm reaches its end, such a one will be reborn into the human world as a wheel-turning king who will unite all within the four continents. Due to the sovereignty of his awesome virtues, he will securely establish limitless hundreds of thousands of sentient beings in the way of the ten wholesome precepts.

"Or, such a one will be born into a great family of *kṣatriyas*, brahmins, or learned laymen, with abundant wealth, jewels, and granaries and storehouses filled to overflowing. His appearance will be extremely majestic, and he will have a complete array of retainers. He will be intelligent and wise, brave and strong, imposing and fierce like a great master of martial arts.

"Or, even if such a one is born as a woman, if she hears the name of the Lord Master of Healing, the Lapis Lazuli Tathāgata, and with utmost sincerity she accepts it and holds to it, then in subsequent lives this person will never again be born as a woman."

A MYSTIC FORMULA FOR DISPELLING DISEASE AND SUFFERING[10]

["Then, Mañjuśrī, when this Master of Healing, the Lapis Lazuli Radiance Tathāgata attained enlightenment, due to the force of his fundamental vows he was able to observe all sentient beings. Some suffered from various diseases and were emaciated, feverish, jaundiced, and so on; others were in the thrall of noxious poisons of repugnant demons; further, others were (naturally) short-lived or were on the brink of untimely death. He sought to cause all these diseases and sufferings to be ended, and to fulfill all desires.

["At that point, the Lord entered into the *samādhi* named 'Dispeller of the Afflictions of All Beings.' Having entered this *samādhi,* a great brilliant light shone from the *ūrṇā* between his eyebrows, and from its midst a great *dhāraṇī* resounded: *'Namo bhagavate bhaiṣajyaguru-vaiḍūrya prabhā-rājāya tathāgatāya arthate samyak-saṃbuddhāya tadyathā. Oṃ bhaiṣajye bhaiṣajye bhaiṣajya-samudgate svāhā.'*[11]

["Then after this *dhāraṇī* was uttered, from the midst of this light, there was a great rumbling and shaking of the earth and a great radiance shone forth. Illnesses and miseries were removed from all beings, and they all became peaceful and joyous.

["O Mañjuśrī, if there is a good son or daughter who is ill, for the sake of that person you should wholeheartedly constantly clean and bathe him. You should provide for him food, medicine, and water from which all insects have been strained, having recited the *dhāraṇī* over it 108 times. Upon swallowing these substances, all the sufferings of disease will be dispelled. If this person seeks something, with utmost sincerity he should think of the *dhāraṇī* and recite it. In this way, he will obtain all that he seeks, be free of illnesses, and have a long life. At the end of his life, this person will be reborn into the realm of the Buddha (of Healing). He will achieve the non-regressing state and reach enlightenment.

["This is why, Mañjuśrī, good sons and daughters should, with utmost sincerity, diligently revere and worship that Master of Healing, the Lapis Lazuli Radiance Tathāgata, and they should ever hold this *dhāraṇī,* never allowing it to be lost.

["Next, Mañjuśrī, any sons or daughters of pure faith who hear all the names of the Master of Healing, the Lapis Lazuli Radiance Tathāgata, Arhat, Perfectly Enlightened One, should—having heard them—recite them and hold to them. At dawn, they should clean their teeth with sticks of wood, bathe, and purify themselves.

With various fragrant flowers, incense, perfumed unguents, and with music from all instruments, they should worship an image (of that Buddha). They should personally copy this *sūtra* or have others do so, and they should wholeheartedly accept it, hold to it, and listen to its principles. They should offer *pūjā* worship to the master of the teachings (who explicates the principles), and should offer to him all the necessities of life, making sure that he lacks none of these. Having done so, they will be covered by the protective thoughts of the Buddhas. All that they seek shall be fulfilled, and they will reach enlightenment."]

WORSHIP OF THE BUDDHA OF HEALING AND ITS BENEFITS

Then the youth Mañjuśrī saluted the Buddha and said: "O Lord, I aspire that in the age of the replica teachings, by all sorts of means, I shall cause the good sons and daughters of pure faith to hear the name of the Lord Master of Healing, the Lapis Lazuli Radiance Tathāgata. Even during their sleep, I will awaken their ears with the Buddha's name.

"O Lord, they should accept this *sūtra* and hold to it, read it, and recite it. Furthermore, they should lecture on it and explicate its points to others. They themselves should copy it or have others copy it, and worship and pay reverence to the *sūtra* with all sorts of fragrant flowers, perfumed unguents, powdered incense, burning incense, garlands, necklaces, banners, a canopy, drums and music, and they should perform *pūjā* with a five-colored cloth cover for it. They should sweep the site, sprinkle water to purify the area, and then set up a tall throne and securely place the *sūtra* on it. At that time, the Four Great *Deva* Kings together with their retinue overflowing with countless hundreds of thousands in the *deva* assembly will all go to this place of *pūjā* and guard and protect it.

"O Lord, if in this place where the *sūtra* is precious and popular there are those who are able to accept and hold to it, then by means of the merits of the fundamental vows of the Lord Master of Healing, the Lapis Lazuli Radiance Tathāgata and through hearing his name, one should know that in this place there no longer shall be untimely deaths. Also, never again in this place will evil ghosts and demons snatch away the vital spirits of men. Those who have suffered thusly will once again regain their original peace and joy of body and mind."

The Buddha told Mañjuśrī: "So it is, so it is. [It shall be] exactly as you say, Mañjuśrī. If there are any good sons and daughters of pure faith who wish to worship in *pūjā* that Lord Master of Healing, the Lapis Lazuli Radiance Tathāgata, first they should make an image of that Buddha's form, set up a pure throne, and securely place the image on it. They should scatter all sorts of flowers there, burn various incenses, and they should gloriously adorn the site with various banners and pennants. For seven days and seven nights they should accept and hold to the eight-fold vows, eat pure food, bathe in fragrant and pure water, and wear new and clean clothing. They should give birth to the unstained, single-minded state, with no thought of anger or harm. Towards all sentient beings, there should arise the thoughts of blessings and benefits, peace, loving kindness, sympathetic joy, and equanimity. They should play musical instruments and sing praises while circumambulating to the right of the Buddha image. Furthermore, they should recall the merits of that Tathāgata's fundamental vows and study and recite this *sūtra.* They should think only of its principles and lecture on the *sūtra,* elucidating its main points.

"It will follow that all those joyous things which are sought shall come to pass. If long life is sought, then longevity shall be granted. If wealth and abundance are sought, then that prosperity shall be obtained. If an official position is sought, then it shall be gained, and if a son or daughter is sought, the child will be born.

"Furthermore, if there is a person who suddenly has nightmares, who sees all sorts of evil apparitions, or who encounters monstrous birds which flock together, or if a hundred ominous portents materialize in his home—if that person uses all sorts of marvelous and valuable utensils to perform reverent *pūjā* to that Lord Master of Healing, the Lapis Lazuli Radiance Tathāgata, then the nightmares, evil apparitions, and all inauspicious things will disappear, unable to cause harm.

"If there are any persons who are threatened by water, fire, sword, poison, hanging from a precipice, wicked elephant, a lion, tiger, wolf, bear, poisonous snake, scorpion, centipede or millipede, or mosquito—if such a one is able to recall with perfect sincerity that Buddha and reverently worship him, he will be freed from all dreadful things. If another state invades and disturbs the peace, or if robbers and thieves cause disorder, one who recalls and reverently worships that Tathāgata also will obtain freedom [from these disturbances].

"Next, Mañjuśrī, there may be good sons and daughters of pure faith who—having reached the end of their days—have never served another *deva,* have taken wholehearted refuge in the Buddha, the Teachings, and the Order and accept and hold to the restraining precepts. If among the five precepts, or the two hundred fifty precepts of the monks, or the five hundred precepts of the nuns that such a person has accepted, if any of these precepts that were accepted have been broken, then that person may fear that he will sink into a woesome path. If such a one is able to concentrate solely on the name of that Buddha and reverently worship him, then he certainly will not suffer rebirth in any of the three woesome paths.

"If there is a woman about to give birth who suffers from acute pain, if she is able to praise the name and form and reverently worship that Tathāgata with utmost sincerity, then all her pain will be removed and her child will be born without bodily defect. The appearance of her child will be perfect, and all who see him will exclaim with joy. The child will be endowed with keen sense-organs, intelligence, and tranquility. He will seldom become ill, and non-human beings will never snatch away his vital spirit."

THE IMPORTANCE OF FAITH

At this time the Lord told Ānanda: "All the merits of that Lord Buddha Master of Healing, the Lapis Lazuli Tathāgata, just as I have praised them, are [aspects of] the profound range of spiritual activities[12] of the Buddhas, and they are difficult to comprehend. Do you have faith in them or not?"

Ānanda replied: "O Lord of Great Virtue, no doubts arise in me towards the *vaipulya sūtras* spoken by the Tathāgata. Why is this so? The karma produced by the deeds, words, and thoughts of all the Tathāgatas is entirely pure. O Lord, the discs of the sun and the moon can be caused to sink and fall, and the wonderfully lofty king of mountains [Mount Sumeru] may be caused to shake, but the words of the Buddhas never change.

"O Lord, the roots of faith of sentient beings are incomplete. Though they hear descriptions of the profound ranges of activity of the various Buddhas, these beings of incomplete faith may merely think: 'How can we, just by concentrating on the name of a single Buddha, Master of Healing, the Lapis Lazuli Radiance Tathāgata, thereby obtain such excellent blessings?' From this lack of faith, there arises in turn slander and defamation. In the long night, these beings lose their great beneficial joy and sink into the woesome paths, plunged inexhaustibly into *saṃsāra.*"

The Buddha told Ānanda: "If these sentient beings hear the name of the Lord Master of Healing, the Lapis Lazuli Radiance Tathāgata, and with utmost sincerity accept it and hold to it, and no doubts arise, then they will not fall into a woesome path.

"Ānanda, it is difficult to have faith in and comprehend the profound practices of the Buddhas. You now are able to accept them, and you should know that this has been caused by the awesome power of the Tathāgatas. Ānanda, the *śrāvakas, pratyekabuddhas,* the Bodhisattvas who have not yet climbed the stages [of development], and all the others are unable to have faith in them and comprehend them with such sincerity. It is only the Bodhisattva with one remaining birth [who can do so].

"Ānanda, a human incarnation is difficult to obtain. It is also difficult to obtain faith in the Three Jewels, and to revere, honor, and respect them. It is even more difficult to be granted the opportunity to hear the name of the Lord Master of Healing, the Lapis Lazuli Radiance Tathāgata. Ānanda, if I were to describe the boundless Bodhisattva practices, the limitless excellent and clever means, the infinitely vast great vows of that Master of Healing, the Lapis Lazuli Radiance Tathāgata—if I were to describe these for an aeon or even longer, that period would soon be exhausted. The practices, vows, and excellent skillful means of that Buddha are inexhaustible."

SAVING THOSE ON THE BRINK OF DEATH OR DISASTER

At that time in the assembly, there was a Bodhisattva-mahāsattva named "Saving Deliverance."[13] He rose from his seat and circumambulated the Buddha, baring his right shoulder. Kneeling with his right knee to the ground, he bowed with palms clasped together and addressed the Buddha: "O Lord of Great Virtue, in the era of the replica teachings, there will be sentient beings who are distressed by various kinds of suffering, emaciated by lengthy illnesses. Unable to eat or drink, their throats parched and their lips dry, every direction in which they look seems dark. The signs of death appear, and parents, relatives, friends, and acquaintances will gather around such a person with lamentations and weeping.

"Then, while his body lies in its original position, he is seized by the messengers of Yama who lead his spirit consciousness before that King of the Law. The inborn spirits attached to all sentient beings, who record whether each being's conduct is good or bad, will then hand down these records in their entirety to Yama, King of the Law. Then, the King will interrogate this person, and he will sum up the person's deeds. According to the positive and negative factors, he shall judge him.

"If that sick person's relatives, close friends, and acquaintances are able to take refuge in the Lord Master of Healing, the Lapis Lazuli Radiance Tathāgata for that person's sake, and if they ask an assembly of monks to recite this scripture, light the seven-storied lamps and suspend the five-colored life-prolonging spirit banner—then that person's consciousness may be returned to his body [immediately]. He will clearly remember what he has experienced, as if it were a dream.

"If his consciousness returns after passing through seven, twenty-one, thirty-five, or forty-nine days, he will feel as if he is awakening from a dream, and he will remember that he has received the fruits and retributions of his good and bad karma. Due to his personally witnessing and experiencing the fruits and retributions of his karma, and since he reached this life with difficulty, he will not create bad karma for himself [in the future].

"Because of this, good sons and daughters of pure faith, you all should accept and hold to the name of the Master of Healing, the Lapis Lazuli Radiance Tathāgata and, accordingly, revere and worship him with effort to the utmost of your capacity."

Then Ānanda inquired of the Bodhisattva Saving Deliverance: "Good son, please explain how one should revere and worship that Lord Master of Healing, the Lapis Lazuli Radiance Tathāgata? How should one construct the life-prolonging banner and lamps?"

The Bodhisattva Saving Deliverance replied: "O Virtuous One, if you desire to deliver a sick person from the pain of disease, for the sake of this person you should accept and hold to the eightfold vows for seven days and seven nights. You should collect together food, drink, and other property and, in accordance with your means, provide a *pūjā* offering to the community of monks.

"You should worship with a *pūjā* offering that Lord Master of Healing, the Lapis Lazuli Radiance Tathāgata, six times during the day and night. Read and recite this *sūtra* forty-nine times. Light forty-nine lamps and make seven images of the form of that Tathāgata. In front of each image arrange seven lamps. Make each lamp as large as a cartwheel, and for forty-nine days let their shining light ceaselessly burn. Make a five-colored, variegated banner forty-nine hand-lengths in height. You should release forty-nine living creatures of varied species. Then the sick person will be able to obtain passage through this danger, and he will be removed from the grasp of evil demons.

"Furthermore, Ānanda, in the case of a *kṣatriya* king properly enthroned by means of the *abhiṣeka* rite, when calamities and troubles arise—such as an epidemic among the people, invasion of the state, internal rebellion, an adverse delineation of the stars, a lunar or solar eclipse, unseasonal winds and rains, or the lack of rain in its proper season—there should arise in that properly enthroned *kṣatriya* king the thought of compassion and pity towards all sentient beings. He should pardon all who are incarcerated. Relying on the method of *pūjā* described above, he should worship the Lord Master of Healing, the Lapis Lazuli Radiance Tathāgata.

"Due to these good roots and the force of that Tathāgata's

fundamental vows, his state will be caused to become tranquil. The winds and rains will occur at their proper seasons, and the crops will all ripen. All sentient beings will be healthy and will be gladdened and joyous. In his state, there will be no tyrannical *yakṣas,* nor sentient beings with various spiritual distresses. All negative omens will be removed, and the *kṣatriya* ruler will have a long life, handsomeness, and vitality free from disease. His sovereign rule will be prosperous.

"Ānanda, if the ruler, the queen and lesser consorts, the heir apparent and other princes, the great ministers, court attendants and ladies, the provincial officials, and the masses are troubled by the suffering of disease or other calamities, they also should make and set up five-colored spirit banners and kindle lamps, seeing that they burn continuously. They should release various living creatures, scatter flowers of varied colors, and light various famous incenses. They will then obtain freedom from all diseases and liberation from all difficulties."

At that point, Ānanda asked the Bodhisattva Saving Deliverance, "Good son, how can one increase the life of one whose span is already exhausted?"

The Bodhisattva Saving Deliverance said: "O Virtuous One, how can you not have heard the Tathāgata speak of the nine untimely deaths?[14] This is why I am encouraging you to make the life-prolonging banners and lamps and to cultivate the various auspicious virtues. By cultivating the auspicious, one thereby lives to the fullest extent of his life-span, and does not experience suffering and distress."

Ānanda asked, "What are the nine untimely deaths?"

The Bodhisattva Saving Deliverance replied: "There may be sentient beings who have contracted an illness, which—though minor—goes untreated through lack of both medicine and physician. Or, the person may meet a doctor who gives him the wrong medicine. Such persons actually should not die, yet they are caused to have untimely deaths. Furthermore, a person may have faith in materialistic and demonic heretics, masters of black magic. The false explanations of calamities and blessings which they provide will lead to fearful actions. Since this [misled] person cannot discern correctly with his own heart, he asks divinatory questions in his search for good fortune, and he kills all sorts of living creatures to propitiate spirits. He calls the spirits of the waters and begs for blessings, desiring to lengthen his years. In the end, he is unable to obtain this. Stupid and confused, believing in false and inverted views—it follows that such a person is led to an untimely death and enters into a hell with no definite time of release. These are what is known as the first untimely death.

"The second untimely death is by execution according to the ruler's laws. The third is when someone goes out on hunts or pleasure excursions and engages in debauch and drunkenness to excess, with no limits. His vital spirit is snatched away by a [demonic] non-human being, thus causing untimely death. The fourth untimely death is burning by fire. The fifth is by drowning in water.

"Some are devoured by wild beasts, thus causing the sixth untimely death. The seventh untimely death is by falling off a mountain precipice. The eighth untimely death is caused by harm from poisonous herbs, hateful entreaties [spells], and magical incantations causing corpses, devils, and other such things to arise. The ninth is caused by starvation and dehydration due to not obtaining food and drink.

"This is the Tathāgata's summary explanation of the nine types of untimely deaths. Beyond these, there are, in addition, limitless other untimely deaths which would be altogether difficult to expound upon.

"Next, Ānanda, that King Yama is in charge of the entering of names in the register of all persons in the world. If there are any sentient beings who are not filial, who have committed the five disobediences,[15] who have broken and defiled the Three Jewels, who have infringed upon the laws of the ruler and subjects, and who have slandered faith in the precepts, then the King of the Law, Yama, will punish them in accordance with his examination of the severity of the crimes. This is why I now am urging all sentient beings to kindle lamps, make banners, and give rise to the cultivation of that which is auspicious. This will cause sentient beings to pass over suffering and distress, to avoid meeting with all sorts of difficulties."

THE YAKṢA GENERALS AND THEIR PLEDGE

At that time in the assembly, there were Twelve Great *Yakṣa* Generals seated together in the meeting. Their names are: Kumbhīra, Vajra, Mihira, Aṇḍīra, Anila, Saṇḍila, Indra, Pajra, Makura, Kinnara, Catura, and Vikarāla.[16] Each of these Twelve *Yakṣa* Generals has seven thousand *yakṣas* in his troops.

They raised their voices together and addressed the Buddha: "O Lord, we now, having received the Buddha's awesome force, have been granted the hearing of the name of the Master of Healing, the Lapis Lazuli Radiance Tathāgata. Never again will we have the fear of sinking into a woesome path. Together, we all have the same thought: we will take utmost refuge in the Buddha, the Teachings, and the Order. We aspire to bear responsibility to do acts of righteous benefit, enrichment, peace and joy for all sentient beings, no matter in what village, town, capital, or forest grove of retirement they dwell.

"As to those who circulate this *sūtra* or who further accept and hold to the name of the Master of Healing, the Lapis Lazuli Radiance Tathāgata and revere and worship him, we will cause them to be freed from all suffering and difficulties. All the desires of these persons will be caused to be fulfilled. Those who seek release from the distress of illness should also read and recite this *sūtra.* Taking a five-colored rope, they should knot our names into it, untying the knots when their wishes are fulfilled."

At that point, the Lord praised all the Great *Yakṣa* Generals saying: "Excellent, excellent, Great *Yakṣa* Generals! When you think of repaying the merciful blessings of the Lord Master of Healing, the Lapis Lazuli Radiance Tathāgata, you should ever serve all sentient beings in the way you have described, bringing to them blessings and benefits, peace and joy."

NAMING THE SŪTRA AND CONCLUSION

Then Ānanda asked the Buddha, "O Lord, what name should be given to this teaching and how should we uphold it?"

The Buddha told Ānanda: "The name of this teaching is 'The Merits of the Fundamental Vows of the Master of Healing, the

Lapis Lazuli Radiance Tathāgata.' It is also called 'Sacred Formula of the Binding Vows of the Twelve *Deva* Generals to Enrich All Sentient Beings.' It is also called 'Tearing Away All Karmic Veils.' In this way, you should uphold it."

After the Lord finished speaking, all the Bodhisattva-mahāsattvas, the great *śrāvakas,* the king of the state, great ministers, brahmins, learned laymen, *devas, nāgas, yakṣas, gandharvas, asuras, garuḍas, kiṃnaras,* and beings human and non-human—all in the entire great congregation who heard the Buddha's teaching rejoiced. They faithfully accepted and put into practice the teachings of the *sūtra* of the merits of the fundamental vows of the Master of Healing, the Lapis Lazuli Radiance Tathāgata.

1. These opening phrases are found in the Sanskrit manuscript versions of the *Bhaiṣajya-guru vaiḍūrya-prabha-rāja-sūtram,* Nalinaksha Dutt, ed. *Gilgit Manuscripts,* vol. I (Srinagar, Kashmir: 1939), p. 1 (unless otherwise noted, page numbers refer to the numbering of the Sanskrit text). The Chinese text used, upon which this translation is principally based, was copied in 765 C.E. It was found by Sir Mark Aurel Stein at Tun-huang early in this century, and now is in the collection of the British Museum (Stein ms. 2616, Giles catalog 3574).
2. Though the Chinese text (p. 405A) has only half the compound for "arhat," *ying* (instead of *ying-kung*), the Sanskrit text (p. 2) has "arhat." This peculiar omission is found in many of the Healing Buddha texts, including the *Sūtra on the Merits of the Fundamental Vows of the Seven Buddhas, the Lapis Lazuli Radiance Masters of Healing* (T. 451).
3. There are a number of lists of these thirty-two principal marks and eighty secondary marks, which differ in minor aspects. In Alex Wayman's article "Contributions regarding the thirty-two characteristics of the great person" (*Sino-Indian Studies* V, 1957 [Liebenthal Festschrift], pp. 243–260), it is noted that analysis of the characteristics or marks (*lakṣaṇa*) of the body to foretell the destiny of a child was an Indian practice predating Buddhism. Among the primary marks of the great man, often depicted in Buddhist art, are those such as: the *uṣṇīṣa,* a bulge on the top of the head indicating authority; the *ūrṇā,* a curl of silver hair between the eye-brows (depicted in images as a slight bulge

at the location of the "third-eye"); hands and feet marked by a wheel rim; webs joining the fingers and toes on the hands and feet.

4. To commit no faults, to act in a wholesome manner, and to seek to benefit all sentient beings.

5. Two aspects are referred to here: the physical difficulties and sorrows which women were subject to in an age when medical treatment was often primitive, and the apparent low social status of women in the region where this text was first composed. For more on this, see p. 64.

6. Literally "there have been no women there." My rendering of this phrase in a non-literal manner is due to the encouragement of all "good sons and daughters" to vow to be reborn in the paradise, this statement occurring a mere two paragraphs after the phrase in question.

7. Gold, silver, lapis lazuli, quartz crystal, agate, carnelian, and ruby or red pearl.

8. The eightfold vows include: no killing, no stealing, no improper sexual conduct, no false speech, no alcoholic drinks, no cosmetics or personal adornments, sleeping on a mat on the ground, and no food after noon.

9. The names of the eight Bodhisattvas are: Mañjuśrī, Avalokiteśvara, Mahāsthāmaprāpta, Akṣayamati, "Precious Sandal Blossom" (this Bodhisattva is not well-known; his name has no standard Sanskrit equivalent), Bhaiṣajya-rāja, Bhaiṣajya-samudgata, and Maitreya. Though not mentioned either in this Chinese version of the *sūtra* or the Sanskirt manuscript, they are specifically named in chapter twelve of the *Abhiṣeka-sūtra*, T. XXI, 1131, p. 534A.

10. This section, though found neither in the Tun-huang version of Hsüan-tsang's translation nor in the Sanskrit manuscript remains, can be found in slightly altered form in the later expanded version of this *sūtra*, the scripture of the Seven Healing Buddhas (Translation IV). It is also popularly incorporated into modern versions circulated among Chinese Buddhists, including a version in my possession recently published in Hong Kong. It is included in Walter Liebenthal's translation, *The Sūtra of the Lord of Healing* (Peking: 1936), and is also found in a Chinese version of the *sūtra* circulated in Peking in the early 1930s, found in the collection of the late Prof. F. D. Lessing.

11. This can be translated as: "I honor the Lord Master of Healing, the King of Lapis Lazuli Radiance, Tathāgata, Arhat, Perfectly Enlightened One, saying: To the healing, to the healing, to the supreme healing hail!"

12. *hsing-chu* is the equivalent of the Sanskrit *gocara* ("range, abode, field of action"), Sanskrit text, p. 21.

13. *Chiu-t'o* is the equivalent of the Sanskrit Trāṇamukta. In the Sanskrit text, p. 23.
14. "Untimely" also carries the connotation of "violent."
15. *Pañcāntarya:* patricide, matricide, killing an arhat, shedding the blood of a Buddha, and destroying the harmony of the Saṃgha.
16. These are tentative reconstructions based on traditional Sino-Japanese understanding of the text. For variants, see Dutt's Sanskrit edition and his notes, pp. 29–30.

TRANSLATION IV

Sūtra on the Merits of the Fundamental Vows of the Seven Buddhas of Lapis Lazuli Radiance, the Masters of Healing

(Yao-shih liu-li-kuang ch'i-fo pen-yüan kung-te ching)

From the Chinese version of the Tripiṭaka Master I-ching (T'ang, 707 C.E.), T. XIV, 451.

INITIAL SECTION

Thus have I heard; once when the Lord was traveling throughout the states in order to transform the inhabitants, he arrived at the city of Vaiśālī and dwelt at the base of a tree from which music resounded. Together with him was an assembly of great monks totaling eight thousand. Also, there were thirty-six thousand Bodhisattva-mahāsattvas, such as the Bodhisattva Gentle Glory (Mañjuśrī), the Bodhisattva Observer of the Cries of the World (Avalokiteśvara), the Bodhisattva Loving Kindness (Maitreya), the Bodhisattva Well Appearing (Subhūti), the Bodhisattva Great Wisdom, the Bodhisattva Clear Wisdom, the Bodhisattva Mountain Peak, the Bodhisattva Eloquent Peak, the Bodhisattva Grasps the Wondrously Lofty Peak, the Bodhisattva Unfailing Transcendence, the Bodhisattva Subtle and Wondrous Voice, the Bodhisattva Ever Reflecting, the Bodhisattva Holder of the Thunderbolt (Vajradhara), and other great Bodhisattvas who are supreme leaders like them.[1]

Also in attendance were the king of the state, his great ministers, brahmins, learned laymen, *devas, nāgas,* and others of the eight classes of beings human and non-human.

This boundlessly great assembly respectfully gathered around in a circle, and the Buddha spoke to them about the Dharma. From beginning, middle, to end, the intent of his apt phrases was excellent and skillful. His entirely pure words matched the purity of his conduct. He pointed out the benefits and joys [of the Way], and all were caused to become completely endowed with the subtle and sublime practices and vows, and [entered upon] the path of the great enlightenment.

Then, the Prince of the Dharma, the Bodhisattva-mahāsattva Mañjuśrī, inspired by the awesome spiritual influence of the Buddha, arose from his seat, baring his right shoulder [as a gesture of respect]. He knelt with his right knee on the ground, clasped his palms together, and reverently addressed the Buddha, saying: "O Lord, today there are boundless humans and *devas* in the great assembly. They have all gathered together like a cloud in order to hear the Dharma. It is only you, O Lord Buddha, who knows of all the Buddha-fields, since you have passed through aeons as incalculable as grains of dust and sand, from that moment when you first expressed the aspiration to attain enlightenment up to now. For our sake and for the sake of beings of the future age of the replica teachings, we wish that with love and compassion you may expansively describe the names of the various Buddhas, the merits of their fundamental vows, the adornments of their realms, and their clever methods [for teaching the Dharma]. Cause the karmic fetters of all your listeners to be removed and eliminated so that they may attain the enlightenment from which there is no turning back."

Then the Lord praised the Bodhisattva Mañjuśrī, saying: "Excellent, excellent, Mañjuśrī. Due to your thoughts of great compassion and pity, all the boundless sentient beings hindered by karmic fetters, all suffering with the sorrows of various diseases, and all beings with piteous afflictions will obtain peace and joy due to your request. Your exhortation that I expound on the names of the various Buddhas, on the merits of their fundamental vows, and on the adornments of their realms stems from my awesome spiritual powers, which have caused you to raise this question. You now should listen carefully, and with utmost attention consider what I have to say."

Mañjuśrī responded, "I sincerely desire that you speak to us. We will listen with great joy."

THE BUDDHA AUSPICIOUS KING

The Buddha told Mañjuśrī: "In the East, beyond as many Buddha-fields as there are four times the number of grains of sand in the Ganges River, there is a realm named Radiant Victory. The Buddha is known by the apt name of Auspicious King Tathāgata, Arhat,[2] Perfectly Enlightened One, Perfect in Mind and Deed, Well-Gone, He Who Knows the World, Unsurpassed Being, Tamer of Passions, Teacher of *Devas* and Men, Buddha, Lord. Surrounding him, there are countless millions of Bodhisattvas, all of whom have reached the stage from which there is no regression. At this moment, he is discoursing on the Dharma, securely seated upon a lion throne, which is marvelously adorned with the seven precious things.

"Mañjuśrī, that Buddha-land is pure, and it is gloriously adorned. A hundred thousand *yojanas* in length and breadth, its soil is made of the gold of the Jambunadi River, even and smooth. The air is like a celestial fragrance. In that land, there are none of the woesome paths of existence, nor is there any temptation.[3] Also, there is no rubble [strewn upon the ground],[4] no sand or stones, nor are there brambles or thorns. There are jeweled trees arranged in an orderly fashion, and the fruits of their blossoms are nourishing and plentiful. There are many bathing pools, with steps adorned by gold, silver, pearls, and various other gems. Mañjuśrī, in that land the Bodhisattvas are born in lotus blossoms made of the seven precious substances. Because of [all] this, the good sons and daughters of pure faith should vow to be reborn in the realm of that Buddha.

"Mañjuśrī, when that Buddha, Tathāgata, Arhat, Perfectly Enlightened One first aspired to set out upon the Bodhisattva Path, he made eight great vows. What are these eight?

"*First Great Vow:* 'I vow that when I attain supreme enlightenment in a future age, if there are any beings whose bodies are constrained and pressed upon by the sufferings of disease, such as the afflictions of fevers, malaria, and black magic arising from repugnant demons, spirits of corpses, and so on—if such persons are able to call out my name with perfect sincerity, due to my spiritual force[5] all their diseases and sufferings will be removed, and they will personally experience supreme enlightenment.'

"*Second Great Vow:* 'I vow that when I attain enlightenment in a future age, if there are any sentient beings who are blind, deaf, mute, who are leprous, suffer from delirium, or who are distressed by any disease—if such beings are able to call out my name with perfect sincerity, due to my spiritual force they will be fully endowed with perfect sense faculties, they will be rid of all disease, and they will reach enlightenment.'

"*Third Great Vow:* 'I vow that when I attain supreme enlightenment in a future age, if there are any sentient beings who are bound and compelled by desire, anger, and ignorance, who unceasingly commit crimes and participate in various negative practices, who slander the genuine Teachings and do not cultivate the perfections,[6] who indeed shall sink to the hells and be subject to suffering and pain—if such beings call out my name with perfect sincerity, due to my spiritual force I will cause a halt to their unceasing crimes and I will cause them to be rid of all their karmic fetters. These sentient beings will not sink to the woesome paths of existence but will constantly receive human or *deva* incarnations of rare peace and joy, and they will reach enlightenment.'

"*Fourth Great Vow:* 'I vow that when I attain enlightenment in a future age, if there are any sentient beings who lack clothing, food, necklaces, bedding, property, precious things, fragrant flowers, or music—if such beings are able to call out my name with perfect sincerity, due to my spiritual force whatever was lacking in their lives will be obtained in ample quantity, and they will reach enlightenment.'

"*Fifth Great Vow:* 'I vow that when I attain enlightenment in a future age, if there are any sentient beings who have had their bodies bound in chains and have been put in wooden cangues, and who have suffered as a result of the whip—if such beings are able to call out my name with perfect sincerity, then due to my spiritual force they will obtain release from all these afflictions, and they will reach enlightenment.'

"*Sixth Great Vow:* 'I vow that when I attain enlightenment in a future age, if there are any sentient beings who are in a place of danger, under attack by evil beasts such as bears, leopards, wolves, pythons, cobras, or scorpions, and if at that grave moment when the creature who seeks to cut off that being's life lets out a great roar, if at that grave moment these sentient beings are able to call out my name with perfect sincerity, then due to my spiritual force they will obtain release from all fear, and compassion will arise in all these evil beasts. They will always have peace and joy, and they will reach enlightenment.'

"*Seventh Great Vow:* 'I vow that when I attain enlightenment in a future age, if there are any sentient beings who engage in quarrelsome debates and lawsuits, thus producing grief and anger—if such persons are able to call out my name with perfect sincerity, then due to my spiritual force the quarrels and lawsuits will be dispersed, each party will have compassion upon the other, and they will reach enlightenment.'

"*Eighth Great Vow:* 'I vow that when I attain enlightenment in a future age, there may be sentient beings who, when setting out upon a river or sea, meet with a great ill wind which blows their boat or ship beyond islands or the shore, making return so difficult that they become grief-stricken and alarmed. If they are able to call out my name with perfect sincerity, then due to my spiritual force they will attain their wish and reach a tranquil haven where they will receive all joyful things, and they will reach enlightenment.'

"O Mañjuśrī, these are the eight subtle and sublime great vows which were expressed by that Buddha, Tathāgata, Arhat, Perfectly Enlightened One when he set out upon the Bodhisattva Path. Since that Lord first made these resolves, by the force of his *samādhi* he has perfected sentient beings and worshipped the various Buddhas and their glorious and pure Buddha-fields. His retinue of Bodhisattvas is complete, and their auspicious virtues are inconceivable. If you tried to recite the names of all the *śrāvakas* and *pratyekabuddhas* present there, you could recite their names for many aeons, yet the list would still be incomplete. This list does not even include the [vast number of] Bodhisattvas in his retinue who will become Buddhas in their next incarnation.

"Mañjuśrī, if there are any good sons or daughters of pure faith, if there are any kings, great ministers, wealthy sponsors, or learned laymen who aspire to the rare and auspicious termination of all their afflictions, they should call out the name of that Buddha and recite this *sūtra.* With perfect sincerity, they should honor and reverently worship that Buddha. All the veils of their negative karma and all their diseases and sufferings will be dispelled. Whatever they seek will be received to their satisfaction. They will attain to the state from which there is no regression. They will reach enlightenment."

THE BUDDHA SOVEREIGN KING, MAJESTIC LIGHT AND SOUND OF THE MOON-JEWEL INSIGHT

"Next, Mañjuśrī, in the East, past as many Buddha-fields as there are five times the amount of grains of sand in the Ganges River, there is a realm known as "Marvelous Gem." The Buddha is named Sovereign King, Majestic Light and Sound of the Moon-Jewel Insight Tathāgata, Arhat, Perfectly Enlightened One. There are untold millions of Bodhisattvas surrounding him as he presently discourses on the Teachings, explaining the subtle, sublime, and deep principles of the vast Mahāyāna.

"Mañjuśrī, when that Buddha first expressed the aspiration to set out upon the Bodhisattva Path, he made eight great vows. What are these eight?

"*First Great Vow:* 'I vow that when I attain enlightenment in a future age, if there are any sentient beings engaged in farming or commercial activities which cause disturbances in their hearts, who, though they aspire to cultivate the rare and good teachings of enlightenment, are unable to escape from the round of birth and death, each on the verge of boundless distress—if such persons are able to call out my name with utmost sincerity, due to my spiritual force they will be provided with clothing, food and drink, and property, and according to their desires they will be amply supplied with gold, silver, and precious things. All the wholesome roots will be increased, and they will not abandon the aspiration to attain enlightenment. They will be freed from the sufferings of the woesome paths and from their delusions. They will reach enlightenment.'

"*Second Great Vow:* 'I vow that when I attain enlightenment in a future age, if there are any beings within the realms of the Ten Directions who are subject to great distress, their bodies pressed upon by heat, cold, hunger, and thirst—if they are able to call my name with utmost sincerity, then due to my spiritual force the karma due to faults committed in past lives will all be removed. They will cast off their afflictions, receiving the joys of [birth as] humans or *devas,* and they will reach enlightenment.'

"*Third Great Vow:* 'I vow that when I attain enlightenment in a future age, if there are any females within the realms of the Ten Directions to whom the vexations of licentious passions constantly return to their minds, and who repeatedly become pregnant and truly detest this, who suffer great distress when they reach the time of childbirth—if my name should pass through their ears for but a moment, and if they further call it out and retain it in their minds, then due to my spiritual force all their sufferings will be removed. After abandoning their present bodies [at the end of this life], they will always be reborn as men, and they will reach enlightenment.'

"*Fourth Great Vow:* 'I vow that when I attain enlightenment in a future age, if there are any sentient beings who together with parents, brothers, sisters, wives, retainers, relatives, or friends travel through a dangerous and difficult region and are caused distress by being hunted down by thieves—if such persons have heard my name for but a moment, and if they again call it out and retain it in their minds, then due to my spiritual force they will be freed from all their troubles, and they will reach enlightenment.'

"*Fifth Great Vow:* 'I vow that when I attain enlightenment in a future age, if there are any beings who travel in the darkness of night in order to carry out their work and are harassed by negative spirits to their utter grief and suffering—if such persons have heard my name for but a moment, and if they again call it out and retain it in their minds, then due to my spiritual force they will meet with light arising out of that darkness. In those negative spirits, there will arise thoughts of loving kindness and compassion, and these persons will reach enlightenment.'

"*Sixth Great Vow:* 'I vow that when I attain enlightenment in a future age, if there are any beings who engage in vile and negative practices and do not believe in the Three Jewels, whose insight is sparse, who do not cultivate the wholesome teachings, neither cultivating studies of the sense organs and their faculties, the way of enlightenment, proper mindfulness and *samādhi,* nor of total self-control—if such beings are able to call out my name with utmost sincerity, then due to my spiritual force their insight will gradually increase. They will cultivate studies of the thirty-seven *bodhipakṣya dharmas,* develop profound faith in the Three Jewels, and they will reach enlightenment.'

"*Seventh Great Vow:* 'I vow that when I attain enlightenment in a future age, if there are any beings whose thoughts dwell on desire and coarseness, who practice and abide in the Two Vehicles [of the *śrāvaka* and the *pratyekabuddha*], who turn their backs on the peerless, excellent, and sublime enlightenment—if such beings are able to call out my name with utmost sincerity, they will abandon their views of the Two Vehicles. Turning towards the supreme awakening, they will attain the state from which there is no regression, and they will reach enlightenment.'

"*Eighth Great Vow:* 'I vow that when I attain enlightenment in a future age, if there are any beings who, at the time of the imminent end of an aeon, when the fires of passion arise [to destroy the world], generate great sorrow and fear, suffering, weeping and wailing; and if, due to the force of the negative karma created in their past lives they are subject to these sufferings, with no place of refuge—if they are able with perfect sincerity to call out my name, all sorrows and sufferings will disappear. They will be immersed in the joys of clarity and coolness. At the end of their present lives, these persons will be reborn in lotus blossoms in my Buddha-land. Constantly cultivating wholesome teachings, they will reach enlightenment.'

"Mañjuśrī, these are the eight types of subtle and sublime great vows, which were expressed by that Buddha, Tathāgata, Arhat, Enlightened One, when he set out upon the Bodhisattva Path. Further, the Buddha-field where that Tathāgata dwells is vast and extensive, and the awesome and pure land is as flat as the palm of my hand. The trees there, bearing a heavenly and sublime fragrance, grow in orderly rows. Heavenly flowers cover the grounds, and celestial music constantly resounds. Marvelous celestial bells are hung everywhere. The lion throne [of the Buddha] is gloriously adorned with heavenly gems, and the steps of the various marvelous bathing ponds are also adorned with celestial gems. The soil is soft, without any [gravel or] rubble.

"There is no temptation there, nor any of the afflictions. All who dwell there are Bodhisattvas who have reached the non-regressing stage, and all are born in lotus blossoms. If a person thinks of food, drink, clothing, or any other goods, then, at that moment, these things manifest before the person, in accord with his wishes. This is why the realm is called 'Marvelous Gem.'[7]

"Mañjuśrī, if there are any sons or daughters of pure faith, any kings of states, princes, great councillors or lesser ministers, queens, or court ladies who, with diligence and utmost sincerity, reverently worship that Buddha six times during the day and night and call out his name; if they make an image [of that Buddha] and reverently offer fragrant flowers, music, burning incense, powdered incense, fragrant unguents; if they maintain the eightfold vows with glorious purity for seven days; if there arises in them thoughts of loving kindness and compassion towards all living things, and they vow to be reborn in that Buddha-land, then that Lord Buddha and the various Bodhisattvas will hold these persons in their protective thoughts. They will be purified of all the karma due to their faults. They will attain the non-regressing state of supreme enlightenment, having gradually attained the state where desire, anger, and ignorance are trivial. They will not contract any of the various diseases, and so their spans of life will be extended. Whatever they seek shall be as they wish. As to quarrelsome enemies, joy will arise in them all.

"After such a person abandons his body, he will go to that [Buddha-] land and will be reborn in a lotus blossom. At the moment when he is to be born, his mindfulness, *samādhi*, and control over passions will be entirely lucid. Mañjuśrī, you should know that the infinite merits of the name of that Buddha are such that if one hears it, whatever is desired will become manifest."

THE BUDDHA RADIANT GEM OF GOLDEN HUE, PERFECTED IN THE SUBLIME PRACTICES

"Next, Mañjuśrī, in the east, beyond as many Buddha-fields as six times the number of grains of sand in the Ganges River, there is a realm called 'Wholly Complete Incense Heap.' The Buddha there is named 'Radiant Gem of Golden Hue, Perfected in the Sublime Practices Tathāgata, Arhat, Perfectly Enlightened One.' Boundless millions of Bodhisattvas encircle him as he presently discourses on the Teachings.

"Mañjuśrī, when that Buddha first set out upon the Bodhisattva Path, he made four great vows. What are these four?

"*First Great Vow:* 'I vow that when I attain enlightenment in a future age, if there are any beings who engage in various types of butchery and harm, cutting lives short, who, due to this bad karma, are subjected to the sufferings of rebirth in a hell realm; or if such persons are reborn as humans, they have a short life with many illnesses, or they meet with the harm of flood, fire, swords, or poison, and thereby meet with painful death—if such a person hears my name and with perfect sincerity calls it out and retains it in his mind, then due to my spiritual force all his bad karma will be eliminated. Free of illness, he will have a long life, not meeting with an untimely death, and he will reach enlightenment.'

"*Second Great Vow:* 'I vow that in a future age when I attain enlightenment, if there are any beings who create bad karma by stealing property from others and are thus bound to sink to a woesome path of existence, or, although obtaining rebirth as humans, find themselves born into impoverished families lacking clothing and food and constantly subjected to various sufferings—if such persons hear my name and with utmost sincerity call it out and retain it in their minds, then due to my spiritual force all their negative karma will be eliminated. They will never be lacking in clothing, food, and drink, and they will reach enlightenment.'

"*Third Great Vow:* 'I vow that when I attain enlightenment in a future age, if there are any beings who insult each other and treat each other rudely as if they were enemies—if such persons hear my name and with utmost sincerity call it out and retain it in their minds, then due to my spiritual force there will arise in each person thoughts of loving kindness, like that of a father and mother [towards their children] and they will reach enlightenment.'

"*Fourth Great Vow:* 'I vow that when I attain enlightenment in a future age, if there are any beings who are bound by desire, anger, and delusion, if there are any monks, nuns, laymen or laywomen—any in the seven categories[8]—who offend against the restraining items for study given by the Tathāgata and thus create negative karma, who are about to fall to the hells and suffer bitter retribution—if these persons hear my name and with perfect sincerity call it out and retain it in their minds, then due to my spiritual force all their negative karma will be eliminated and their afflictions will be cut off. Honoring the precepts of moral purity, they will be well able to guard their deeds, words, and thoughts. Throughout eternity they will never regress, and they will reach enlightenment.'

"Mañjuśrī, those are the four types of subtle and sublime great vows which were expressed by that Buddha, Tathāgata, Arhat, Perfectly Enlightened One, when he first set out upon the Bodhisattva Path.

"Mañjuśrī, the Buddha-field where that Tathāgata dwells is vast and extensive, glorious and pure. The ground is as level as the palm of my hand, and is entirely made of gems. The air is always fragrant, like marvelous sandalwood. Further, the paths are marked out by rows of fragrant trees, and everywhere heavenly and marvelous pearls, jewels, and *maṇi* gems are suspended. There are many bathing ponds, which are adorned with celestial gems. Fragrant waters fill them, and all their merits are complete. At the four borders, there are hung marvelous colored paintings. The thoroughfares and streets, the eight paths—wherever they lead—are gloriously adorned.

"None of the beings there have any of the afflictions, nor do they have grievous and piteous sufferings. Also, there is no temptation there. Many abide within the various stages of the Bodhisattva assembly. Excellent and sublime musical sounds are not produced from instruments but resound spontaneously: they are the extensive preachings on the subtle and marvelous profound

Teachings of the Mahāyāna. If there are any beings who hear these sounds, they will attain to the supreme enlightenment from which there is no regression.

"O Mañjuśrī, due to the force of that Buddha Tathāgata's former vows and his apt and clever expedient means, that Buddha-field was made complete. Making his glorious adornments perfect, [the Buddha] sat upon the throne of enlightenment and had the following thought: 'In the future ages, suppose that there are beings who are bound by desire, anger, and delusion, who are beset by disease, who are taken advantage of by resentful persons, or who are about to suffer untimely death, and further, who are about to fall to the hells due to their bad karma and will be subject to great suffering.' That Buddha, seeing those suffering beings, uttered this *dhāraṇī* to tear away their karmic veils. Because he causes them to accept and hold to the *dhāraṇī,* in that same life they will obtain great benefits, and they will be far distant from all sufferings, abiding in enlightenment. This is the *dhāraṇī* he uttered, saying:

Tan-chih-t'a-hsi-t'i-hsi-t'i su-hsi-t'i mu-che-erh-mu-ch'a-erh mu-t'i-pi-mu-t'i an-mo-li-pi-mo-pi man-chieh-li-shen-lan-jo-chieh-pi-ho-la-tan-no chieh-pi sa-p'o-o-t'a-p'o-tan-erh po-lo-mo-o-t'a so-tan-erh-mu-na-hsi mo-ho-mu-na-hsi o-pu-ti-o-shih-pu-ti pi-to-p'o-i su-pa-ni pa-lo-kan-mo ch'u-hsieh-ch'u pa-lo-kan-mo-chu-hsieh san-p'o-o-t'i-shu a-po-lo-tsa-ti-sa-pa-mu-lo-chih a-po-ch'a-ti-hsieh-ti che-tu-sha se-tun-p'o-t'o-chu-p'o-hsieh-ti na-mo-so tan-t'a-chieh-to-nan so-ha.

"When the Lord uttered this *dhāraṇī* of great force and brilliance, all the great Bodhisattvas, the Four Great *Deva* Kings, Indra and Brahmā, and others in the assembly praised him, saying: 'Excellent, excellent, O Lord of Great Compassion. You have been able to utter in this way the great and powerful spiritual formula of the Tathāgatas of the Past, for the sake of all the limitless beings who desire abundance, who seek to exhaust the sea of sufferings and climb upon the shores of *nirvāṇa,* with all diseases cured and all desires perfectly fulfilled.' "

The Buddha told the great assembly: "If there are any sons or daughters of pure faith, any kings, princes, great councillors or lesser ministers, queens, or court ladies, who wish to gain blessings and merits; if there arise in them thoughts of respect and faith in this spiritual formula; if they read it, recite it, and explain its meaning to others; if there arises in them the mind of great compassion towards all living beings; if six times during the day and night with fragrant blossoms and brilliant lamps they offer *pūjā* with grave attention, and purify themselves by bathing their bodies; and if they hold to the eightfold vows, and with utmost sincerity think of and recite [the *dhāraṇī*], then limitless karmic fetters—no matter how grave—will be eliminated. In the present life, they will be separated from all afflictions. When they reach the ends of their lives, the various Buddhas will hold them in their protective thoughts, and they will be reborn in a lotus blossom within that Buddha-land, [Wholly Complete Incense Heap]."

THE BUDDHA WITHOUT GRIEF, HE WHO IS MOST EXCELLENT AND AUSPICIOUS

"Next, Mañjuśrī, towards the East beyond as many Buddha-lands as seven times the number of grains in the sand of the Ganges, there is a realm known as Without Grief. The Buddha there is called Without Grief, He Who Is Most Excellent and Auspicious Tathāgata, Arhat, Perfectly Enlightened One. He is presently expounding on the Teachings to the Assembly there.

"The Buddha-field where that Tathāgata dwells is vast and extensive, gloriously pure, as flat as the palm of my hand, and made entirely from gems. The soil is fine, smooth, and soft, and the air is always fragrant. There are no cries of grief or suffering; this land is set apart from all afflictions. Also in that place, there are no woesome paths of existence, nor is any temptation known.

"Everywhere there are bathing ponds with golden steps, all filled with fragrant waters. Jeweled trees grow in rows, flourishing with blossoms and fruits. Excellent and sublime sounds of music do not emanate from instruments, but resound spontaneously. The merits and glorious adornments are like those of the Realm of Utmost Joy in the West, the Land of Infinite Life.[9]

"O Mañjuśrī, when that Lord Buddha first set out upon the Bodhisattva Path, he made four great vows. What are these four?

"*First Great Vow:* 'I vow that when I attain enlightenment in a future age, should there be any sentient beings who are constantly bound and constrained by grief and suffering—if they hear my name and with utmost sincerity call it out and retain it in their minds, then due to my spiritual force all their piteous griefs and all their miseries will cease. Their lives will be long and placid, and they will reach enlightenment.'

"*Second Great Vow:* 'I vow that when I attain enlightenment in a future age, if there are any sentient beings who, having created bad karma, are reborn into places of uninterrupted darkness and suffer miseries within the great hell realms—if those beings heard my name in a former life, I will radiate from my body illuminating rays to those suffering ones in their present incarnations. Due to my spiritual power, when they see these rays, all their veils of karma will be removed. They will be liberated from all their sufferings and will be reborn among men or *devas.* They will receive whatever joys they wish, and they will reach enlightenment.'

"*Third Great Vow:* 'I vow that when I attain enlightenment in a future age, I will aid sentient beings who have created bad karma by murder, thievery, depravity, or immorality. Such beings may in this present incarnation be about to sink to a woesome path of existence, having suffered from beatings by swords and staves. Though such a person may possibly obtain rebirth as a human, his life will be cut short by many illnesses. Such a person, reborn into an impoverished family, lacking clothing, food, and drink, is ever subject to the sufferings of heat and cold, hunger and thirst, his complexion is dull and lacks vibrancy, and none in his circle of acquaintances is virtuous or wise. If such a person hears my name and with utmost sincerity calls it out and retains it in his mind, then due to my spiritual force, whatever he desires—food, drink, and clothing—will all be provided for him in abundance. His body will glow and be attractive, like that of a *deva.* There will be good persons with whom he can associate, and he will reach enlightenment.'

"*Fourth Great Vow:* 'I vow that when I attain enlightenment in a future age, if there are any beings who are constantly haunted and disordered by *yakṣas* and various evil spirits who snatch away their vital spirits and subject them to various sufferings—if such persons hear my name and with utmost sincerity call it out and are mindful of it, then due to my spiritual force the various *yakṣas* and the others will all withdraw and scatter, the mind of loving kindness having arisen in each of them. These persons will be liberated from all sufferings, and will reach enlightenment.'

"O Mañjuśrī, these are the four types of subtle and marvelous great vows made by that Buddha, Tathāgata, Arhat, Perfectly Enlightened One, when he first set out upon the Bodhisattva Path.

"If there are any sentient beings who hear the name of that Buddha and who call out that name six times during the day and night, and worship [that Buddha] with reverence and utmost sincerity, and if, in them, there arises thoughts of loving kindness and compassion towards the places of incarnation of all sentient beings, then the karmic veils of such persons will be removed, and they will be freed from grief and sorrow. Having no illness, their lives will be long, and they will obtain knowledge of their previous incarnations. They will be reborn in lotus blossoms within that Buddha-land, and they will always be guarded and protected by the *devas*.

"O Mañjuśrī, those who call out that Buddha's name are able to generate limitless auspicious karma, as I have described. As to the land of that Buddha, the force of his vows, his glorious adornments, and his surpassing merits, these are things which the *śrāvakas* and *pratyekabuddhas* are unable to understand. Only other Tathāgatas, Arhats, Perfectly Enlightened Ones [can truly know of these.]"

THE BUDDHA THUNDERING SOUND OF THE DHARMA SEA

"Next, Mañjuśrī, in the East, beyond as many Buddha-fields as there are eight times the number of sands in the Ganges River, there is a realm named Dharma Banner. The Buddha there is called Thundering Sound of the Dharma Sea Tathāgata, Arhat, Perfectly Enlightened One. He presently is expounding on the Teachings.

"O Mañjuśrī, the land where that Buddha dwells is pure and unstained. Its soil is level and is made of quartz crystal. Light is always shining there, and the air is perfumed with fragrance. The city walls are made of precious emeralds. The eight thoroughfares are marked by gold and silver borders. The towers and pavillions, the palaces and halls, the towering rafters, the doors and windows, the railings and parapets are all completely adorned with various gems. Jeweled trees of celestial fragrance grow everywhere in orderly rows, and celestial silks hang down from their branches. Also, heavenly bells are suspended in various places. Gentle breezes push against them and subtle tones resound with notes of vast joy, impermanence, the voidness of suffering, and egolessness. All who hear them abandon their desires and attachments, the accompanying habits are gradually abandoned, and they personally experience profound *samādhi.*

"Flowers of celestial and sublime fragrances are scattered upon the ground. On each of the four sides of the land, there are eight bathing ponds. Golden sand is spread upon their bottoms, and they are filled with perfumed water.

"Mañjuśrī, in that Buddha-field there are no woesome paths of existence, and there is no temptation. After being reborn in the lotus blossoms, the beings there suffer no further afflictions.

"When that Buddha Tathāgata first set out upon the Bodhisattva Path, he made four great vows. What are these four?

"*First Great Vow:* 'I vow that when I attain enlightenment in a future age, if there are any sentient beings who are born into families which espouse perverse views, in whom the pure faith in the Buddha, the Teachings, and the Order does not arise, who are far distant from the aspiration to attain supreme enlightenment—if such beings hear my name and with utmost sincerity call it out and retain it in their minds, then due to my spiritual force their unenlightened perverse "wisdom" will be dispersed in the space of a day and night. They will profoundly generate a true faith in the Three Jewels, never again regressing, and they will reach enlightenment.'

"*Second Great Vow:* 'I vow that when I attain enlightenment in a future age, should there be any beings who are born in border regions, who, since they grow close to bad friends, create for themselves all sorts of negative karma, who do not cultivate wholesome things, who have never even heard the names of the Three Jewels, who sink to the three woesome paths of existence following their deaths—if such beings hear my name for but a moment, due to my spiritual force their karmic veils will be removed. They will meet with good acquaintances, they will not fall to woesome paths of existence, and they will reach enlightenment.'

"*Third Great Vow:* 'I vow that when I attain enlightenment in a future age, if there are any sentient beings who lack clothing, food, drink, bedding, medicine, and other necessities for life, and, because of these causes and conditions, there arises great suffering and grief resulting in the creation of bad karma as they [desperately] seek for these things—if they hear my name and with utmost sincerity call it out and retain it in their minds, then due to my spiritual force they will be provided with whatever they lack, as they think of it, and they will reach enlightenment.'

"*Fourth Great Vow:* 'I vow that when I attain enlightenment in a future age, should there be any beings who, due to negative karma from past lives, quarrel and debate with one another, who are unforgiving and grudging in their actions, who wound each other with bows and arrows, swords and staves—if such persons hear my name and with utmost sincerity call it out and retain it in their minds, then due to my spiritual force there will arise in each one the mind of loving kindness, and they will not harm each other [again]. Unwholesome thoughts will never arise in them again—how much less will they desire to kill their former enemies. They will constantly practice joyful giving, and they will reach enlightenment.'

"O Mañjuśrī, these are the four types of subtle and sublime vows made by that Buddha, Tathāgata, Arhat, Perfectly Enlightened One, when he first set out upon the Bodhisattva Path. If there is a son or daughter of pure faith who hears the name of that Buddha and with utmost sincerity reverently and diligently worships him, and receives his name, holds to it, retains it in his mind, and recites it, then his karmic veils will be removed and he will never turn back from the aspiration to attain enlightenment. He will gain knowledge of all his past lives, and he will always be able to meet a Buddha wherever he is reborn in the future. Such a person will have a long life, free from illness, and, at the end of his life, he will be reborn in that Buddha-land. Clothing, food, drink, and the necessities of life will be supplied as he thinks of them, and nothing will be lacking.

"Mañjuśrī, that Lord Buddha completely endows beings in this way with boundless merits. Because of this, all sentient beings will ever think of him, never forgetting [his name]."

THE BUDDHA VICTORIOUS WISDOM OF THE DHARMA SEA, HE WHO ROAMS FREELY BY HIS SPIRITUAL POWERS

"Next, Mañjuśrī, in the East, beyond as many Buddha-fields as nine times the number of sands in the Ganges River, there is a realm named Wholesome Abode in the Sea of Jewels. The Buddha is called Victorious Wisdom of the Dharma Sea, He Who Roams Freely by His Spiritual Powers, Tathāgata, Arhat, Perfectly Enlightened One. He presently is discoursing on the Teachings.

"Mañjuśrī, when that Buddha Tathāgata first set out on the Bodhisattva Path, he made four great vows. What are these four?

"First Great Vow: 'I vow that when I attain enlightenment in a future age, should there be any sentient beings who have created negative karma by harming various living creatures in the course of ploughing and farming, or who, in beginning to clear fields, have imposed upon others, or who in battle array with weapons and lances have constantly killed and harmed other beings—if such persons hear my name and with utmost sincerity call it out and retain it in their minds, then due to my spiritual force they will be provided with the necessities of life. They will not [need to] borrow or appeal for things, but will be entirely satisfied in accordance with their wishes. Constantly cultivating all that is wholesome, they will reach enlightenment.'

"Second Great Vow: 'I vow that when I attain enlightenment in a future age, if there are any beings who commit the ten negative acts, the faults of killing and so on, and, if due to these causes and conditions, they are about to sink to the hells—if such persons hear my name and with utmost sincerity call it out and hold it in their minds, they will obtain perfection in the ten wholesome paths, they will not sink to the woesome paths of existence, and they will reach enlightenment.'

"*Third Great Vow:* 'I vow that when I attain enlightenment in a future age, if there are any beings who do not have freedom, who are bound in service to others, who endure the suffering and pain of being bound by fetters, wearing a locked cangue, being whipped and beaten, and are punished to the absolute extreme of endurance —if such beings hear my name and with utmost sincerity call it out and hold it in their minds, then due to my spiritual force they will be freed from all perils, and they will reach enlightenment.'

"*Fourth Great Vow:* 'I vow that when I attain enlightenment in a future age, if there are any beings who commit negative acts and have no faith in the Three Jewels, who follow dissolute views and cast aside genuine principles, who are fond of the followers of heretical teachings, who slander and defame the *sūtras* of the Buddha, saying that they are not sacred speech, who revere, accept, and hold to the scriptures of other paths, who themselves cause others to become entirely deluded, who are about to sink to the hells with no escape for an indeterminate time, or if they should obtain human birth, it is in one of the eight places of difficulty,[10] where they are far distant from the True Way and blind without the eye of wisdom—if such beings hear my name and with utmost sincerity call it out and hold it in their minds, then due to my spiritual force when the end of the life of such a person grows near, with correct thoughts now present, he will be freed from his troubles. He will always be born in the middle kingdom,[11] receiving excellent and marvelous joy, and he will reach enlightenment.'

"O Mañjuśrī, these are the four types of subtle and sublime great vows made by that Buddha, Tathāgata, Arhat, Perfectly Enlightened One, when he first set out upon the Bodhisattva Path. Mañjuśrī, the merits and glorious adornments of the land of that Buddha [are so marvelous that they] cannot be compared to even the most marvelous gems of other Buddha lands."

THE BUDDHA MASTER OF HEALING, OF LAPIS LAZULI RADIANCE

"Next, Mañjuśrī, in the East, beyond as many Buddha-fields as ten times the number of grains of sand in the Ganges River, there is a realm named Pure Lapis Lazuli. The Buddha there is called Master of Healing, the Lapis Lazuli Radiance Tathāgata, Arhat, Perfectly Enlightened One. Mañjuśrī, when that Lord Buddha first expressed his aspiration to enter upon the Bodhisattva Path, he made twelve great vows. What are these twelve?

"*First Great Vow:* 'I vow that when I attain enlightenment in a future age, the brilliance radiating from my body will illumine boundless realms. This body will be excellently adorned with the thirty-two primary marks and the eighty secondary marks [of the great man]. I will cause all beings to wholly resemble me.'

"*Second Great Vow:* 'I vow that when I attain enlightenment in a future age, my body will be like lapis lazuli, with a purity penetrating within and without. The radiance, vast and great, will fill all the regions, the glorious adornment of my blazing aureole surpassing the sun and moon in brilliance. Even those in the hells within the periphery of the Iron Mountains will be able to see me, and I, them.[12] In this world, I will illumine the way of all those who travel about in the darkness of night. When these beings see my radiance, all that is concealed will be illumined, so that they may proceed with their concerns.'

"*Third Great Vow:* 'I vow that when I attain enlightenment in a future age, with infinite and boundless insight and means, I will cause all sentient beings to obtain without surcease all the necessities of life.'

"*Fourth Great Vow:* 'I vow that when I attain enlightenment in a future age, should there be any sentient beings who tread upon heretical paths, I will cause them all to walk upon the genuine path to enlightenment. If they practice the ways of the *śrāvaka* or *pratyekabuddha,* I will cause them to securely abide within the teachings of the Mahāyāna.'

"*Fifth Great Vow:* 'I vow that when I attain enlightenment in a future age, if there are any sentient beings who cultivate and practice the pure conduct of my teaching, I will cause them all to maintain the precepts without breaking them, to gain excellent defenses against breaking the precepts, against acts of body, speech, or mind [so grave] that they would sink to a woesome path of existence. Should they break any of the precepts, having heard my name, they should concentrate on it, accept it, and hold to it, and with utmost sincerity again vow to be chaste. [Due to my spiritual force] they will regain their purity, and they will reach enlightenment.'

"*Sixth Great Vow:* 'I vow that when I attain enlightenment in a future age, if there are any sentient beings whose sense faculties are incomplete, who are ugly, stupid, rheumatic, deaf, blind, mute, bent, lame, hunchbacked, leprous, insane, bound and constrained by the sufferings of all sorts of diseases—if such persons hear my name and with utmost sincerity call it out and hold it in their minds, then they will all receive that which is auspicious and glorious, and they will be cured of all disease.'

"*Seventh Great Vow:* 'I vow that when I attain enlightenment in a future age, if there are any sentient beings who are impoverished, beset by troubles and suffering, who have no place of refuge, who are sick with disease and have neither medicine nor physician—if they should hear my name for but a fleeting moment, they will be cured of all their diseases, their families will increase and flourish, lacking neither wealth nor property. They will be peaceful and joyous in body and mind, and they will reach enlightenment.'

"*Eighth Great Vow:* 'I vow that when I attain enlightenment in a future age, if there are any women who feel extreme repugnance towards all the sufferings which befall women, and who desire to abandon their female form—if they hear my name and with utmost sincerity call it out and hold it in their minds, then in the present life they will become men endowed with all the marks of the "great man," and they will reach enlightenment.'[13]

"*Ninth Great Vow:* 'I vow that when I attain enlightenment in a future age, I will cause all sentient beings to escape from Māra's net. Further, the followers of the different types of depraved views all will take up, accept, and be caused to generate correct views. I will gradually induce them to cultivate and study the various Bodhisattva practices, and they will reach enlightenment.'

"*Tenth Great Vow:* 'I vow that when I attain enlightenment in a future age, if there are any sentient beings who have been arrested in accordance with the king's laws, who are confined to a gloomy prison, who wear locked cangues, who are whipped and are punished to the extreme; further, should there be any beings who are subjected to numerous matters of suffering and pain, meeting with increasing sorrows and distress, not even having a fleeting moment of joy—if such persons hear my name, then due to the awesome spiritual force of my auspicious virtues they will obtain freedom from all sorrows and suffering, and they will reach enlightenment.'

"*Eleventh Great Vow:* 'I vow that when I attain enlightenment in a future age, if there are any beings who are distressed by the fires of hunger and create negative karma in their search for food—if such beings hear my name and with perfect sincerity call it out and retain it in their minds, I will first enable them to obtain whatever supreme and marvelous food and drink they desire, which they may eat to their satisfaction. Afterwards, by means of the taste of the Teachings, I will cause them to abide in peace and joy, and they will reach enlightenment.'

"*Twelfth Great Vow:* 'I vow that when I attain enlightenment in a future age, if there are any sentient beings whose bodies are unclothed, who meet with distress due to mosquitoes and flies, heat and cold—if such beings hear my name and with utmost sincerity call it out and retain it in their minds, then in accord with this excellent act, they will obtain all sorts of supremely marvelous clothing. I will cause them to be fully satisfied with objects gloriously adorned with gems, and with instrumental music and fragrant blossoms. They will be distant from all misery and distress, and they will reach enlightenment.'

"O Mañjuśrī, these are the subtle, sublime, and supreme vows made by the Master of Healing, the Lapis Lazuli Radiance Tathāgata, Arhat, Perfectly Enlightened One, when he first set out upon the Bodhisattva Path."

[THUS ENDS THE] INITIAL SECTION OF THE SŪTRA ON THE MERITS OF THE FUNDAMENTAL VOWS OF THE SEVEN BUDDHAS OF LAPIS LAZULI RADIANCE, THE MASTERS OF HEALING

FINAL SECTION

Then the Buddha told Mañjuśrī: "If I were to speak for an aeon or even longer than that, I would be unable to fully describe the merits and the glorious adornments of the Buddha-field, and the great vows which the Master of Healing, the Lapis Lazuli Radiance Tathāgata, made when he first set out upon the Bodhisattva Path.

"Now that Buddha-field is entirely pure; it is unstained by desire. There is no temptation there, and since the three woesome paths do not exist in that land, there are no cries of suffering. Its soil consists of pure lapis lazuli. The walls and gates, palaces and halls, corridors and verandas, balconies and windows, draperies and curtains are all made of the seven precious substances. It is just like the merits and glorious adornments of the Realm of Utmost Joy in the West.

"In the land of that Buddha, there are two Bodhisattvas, the first named All-Pervading Solar Radiance and the second named All-Pervading Lunar Radiance. They are the leaders of that immeasurable Bodhisattva assembly, and are well able to maintain the precious treasury of that Buddha's genuine Teachings.

"This is why, Mañjuśrī, sons and daughters of pure faith should aspire to be reborn in the realm of that Buddha."

THE BUDDHA AIDS THOSE WHOSE KARMA HAS LED THEM TO DISTRESS

"Next, Mañjuśrī, there are beings who do not distinguish between good and bad, who only cherish greed and stinginess. They know nothing of spreading charity and of the fruits and rewards of giving. Stupid and dense, they have little insight and lack roots of faith. Amassing much wealth, jewels, and property, they industriously guard and protect [their hoard]. When they see a beggar coming, they become displeased, and if they should fail to protect themselves and are forced to give in charity, they are so profoundly miserly that it is as if they are cutting a piece off their own bodies.

"Furthermore, there are sentient beings who are boundlessly stingy and avaricious. They amass their wealth, and since they do not even spend it on themselves, how could they possibly be able to give it to their parents, wives, children, or to their maid-servants, laborers, or to beggars.

"Such a being, at the end of his present life, will be reborn in the realm of starving ghosts or as an animal. Yet because in a former incarnation as a human such a being heard the name Master of Healing, the Lapis Lazuli Radiance Tathāgata, even though he dwells in a woesome mode of existence, he will be able to recall once again the Tathāgata's name. He will disappear from that realm and be reborn as a human. Obtaining knowledge of his past lives and dreading [return to] the woesome paths, he will no longer take joy in worldly pleasures. He will come to like to practice benevolent charity, and he will praise those who delight in giving. He will have no thoughts of greed with regard to any of his possessions. One after the other, using his head, eyes, hands, feet, blood, flesh and torso, he will be able to distribute charity to all who come seeking it. How much more will he be able to distribute his other property?

"Next, Mañjuśrī, there may be persons who, though they have taken refuge in the Lord and have accepted the various points of his teachings, have not followed the majestic deportment according to the precepts of moral purity and have rejected correct views; there may be those who uphold the precepts and correct views, yet do not seek after learning, and thus fail to comprehend the deep principles of the *vaipulya sūtras* spoken by the Buddha; there may be those who are learned but conceited, who, due to their conceited thoughts, think that they are right and all others are wrong. They come to detest and despise the genuine teachings, becoming companions and associates of Māra: in this way these stupid persons themselves practice heretical views. They repeatedly send boundless millions of sentient beings plunging into the pitfalls of great danger. These persons will sink to the Naraka hell realms or to animal or ghostly rebirth.

"If they have previously heard the name of the Master of Healing, the Lapis Lazuli Radiance Tathāgata, then due to the awesome force of that Tathāgata's fundamental vows, those beings will once again think of the Buddha's name while still in the hell. When that life is ended, they will be reborn as humans. They will obtain correct views, striving zeal, joy of the mind, and self-control [such that all actions are] wholesome. Abandoning the ordinary life and leaving home [to become members of the Order], they will accept and uphold the items to be studied in the Teachings of the Buddha, and they will have nothing to do with that which is offensive and breaks the precepts. They will hold to correct views, become learned, and comprehend the deep principles [of the *sūtras*]. Divorced from pride, they will neither slander the genuine Teachings, nor become companions of Māra. They will gradually cultivate and practice the various aspects of the Bodhisattva Path, and they will reach enlightenment.

"Next, Mañjuśrī, there may be sentient beings who are grudging and greedy, envious and jealous, who create negative karma, who praise themselves while slandering others. These beings will sink to the three woesome paths of existence at the end of their lives. For limitless thousands of years they will suffer all sorts of miseries.

"Then, at the end of such a person's life in the woesome path of existence, he will be reborn among humans, or he may be an ox, horse, camel, or donkey. Constantly whipped and flogged, bound by thoughts of hunger and thirst, he will always be burdened with heavy loads on his back, and will suffer from utmost fatigue.

"If he obtains rebirth as a human, it will be as a menial in someone's household, as a female slave or as a servant, always at the beck and call of others, never free.

"Due to having heard in that previous human incarnation the name of the Master of Healing, the Lapis Lazuli Radiance Tathāgata, due to the force of those good roots, in the present life he will recall the name and retain it in his mind, and with utmost sincerity take refuge in it. Due to the Buddha's spiritual force, he will be released from all his sufferings. His sense organs will become sharp and perceptive, and he will develop insight and become learned. Ever-seeking the victorious Teachings, he will constantly meet wholesome [spiritual] friends. Cutting off the snares of Māra for eternity, he will pierce the shell of ignorance. Exhausting the river of afflictions, he will be freed from all the grievous and piteous sufferings of birth, old age, sickness, and death, and he will reach enlightenment.

"Next, Mañjuśrī, if there are any sentient beings who take delight in schisms, who quarrel and cause irritations between themselves and others; and if, by means of deeds, words, and thoughts they create bad karma; if they constantly further matters which are not beneficial; if they plot revengeful injury; if they summon the spirits of the mountains, forests, tomb mounds, and other such places; if they kill living creatures in order to obtain their blood and flesh as sacrificial offerings to the *yakṣa* and *rākṣasa* demons and others; if they write down the names of the cursed, making images of them, and by means of evil magic curse and harm them; if they practice evil magic to raise ghouls, thus putting an end to the life of the enemy and destroying his body—if these sentient beings have heard the name of this Master of Healing, the Lapis Lazuli Radiance Tathāgata, then they will become unable to harm others by all those evil ways. In all the turnings of their minds, there will arise thoughts of loving kindness and compassion. They will think of benefiting others, of peace and joy, and will be free of harmful intent, rejecting hateful thoughts. They will be delighted and satisfied with whatever they receive.

"Next, Mañjuśrī, there may be some among the four classes of monks, nuns, male lay disciples, female lay disciples, and among the sons and daughters of pure faith, who are able to accept and hold the eightfold vows, observing all their aspects for a year or for three months, and due to these good roots, they expect to be reborn in the Western Realm of Utmost Joy and see there the Buddha of Infinite Life—if they hear the name of the Master of Healing, the Lapis Lazuli Radiance Tathāgata, when the end of their lives draws near, eight Bodhisattvas will ascend by their spiritual powers and come to point the way to that realm.[14] Then such persons will be spontaneously reborn in multi-colored, jeweled blossoms in that realm.

"If there are those who—even though they have been born in this celestial realm and have established wholesome roots in their previous lives—still have not exhausted [their karma], because they have been born in this celestial realm they will never again be born into any of the woesome paths of existence. When their life in the celestial realm comes to an end, they will be reborn as humans.

"Such a one may be born as a wheel-turning king who will unite all within the four continents. With awesome virtues and sovereign power, he will urge and transform boundless hundreds of thousands of sentient beings, causing them to cultivate and study the ten wholesome precepts.

"Such a one may be reborn as a *kṣatriya, brahmin,* learned layman, or noble; with abundant wealth, jewels, and granaries and storehouses filled to overflowing. He will be intelligent and wise, brave and fearless, with great physical strength.

"Or, if such a one is born as a woman and hears the name of the Master of Healing, the Lapis Lazuli Radiance Tathāgata, and if she accepts and holds to it with utmost sincerity, in her subsequent incarnations, this person will never again be born as a woman."

A MYSTIC FORMULA FOR DISPELLING DISEASE AND SUFFERING

"Next, Mañjuśrī, when that Master of Healing, the Lapis Lazuli Radiance Tathāgata, attained enlightenment, due to the force of his fundamental vows, he was able to observe all sentient beings. Some suffered from various diseases and were emaciated, feverish, jaundiced, and so on; others were in the thrall of the noxious ways of repugnant demons; further, some were [naturally] short-lived or were on the brink of untimely death. He sought to cause all these diseases and sufferings to be ended, and to fulfill all desires.

"At that point, that Lord entered into the *samādhi* called 'Dispeller of the Afflictions of All Beings.' Having entered this *samādhi,* a great brilliant light shone from the *ūrṇā* between his eyebrows, and from its radiance resounded a great *dhāraṇī:*

Namo bhagavate bhaiṣajyaguru-vaiḍūrya prabhā-rājāya tathāgatāya arhate samyak-saṃbuddhāya tadyathā. Oṃ bhaiṣajye bhaiṣajye bhaiṣajya-samudgate svāhā.[15]

"Then after this *dhāraṇī* was uttered from the midst of this radiance, there was a great rumbling and shaking of the earth and a great brilliant light shone forth. Illnesses and miseries were removed from all beings, and they all became peaceful and joyous.

"O Mañjuśrī, if there is a good son or daughter who is ill, for the sake of that sick one, you should wholeheartedly clean and bathe him. You should provide him with food, medicine, and water from which all insects have been strained, having recited the *dhāraṇī* over these things 108 times. Upon swallowing these substances, all the sufferings of disease will be dispelled. If that person seeks something, with utmost sincerity he should think of the *dhāraṇī* and recite it. He will obtain all that he seeks, be free of illness, and have a long life. At the end of his life, this person will be reborn into the realm of that Buddha [of Healing], and he will achieve the non-regressing state and reach enlightenment.

"This is why, Mañjuśrī, good sons and daughters should, with utmost sincerity, diligently revere and worship that Master of Healing, the Lapis Lazuli Radiance Tathāgata, and they should ever hold this *dhāraṇī*, never allowing it to be lost.

"Next, Mañjuśrī, any sons or daughters of pure faith who hear all the names previously mentioned of the Seven Buddhas, Tathāgatas, Arhats, Perfectly Enlightened Ones should—having heard them—recite them and hold to them. At dawn, they should clean their teeth with sticks of wood, bathe, and purify themselves. With various fragrant blossoms, powdered incense, burning incense, and perfumed unguents, and with music from all instruments, they should worship images [of the Seven Buddhas]. They should personally copy this *sūtra* or have others do so, and they should wholeheartedly accept it, hold to it, and listen to its principles. They should offer *pūjā* worship to the master of the teachings [who explicates the principles], and should offer to him all the necessities of life, making sure that he lacks none of these. Having done so, they will be covered by the protective thoughts of the Buddhas. All that they seek shall be fulfilled, and they will reach enlightenment."

WORSHIP OF THE BUDDHAS OF HEALING AND ITS BENEFITS

Then the youth Mañjuśrī addressed the Buddha and said: "O Lord, I aspire that in the age of the extinction of the Teachings, by means of all sorts of methods, I will cause the sons and daughters of pure faith to hear the names of the Seven Buddhas, Tathāgatas. In the midst of their sleep, I will cause them to be awakened by [uttering] the names of the Buddhas.

"O Lord, they should accept this *sūtra* and hold to it, read it and recite it. Furthermore, they should lecture on it and explicate its points to others. They should personally copy it or have others copy it, and worship and pay reverence to it. With various flowers, perfumed unguents, powdered incense, burning incense, garlands, necklaces, banners, a canopy, drums, and music, they should offer *pūjā*. With a five-colored cloth, they should make a cover for it.

They should purify the site by sprinkling water and sweeping, and they should place the *sūtra* atop a lofty throne. At this time, the Four Great *Deva* Kings together with their retinue, overflowing with countless hundreds of thousands in the *deva* assembly, all will go to this place of *pūjā,* guard it, and protect it.

"O Lord, if in this place where the *sūtra* is precious and popular there are people who accept it and hold to it, then, due to the merits of the fundamental vows of those Seven Buddha Tathāgatas, and due to the power of the awesome spiritual force [transmitted through] hearing their names, you should know that in this place untimely deaths will never again occur. Also, never again in this place will evil spirits snatch away the vital spirits of men. Those who have suffered thusly will once again regain their original peace and joy of body and mind."

The Buddha told Mañjuśrī: "So it is, so it is. [It shall be] exactly as you say, Mañjuśrī. If there are any sons or daughters of pure faith who wish to worship in *pūjā* these Seven Tathāgatas, first they should construct images of the Seven Buddhas. Placing them on a pure throne, supreme and wondrous, they should offer flowers, burn incense, and they should gloriously adorn the site with banners and pennants. For seven days and seven nights, they should accept the eightfold vows, eat pure food, bathe in fragrant water, and don new and clean clothing. Their hearts should be unstained, without thought of anger or harm. Towards all sentient beings, there should ever arise thoughts of blessings and benefits, loving kindness, sympathetic joy, and equanimity. They should play musical instruments and sing praises of the merits [of the Seven Tathāgatas] while circumambulating to the right of the Buddha-images. Recalling all the fundamental vows of those Tathāgatas, they should read and recite this *sūtra.* Thinking only of its principles, they should lecture on the *sūtra,* elucidating its main points.

"Accordingly, whatever they wish shall come to pass. If they seek long life, then longevity will be granted. If they seek wealth and abundance, then that prosperity shall be obtained. If official position is sought, then it will be obtained, and if they seek a son or a daughter, the child will be born. All that is wished for shall follow.

"Furthermore, if there is a person who suddenly has nightmares, who sees various evil apparitions; if monstrous birds come and flock together; or a hundred ominous portents materialize in his home—if this person uses marvelous and valuable utensils to offer reverent *pūjā* to these Buddhas, then the nightmares, evil apparitions, and all inauspicious things will vanish and disappear, unable to cause harm.

"If there are any persons who are threatened by water, fire, sword, poison, hanging from a precipice, a wicked elephant, lion, tiger, wolf, bear, poisonous snake, scorpion, centipede, millipede, mosquito, or other such thing—if such a person is able to recall with utmost sincerity those Buddhas and reverently worship them, he will be freed from all dreadful things. If another state invades and disturbs the peace, or if robbers and thieves cause disorder, from one who recalls and reverently worships these Tathāgatas, all hate-filled enemies will be turned back and scattered.

"Next, Mañjuśrī, there may be sons or daughters of pure faith who—having reached the end of their days—have not served another *deva,* have taken wholehearted refuge in the Buddha, the Teachings, and the Order, and have accepted and held to the restraining precepts. If among the five precepts, the ten precepts, the four hundred Bodhisattva precepts, the two hundred fifty precepts of the monks, or the five hundred precepts of the nuns that such a person has accepted, if any of these precepts which were accepted have been broken, then that person may fear that he will sink to a woesome path of existence. If such a one is able to concentrate solely on the names of these Buddhas and reverently worship them, then he certainly will not suffer rebirth in any of the three woesome paths of existence.

"If there is a woman about to give birth who suffers from acute pain, and if she is able with utmost sincerity to call out the names, worship and praise, and reverently offer *pūjā* to the Seven Buddhas, Tathāgatas, then all her suffering will be removed. The appearance of her child will be perfect, and all who see him will exclaim with joy. The child will be endowed with keen sense-organs, intelligence, few illnesses, and tranquillity. Non-human beings will never snatch away the vital spirit of such a child."

THE IMPORTANCE OF FAITH

The Lord told Ānanda: "All the merits of the names of these Seven Tathāgatas, just as I have praised them, are [aspects of] the profound range of spiritual activities of the Buddhas, and they are difficult to comprehend. You should not have any doubts about them."

Ānanda replied: "O Lord, no doubts arise in me with regard to the *vaipulya sūtras* spoken by the Buddha. Why is this so? There is nothing baseless about the karma produced by the deeds, words, and thoughts of all the Tathāgatas. O Lord, the discs of the sun and moon can be caused to sink and fall, and the wonderfully, lofty king of mountains [Mount Sumeru] may be caused to shake, but in the end the words of the Buddhas will never change.

"O Lord, now the roots of faith of [most] living things are incomplete. Though they hear descriptions of the profound ranges of spiritual activity of the Buddhas, these beings of incomplete faith may merely think: 'How can it be that by merely concentrating on the names of the Seven Buddhas, one can obtain all these blessings and excellent benefits?' From this lack of faith, there arises in turn slander and defamation. In the long night, these beings lose their great beneficial joy and sink into the woesome paths of existence."

The Buddha told Ānanda: "If these sentient beings hear the names of the various Buddhas, they will no longer remain in the woesome paths of existence. Eliminating karma alone will not enable a being to gain rebirth [out of these woesome paths. The aid of the Buddhas is essential.]

"Ānanda, it is difficult to be able to have faith in and comprehend the profound range of activities of the Buddhas. You are able to faithfully accept them, and you should know that this is due to the awesome powers of these Tathāgatas. Ānanda, none of the *śrāvakas* or *pratyekabuddhas* are able to understand this. Only Bodhisattvas with one remaining birth [are able to comprehend this profound matter].

"Ānanda, a human incarnation is difficult to obtain. It is also difficult to be able to obtain faith in the Three Jewels, and to revere, honor, and respect them. To be granted the opportunity to hear the names of the Seven Buddhas, Tathāgatas, is even more difficult than that. Ānanda, if I were to describe the boundless Bodhisattva practices of these Tathāgatas, the limitless clever means, the infinitely vast great vows—if I were to describe these practices, vows, and these excellent and clever means for an aeon or longer, I would be unable to fully describe them."

SAVING THOSE ON THE BRINK OF DEATH OR DISASTER

At that time in the assembly, there was a Bodhisattva-mahāsattva named "Saving Deliverance." He rose from his seat and, baring his right shoulder, he knelt with his right knee on the ground. Clasping his palms together, he addressed the Buddha, saying: "O Lord, when the time arises in the future where the Teachings will be in replica form, there will be sentient beings constrained and vexed by various diseases and sufferings. Their bodies emaciated, unable to eat or drink, their throats parched and their lips dry, it will seem dark in every direction they look. The signs of death will appear. Parents, relatives, friends, and acquaintances will gather around such a person with lamentations and weeping.

"Then, while his body lies in its original position, he will be seized by the messengers of Yama, King of the Law, and be led to that King. The inborn spirits attached to all sentient beings who record whether the being's conduct is good or bad will, at that time, hand down these records in their entirety to Yama, King of the Law. Based on the Laws, the King will interrogate the person about his actions, and he will judge him according to the positive and negative factors.

"If, at this time, that sick person's relatives, close friends, and acquaintances are able to take refuge in the Buddhas [of Healing] for his sake, and if they offer *pūjā* with all sorts of glorious adornments according to proper methods, then the spirit consciousness of that sick person will regain its original vitality as if waking from a dream, having passed through seven, fourteen, or even forty-nine days of unconsciousness. He will remember that he has received the fruits and retribution of his good and bad karma. Due to his personal experience, he will see that the concept of karmic retribution is not specious, and since he reached this life with difficulty, he will not create bad karma for himself.

"Because of this, sons and daughters of pure faith, you should accept and hold to the names of the Seven Buddhas, and revere and worship them according to your capacities."

Then the Venerable Ānanda asked the Bodhisattva Saving Deliverance, "Good son, what is this method for the reverent worship of these Seven Buddhas?"

The Bodhisattva Saving Deliverance answered: "O Virtuous One, if you wish to cause a sick person to be freed from his misery and distress, you should accept and hold to the eightfold precepts for the sake of that person for seven days and seven nights. You should collect together food, drink and other property and, in accordance with your means, offer *pūjā* to the Buddhas and the community of monks.

"You should reverently worship the Seven Buddhas, Tathāgatas, with *pūjā* offerings six times during the day and night. Read and recite this *sūtra* forty-nine times. Light forty-nine lamps and make images of the Tathāgatas, seven in all, placing seven lamps before each image. These lamps should be round like cartwheels, and their shining light should burn ceaselessly for forty-nine nights. Make a banner of variegated colors from forty-nine pieces of material, pieced together into one length. You should release forty-nine living creatures. By doing these things, you will be able to repel misery and suffering, and the sick person will not be in the grasp of negative spirits.

"Ānanda, O Virtuous One, this is the method for worship of these Tathāgatas. If you call out the name of one among these Seven Buddhas and worship him, you will obtain limitless blessings, and whatever you seek and wish for shall be fulfilled. How much more complete will these blessings be if you are able to perform the entire *pūjā* worship.

"Next, Ānanda, O virtuous One, in the case of a *kṣatriya* king who is properly enthroned by means of the *abhiṣeka* rite, when calamities and troubles arise—such as an epidemic, invasion of the state, internal rebellion, adverse delineation of the stars, lunar or solar eclipse, unseasonal winds or rains, drought during the rainy season—then, at that time, there should arise in that properly enthroned *kṣatriya* king thoughts of loving kindness and compassion towards all beings. With great mercy, he should pardon and release from their gloomy difficulties all those distressed beings [in his prisons], and he should worship the Buddhas using the method of *pūjā* described above.

"Due to these good roots and due to the force of those Tathāgatas' fundamental vows, his state will be caused to be tranquil. The winds and rains will occur at their proper seasons, and the crops will ripen. In this state all beings will be healthy, peaceful, and joyous. Further, there will be no tyrannical *yakṣas* or other such beings who would cause spiritual distress among the people. All negative manifestations will be entirely removed, and the properly enthroned *kṣatriya* king will have a long life, handsomeness, and vitality free from diseases. [He will retain his] sovereign rule.

"Ānanda, O Virtuous One, if the ruler, the queen and lesser consorts, the heir apparent and other princes, the great ministers, court attendants and ladies, the provincial officials, and the masses suffer from disease or other calamities, they also should construct images of the Seven Buddhas. They should read and recite this *sūtra*, kindle lamps, make banners, set free various living creatures, and with utmost reverence perform *pūjā* by burning incense and offering flowers. They will thus obtain the elimination of disease and suffering, and gain freedom from all difficulties."

At that point the Venerable Ānanda asked the Bodhisattva Saving Deliverance, "Good son, how can one increase the life of one whose span is already exhausted?"

The Bodhisattva Saving Deliverance replied: "O Virtuous One, how can you not have heard the Tathāgata speak of the nine untimely deaths? It is because of this that the Lord uttered the *dhāraṇī* for healing and [taught] the accompanying practices for healing, such as lighting the lamps, making banners, and cultivating the auspicious actions. By cultivating the auspicious, one can thereby extend one's span of life."

Ānanda asked, "What are the nine untimely deaths?"

The Bodhisattva Saving Deliverance said: "First, there may be sentient beings who have contracted an illness which, though minor, goes untreated through lack of both medicine and physician. Or, a person may meet a physician who does not give him his medicines: though such persons actually should not die, still they suffer untimely deaths. Furthermore, a person may have faith in materialistic and demonic heretics, masters of black magic. The false explanations of calamities and blessings that they provide will lead to fearful actions. Since this [misled] person cannot discern correctly with his own heart, he asks divinatory questions to ascertain whether his fortune is good or bad, and he kills various living creatures to propitiate spirits. He calls the various spirits of the waters and begs for blessings and pity upon him, desiring to lengthen his years. In the end, this is something which he is unable to obtain. Accordingly, delusions and inverted views cause his untimely death. Such a person enters into the hells, without any known time of release.

"The second untimely death is by execution according to the ruler's laws. The third—someone goes out on hunts or pleasure excursions and engages in debauch and drunkenness to excess with no limits. His vital spirit is snatched away by a non-human [demonic] being, thus causing untimely death. The fourth untimely death is burning by fire, and the fifth untimely death is drowning in water.

"Some are devoured by wild beasts, thus causing the sixth untimely death. The seventh untimely death is by falling off a mountain precipice. The eighth untimely death is caused by harm from poisonous herbs, hateful entreaties (spells) and magical incantations which cause corpses, devils, and other such things to arise. The ninth is caused by starvation and dehydration due to not obtaining food or drink.

"This is the Tathāgata's summary explanation of the nine types of untimely deaths. Beyond these, there are, in addition, limitless other untimely deaths that would be altogether difficult to expound upon.

"Next, Ānanda, that King Yama is in charge of entering the names in the register of all persons in the world. If there are any sentient beings who are not filial, who have committed the five disobediences, who have broken and defiled the Three Jewels, who have infringed upon the laws of the ruler and subjects, and who have broken the precepts, then the King of the Law, Yama, will punish them in accordance with his examination of the severity of the crimes. This is why I am now urging sentient beings to kindle lamps, make banners, release creatures, and cultivate that which is auspicious. This will enable beings to pass over suffering and distress, and to avoid meeting with all sorts of difficulties."

THE TWELVE YAKṢA GENERALS AND THEIR PLEDGE

At that time in the assembly, there were Twelve Great *Yakṣa* Generals seated together. Their names were: Great General Kumbhīra, Great General Vajra, Great General Mihira, Great General Anila, Great General Manila, Great General Sanila, Great General Indra, Great General Pajra, Great General Makura, Great General Kinnara, Great General Catura, and Great General Vikarāla. Each of these great *yakṣa* generals had 7,000 *yakṣas* in his troops.

They raised their voices together and addressed the Buddha: "O Lord, having received the Buddha's awesome force, we now have been granted the hearing of the names of the Seven Buddha Tathāgatas. Never again will we have the fear of sinking to a woesome path of existence. Together, we all have the same thought: we will take utmost refuge in the Buddha, the Teachings, and the Order. We aspire to bear responsibility to do acts of righteous benefit, enrichment, peace and joy for all sentient beings, in whatever place they may dwell, be it city, town, or forest grove of retirement.

"We and our troops shall guard and protect those who circulate this *sūtra,* who read it and recite it, and who further accept and hold to the names of the Seven Buddhas and reverently worship them. We will cause them to be freed of all difficulties. All the desires of these persons will be caused to be fulfilled. Those who seek release from the distress of illness should also read and recite this *sūtra.* They should take a five-colored rope and knot our names into it, untying the knots when their wishes are fulfilled."

At that point the Lord praised the Great *Yakṣa* Generals, saying: "Excellent, excellent, Great *Yakṣa* Generals! When you think of repaying the merciful blessings of the Seven Buddha Tathāgatas, you should ever serve all sentient beings in the way you have described, bringing to them blessings and benefits, peace and joy."

THE SEVEN HEALING BUDDHAS MANIFEST TO DISPEL DOUBTS

In the assembly at that time, there were many *devas,* possessors of rare insight. These *devas* had the following thought, "How can it be that by fleetingly hearing the names of the present Tathāgatas of Buddha-realms far distant beyond calculation,[16] one can be granted protection without bounds, and rare blessings?"

Then Śākyamuni Tathāgata, knowing the thoughts in the minds of the *devas,* entered into the profound and sublime *samādhi* known as "Summoning all Tathāgatas." Having entered into that *samādhi,* all of the three thousand myriads of realms shook in six ways, and there rained down marvelous celestial flowers and heavenly incense powders. When those Seven Tathāgatas saw these signs, each came from his realm to the *Sahā*-world.[17]

The Seven Tathāgatas and Śākyamuni Tathāgata greeted each other,[18] and then, due to the force of the fundamental vows made by the Buddhas in past lives, each of them was securely seated upon a lion throne gloriously adorned with celestial gems. The Bodhisattva assembly, the *devas, nāgas,* and eight classes of human and non-human beings, the king of the state, princes, queen, and court ladies, all the great ministers, brahmins, rich men, and learned laymen gathered around the Tathāgatas, in front and behind them, and the Tathāgatas spoke on the Teachings for them.

When the *devas* saw those Tathāgatas, they all clustered together. Due to this event of great rarity, their doubts were excised. Exclaiming with joy at the unprecedented nature of this event, they unanimously spoke in praise, "Excellent, excellent, Śākyamuni. You have abundantly benefited us. To remove our thoughts of doubt, you have caused the Tathāgatas to come to this place."

Then the *devas,* each according to his own capacity, offered *pūjā* to the Tathāgatas with flowers of wondrous fragrance, necklaces, and celestial instrumental music. They circumambulated to the right of the Buddhas seven times, clasped their palms together, worshipped and honored them, saying in praise: "Rare indeed, rare indeed are the Buddha Tathāgatas, whose profound realms are inconceivable. Due to the force of their vows made in past lives, and their excellent and clever methods, they have manifested together in this way. It is a rare and unusual sign."

Then all in the great assembly made individual vows, wishing that all sentient beings might attain the excellent *samādhi* like that of the Tathāgata.

THE MYSTIC FORMULA OF THE SEVEN BUDDHAS

At that point, Mañjuśrī rose from his seat and clasped his palms together in reverence. After circumambulating the Buddhas seven times and worshipping at their feet, he addressed the Lords, saying: "Excellent, excellent! The force of the Tathāgatas' *samādhi* is inconceivable. Due to the force of your fundamental vows, your excellent and adept methods can perfect all beings. We sincerely desire that you reveal to us the spiritual formula of great force, which is able to induce unfortunates of future ages—who are bound by the sufferings of disease, whose astrological configurations cause them all sorts of difficulties, who suffer from pestilence and disease, anger and woe, who tread upon a path of depravity, who meet with various fearful things—to take refuge and cause them to obtain peace and tranquility. If there are sentient beings who write this spiritual formula or have others copy it out, who accept it and hold to it, read it, recite it, and extensively disseminate it among others, they will constantly be covered by the protective thoughts of the Buddhas. The Buddhas themselves will manifest their bodies and cause these beings to have all their wishes fulfilled. These beings will neither sink to a woesome path of existence, nor suffer an untimely death."

At this point, the Tathāgatas praised Mañjuśrī, saying: "Excellent, excellent. It is our awesome spiritual force which causes you to urgently request us to reveal the spiritual formula by which these sentient beings, for whom you have pity, may be separated from their various sufferings and troubles. You now should listen carefully and with wholesome thoughts be mindful of our words; for we shall reveal it to you.

"O Mañjuśrī, there is a great spiritual formula named 'Lapis Lazuli Radiance Force of the *Samādhi* of the Tathāgatas.' If there are any sons or daughters who write it out, who read and recite it, who reverently offer *pūjā* to it in worship, who generate the mind of great compassion towards all sentient beings, then all their desires will be fulfilled. The various Buddhas will manifest their forms and will hold them to their protective thoughts. They will be separated from all their obstructions and afflictions, and they will be reborn in a Buddha-realm."

At this time the Seven Tathāgatas uttered the *dhāraṇī* in unison: "Tan-chih-t'a chu-mi-chu-mi-ch'ing-ni-ni-shen mu-ti-mu-ti chi-o-ta-t'a-ch'ih-to-san-mo-ti-o-ti-se-ch'ih-ti o-ti-mu-ti-p'o-li p'o-po-shu-tan-erh sa-p'o-p'o-po-na-shih-yeh tun-ti-tun-t'u ch'ang-ta-mi-wu-mi-tuan-mi fu-shih-ch'i-ta-lo po-li-shu-tan-erh-yun-mi-ni-yun-mi mi-lu-mi-lu mi-lu-hsi-chieh-lu-sa-p'o-ko-lo mi-yao-tu ni-p'o-lai-erh p'o-t'i-su-p'o-ti fu-t'o-t'o-o-t'i se-ch'a-ni-no-ho lo-yo-tu-mi sa-p'o-ti-p'o san-mi-o-san-mi-san-man-t'ien han-lan-tu-mi p'o-fu-t'o p'u-t'i-sa-ch'ui shan-mi-shan-mi po-la-ku-mi-man tu-mi sa-p'o-i-ti-wu-p'o-to-p'o-sa-p'o-pi-ho-ta-yeh sa-p'o-sa-ch'ui-nan-che-pu-ni-pu-lan-ni-pu-yeh-mi sa-p'o-a-she p'i-liu-li-yeh po-li-ti-p'o-hsi sa-p'o-po chu-yang-chieh-lu-so-ha."

When the Seven Buddhas uttered this *dhāraṇī*, an all-pervading radiant light appeared, the great earth shook and trembled, and various divine transformations appeared all at once. All in the great assembly saw these events, and each according to his capacity offered to those Buddhas flowers of heavenly fragrance, perfumed unguents, and powdered incense. They chanted together words of praise and circumambulated the Buddhas to the right seven times.

Those Lord Buddhas chanted together, saying: "All of you in the great assembly should know that if there are any good sons or daughters; if there are any kings, princes, queens or court ladies, great ministers, officials or commoners; should there be any of these who accept and hold to, read and recite, listen to and disseminate this *dhāraṇī;* if, with flowers of marvelous fragrance, they worship this scripture; if they don new and clean clothing and maintain the eightfold vows in a pure place; and if they constantly generate loving kindness and compassion towards all sentient beings—offering *pūjā* in such a manner—they will obtain limitless blessings.

"Further, if there are any persons who have made prayers, they should make images of these Seven Buddhas. In a pure place, they can offer *pūjā* with various fragrant blossoms, by hanging a canopy made of silken banners, by offering supremely marvelous food and drink, and by playing instrumental music. Such a person should further offer *pūjā* to all the Bodhisattvas and to various *devas*. Before the Buddha images, sitting in an upright and proper manner, he should recite the *dhāraṇī.* For seven days, he should hold to the eightfold vows. Having recited the *dhāraṇī* fully 1,008 times, those Tathāgatas and Bodhisattvas will hold him in their protective thoughts. The Bodhisattva Holder of the Thunderbolt (Vajradhara) and various other spirit beings such as Indra, Brahmā, the Four *Deva* Kings, and others, will all come crowding together to protect this person. All the karmic obstructions incurred through the five grave acts leading to rebirth in the Avīci hell[19] will be entirely eliminated. This person will have no illness, his span of life will be lengthened, and he also will suffer neither untimely death, nor plague, nor pestilence.

"If thieves and robbers from some other place seek to invade a region, belligerent and in battle array, disputatious, and seeking pretext for quarrels; or if the inhabitants are famished due to drought or flood, these frightful situations and others like them will be removed. [Between the enemies] there will arise thoughts of loving kindness, like that of parents [towards children]. Whatever is sought for will be granted as they think of it."

THE MYSTIC FORMULA OF VAJRADHARA, INDRA, BRAHMĀ, AND THE FOUR DEVA KINGS

Then Holder of the Thunderbolt Bodhisattva, Indra, Brahmā, and the Four *Deva* Kings rose from their seats, reverently clasped their palms together, prostrated at the feet of Śākyamuni, and addressed him, saying: "O Lord, we and all others in the great assembly have heard of the rare merits of the fundamental vows of the Buddhas, we have seen these Buddhas, who through their loving kindness and compassion have come to this place, causing us and all sentient beings to personally be inspired to offer *pūjā.* O Lord, if there are places where this scripture and the names, *dhāraṇīs,* and teachings of the Seven Buddhas are circulated, worshipped, and copied out, then we—being inspired by the Buddha's awesome force—will go to those places and protect them. Whether it be the king of a state or a great minister, [an inhabitant of] a city or village, a man or woman, we will not let such persons be vexed by sufferings or disease. They will ever attain peace and tranquillity, having goods and food in flourishing abundance. This will be our response to the grace of the Buddhas.

"O Lord, we have personally made these independent and important aspirations in your presence. If there is any son or daughter of pure faith who seeks to hold us in his mind, that person should recite this *dhāraṇī.*" They then uttered the following formula:

"Tan-chih-t'a wu-mo-chu tan-lo-chu ma-ma-chu-chu-lu ha-hu-hsi-mu-lo-mu-lo-mu-lo chin-shu-lu so-ha."

"If there are any sons or daughters of pure faith, any kings of states, princes, great ministers or councillors, queens, or court ladies, who recite the names of the Seven Buddhas and this *dhāraṇī,* who read and recite them, copy out and reverently worship them, then, in their present lives, they will obtain longevity and freedom from disease. Far distant from all distress, they will not sink to the three lowest paths of existence. Attaining to the non-regressing state, they will reach enlightenment.

"They will be reborn in the Buddha-land of their choice, constantly seeing the Buddhas. They will obtain knowledge of their previous lives, correct mindfulness, correct *samādhi,* and full control over their passions. There will be nothing with which they will not be fully endowed.

"If someone contracts a feverish disease [caused by] a malevolent demon, he should copy out this *dhāraṇī* and tie it behind his elbow. When the disease has been sent [out of the patient's body], then the *dhāraṇī* should be placed in a pure site."

VAJRADHARA'S SPECIAL DHĀRAṆĪ

Holder of the Thunderbolt Bodhisattva, going to where the Seven Buddhas were seated, circumambulated them three times, keeping them to his right. Before each of them he repeated his worship and said, "O Lord, I sincerely wish that you bestow your loving kindness, compassion, and protective thoughts upon me. I wish now, for the sake of the abundant sons and daughters of future ages who will uphold this *sūtra,* to further utter a *dhāraṇī* for them."

Then, those Seven Buddhas praised Holder of the Thunderbolt Bodhisattva, saying: "Excellent, excellent, Holder of the Thunderbolt. We will grant you protection and permit you to utter a *dhāraṇī* for the protection of beings in the future. Those who uphold this *sūtra* will be caused to be free of troubles, and whatever they seek will be obtained in full abundance."

Then Holder of the Thunderbolt Bodhisattva uttered this *dhāraṇī:*

"Nan-ma-chi-to-nan san-miao-san-fu-t'o-nan nan-ma-sa-p'o-po-che-lo-to-lo-nan-tan-chih-t'a an-po-che-li po-che-li mo-ho-po-che-li po-che-lo-p'o-she t'o-lai-erh-san-ma-san-ma san-man-o a-po-lai-ti-hsieh-to-po-che-li shan-ma-shan-ma po-lo-shan-man-tu-mi sa-p'o-pi-a-ta-yeh chu-lu-chu-lu sa-p'o-chieh-ma a-fa-lai-na-erh-yo-yeh san-ma-yeh-mu-nu-san-mu-lo-pu-chia-p'an-po-che-lo-p'o-erh-sa-p'o-she-mi-po-li fu-lai-yeh so-ha."

"O Lord, if there are any persons who hold to the names of the Seven Buddhas, who recall the merits of the fundamental vows of those Buddhas, who all uphold this *dhāraṇī,* and read, recite, and disseminate it, then I will cause these persons' desires to be entirely fulfilled, making sure that there is nothing which they lack. If they wish to see me and question me regarding what is good and what is bad, they should copy out this *sūtra,* make images of the Seven Buddhas and an image of myself, Vajradhara Bodhisattva. They should place Buddha relics before the images, and they should perform the various *pūjā* offerings in the manner described previously, worshipping and generously bestowing [objects in offering].

"Towards the places of incarnation of all sentient beings, there should arise thoughts of loving kindness and compassion. The eightfold vows should be accepted. Dividing the day into three periods, they should purify themselves by bathing during each of these periods, changing their clothes each time. From the eighth day of the first half of the month to the fifteenth day, on each day, they should recite the *dhāraṇī* with unwavering minds 108 times.

"I will manifest my form in their dreams and speak with them, and it will follow that whatever they seek will be entirely fulfilled."

Then, in the great assembly, the various Bodhisattvas all chanted, "Excellent, excellent, Holder of the Thunderbolt. This *dhāraṇī* is inconceivable. Truly you have done an excellent thing by uttering it."

Then the Seven Tathāgatas spoke in the following manner: "We will guard the *dhāraṇī* which you have uttered for the sake of those who wish for abundant benefits. All sentient beings will attain peace and joy, and all that they seek shall be fulfilled. We will not permit this *dhāraṇī* to become hidden or lost from the world."

At this time, the Seven Buddhas told the various Bodhisattvas, Indra and Brahmā, and the Four *Deva* Kings: "We now shall entrust this *dhāraṇī* to you, together with this *sūtra*. In five hundred years hence, when the Dharma becomes lost, you should guard and protect this *sūtra*. The benefits of the awesome force of this *sūtra* are manifold. This force can eliminate faults, and cause all wholesome desires to be fulfilled, but it is ineffective for those unfortunate beings who vilify the genuine Teachings and defame the wise and noble ones. If you confer and grant this *sūtra* [to such unworthy ones], you will cause the Teachings to rapidly be destroyed."

Then the Seven Buddha Lords from the East returned to their original places, having accomplished their mission to this great assembly, having made fullest use of this opportunity. Since there were no futher doubts, each returned to his original land. Seated upon their thrones, they suddenly disappeared.

NAMING THE SŪTRA AND CONCLUSION

The Venerable Ānanda then rose from his seat and prostrated himself before the Buddha's feet. With his right knee on the ground, he reverently clasped his palms together and addressed the Buddha, saying, "What is the name of this *sūtra?* How should we accept and uphold it?

The Buddha told Ānanda: "The name of this *sūtra* is 'The Rare and Glorious Adornments, the Merits of the Fundamental Vows of the Seven Buddha Tathāgatas, Arhats, Perfectly Enlightened Ones.' It is also called 'The Questions of Mañjuśrī.' Further, it is called 'The Merits of the Fundamental Vows of the Master of Healing, the Lapis Lazuli Radiance Tathāgata.' It is also called 'The Bodhisattva Holder of the Thunderbolt's Expression of the Vow for the Future Age.' It is called 'The Purification and Removal of All the Veils of Karma.' Further, it is called 'The Fulfillment of All Desires.' Also, it is called 'The Vows of Protection Expressed by the Twelve Great Generals.' With these names you should receive and uphold this *sūtra.*"

When the Lord finished preaching this *sūtra,* all in the great assembly who heard what he had said—the great Bodhisattvas and the assembly of *śrāvakas,* the *devas,* the *nāgas, yakṣas, gandharvas, asuras, garuḍas, kiṃnaras, mahorāgas,* and beings human and non-human—were greatly pleased. They faithfully accepted this teaching and put it into practice.

[THUS ENDS] THE FINAL SECTION OF THE SŪTRA ON THE MERITS OF THE FUNDAMENTAL VOWS OF THE SEVEN BUDDHAS OF LAPIS LAZULI RADIANCE, THE MASTERS OF HEALING

1. Where commonly identifiable, Bodhisattva names have been given in parentheses in their Sanskrit form.
2. As in Part Two, *Translation III,* "arhat" is rendered as one character, *ying,* rather than by the more usual *ying-kung.*
3. Since it is clearly stated in other sections that nuns and laywomen should vow to be reborn in these realms as well as monks and laymen, the phrase "there are no women there" is translated throughout this text as "there is no temptation there."
4. Literally, "broken tiles."
5. Literally: "Due to this force." In a fuller sense it implies: "Due to the force of the generated faith and due to the spiritual force of the Buddha generated in response." For the purpose of clarity and with regard to the conciseness of the Chinese phrase, it is rendered throughout as "due to my spiritual force."
6. The *pāramitās* of the Bodhisattva Path: Perfection of giving (*dāna*), perfection of morality (*śīla*), of forbearance (*kṣānti*), of striving (*vīrya*), of meditation (*dhyāna*), and of insight (*prajñā*).
7. Referring to the *cintāmaṇi* gem, also known as the "wish-granting" gem.
8. Monks, nuns, novice observers of the six precepts, male and female novice observers of the minor precepts, male and female lay observers of the five precepts.
9. The paradise of the Buddha known as Amitābha or Amitāyus.
10. Where it is difficult to see a Buddha or hear his teachings: the hells, hungry ghost realm, as animals, in the northern continent (where all is pleasant), in the *deva* heavens, as one who is deaf, mute, and blind,

as a worldly philosopher, or in the intermediate period between a Buddha and his successor.

11. Madhyadeśa, Central North India.

12. The Iron Mountains form the outer ring encircling the universe. For an illustration of the main features of the ideal universe, see Judith Hanson, trans., Jamgon Kongtrul's *The Torch of Certainty* (Boulder and London: 1977), p. 92.

13. This differs significantly from Translation III, which states that the woman will be transformed into a man through the rebirth process.

14. See Part Two, *Translation III,* fn. 8.

15. Translated as: "I honor the Lord Master of Healing, the King of Lapis Lazuli Radiance, Tathāgata, Arhat, Perfectly Enlightened One, saying: To the healing, to the healing, to the supreme healing, hail!"

16. The text seems to be missing some characters here. Literally: "Beyond these sands of the Ganges River." Probably the original phrase went something like: "Beyond Buddha-realms as numerous as the sands of the Ganges." T. XIV, 451, p. 416C.

17. *Sahāloka,* the world of endurance, that is, this world. Cf. Suzuki, *Studies in the Laṅkāvatāra Sūtra* (London: 1930), p. 452.

18. Literally, "made inquiries of each other," p. 416C.

19. *Pañcāntarya:* patricide, matricide, killing an arhat, shedding the blood of a Buddha, and destroying the harmony of the Saṃgha.

APPENDICES

APPENDIX I

Healing Agents in the Pāli Canon

THE MAHĀVAGGA section VI of the *Vinaya* contains an entire *materia medica* of items sanctioned by the Buddha for the purpose of healing. These special healing agents, being more rare or more difficult to prepare than the five standard medicines, are exempted from rules forbidding storage of property, and they are permitted to be preserved "for as long as life lasts."[1]

A list follows with some common diseases afflicting monks and the cures permitted by the Buddha:

Wind in the stomach: salted sour gruel. This is also permitted to those not ill as a beverage mixed with water.[2]

Wind afflictions (in general): Oil decoctions mixed with strong alcoholic drink. However, the decoction should not be so strong as to cause the patient to become drunk. If the decoction is improperly prepared to immoderate strength, it may be used as an ointment.[3]

Rheumatism of limbs: (listed in order of increasing severity) sweating, sweating by use of herbs, great sweating (rolling in charcoal pit while covered with dust, sand and leaves), sweating by (sprinkling on) hemp water, immersion in a vat of hot water.[4]

Constipation: drink raw lye.[5]

Itch, small boil, running sore, malodorous body: chunams (to bathe or soak the skin). For those who are not ill, dung, clay, or boiled coloring matter can be used.[6] Also, for some skin diseases a perfumed paste can be applied.[7]

Eye diseases: ointments made from substances such as black collyrium, yellow ochre, lampblack, ointment powders from sandalwood, rosebay, black gum, *tālisa* (*flacourtia cataphracta*), nutgrass. In order to apply these ointments and powders properly, as well as to store and preserve them, monks are permitted ointment sticks, small containers, large boxes with lids to store the small containers, and a case that can be tied to wrap up all the paraphernalia. These sticks and containers are not to be made of rare and precious substances.[8]

Jaundice: drink a compound of cow's urine and yellow myrobalan.[9]

Snake-bite: decoctions of the four irregular things are permitted —dung, urine, ashes, clay.[10]

Poison: drink decoction of dung.[11]

Poison as a result of black magic: decoction of mud turned up by a plow.[12]

In addition, various other substances are deemed acceptable. For these, no specific diseases are mentioned. They are as follows:

Tallows (mixed with oil): from beans, fish, alligators, donkeys.[13]

Roots: turmeric, ginger, orris, white orris, garlic, black hellebore, khus-khus, nut-grass, and whatever other medicinal roots are needed. These cannot be served among foods, but are to be retained solely for healing value. Also, small grindstones are permitted in order to prepare medicines pounded off roots.[14]

Astringent decoctions: prepared from nimb-tree, *kutaja* (*wrightia antidysenterica*), *pakkava* (a creeper), *nattamala* tree (*pongamiaglabia*) or whatever other is needed.[15]

Leaves: nimb leaves, *kutaja* leaves, cucumber leaves, basil leaves, cotton tree leaves, or whatever other is necessary.[16]

Fruits: pepper, black pepper, yellow myrobalan, beleric myrobalan, emblic myrobalan, or whatever other.[17]

Resins: especially from hungu (*assafoetida*), or whatever other.[18]

Salts: sea-salt, black salt, rock salt, culinary salt, or red salt.[19]

Sugar is also permitted to those who are ill, while sugar water can be drunk by those in good health.[20]

Under the special circumstances of possession by a non-human spirit being (this is called a "non-human affliction"), raw flesh and raw blood are permitted as medicine. Presumably, these substances are permitted because: (1) the non-human being in control of the monk is the one who actually eats these substances; (2) having eaten these substances, its craving thereby is satiated; and (3) the being leaves the body of the monk.[21]

Among other special treatments is the use of lotus fibers and stalks by Sāriputta to abate his fever. This seems to be a unique remedy especially suited to his needs.[22]

1. I. B. Horner, trans., *The Book of the Discipline (Vinaya-piṭaka)*, vol. IV (*Mahāvagga*) (London: 1951), p. 271. (Hereafter referred to as *Mahāvagga.*)
2. *Mahāvagga*, p. 276.
3. *Mahāvagga*, p. 278.
4. *Mahāvagga*, pp. 278-279.
5. *Mahāvagga*, p. 280.
6. *Mahāvagga*, p. 274.
7. *Mahāvagga*, p. 281.
8. *Mahāvagga*, p. 275.
9. *Mahāvagga*, p. 280.
10. *Mahāvagga*, p. 280.
11. *Mahāvagga*, p. 280.
12. *Mahāvagga*, p. 280.
13. *Mahāvagga*, pp. 270-271.
14. *Mahāvagga*, pp. 271-272.
15. *Mahāvagga*, p. 272.
16. *Mahāvagga*, p. 272.
17. *Mahāvagga*, pp. 272-273.
18. *Mahāvagga*, p. 273.
19. *Mahāvagga*, p. 273.
20. *Mahāvagga*, p. 308.
21. *Mahāvagga*, p. 308.
22. *Mahāvagga*, p. 274.

APPENDIX II

References to Bodhisattvas of Healing in the Chinese Buddhist Canon

BODHISATTVAS whose names indicate special healing abilities appear in a wide range of Mahāyāna texts. Utilizing the comprehensive indices to the *Taishō Shinshū Daizōkyō* edition of the Canon, I have found that Bodhisattvas of Healing (that is, whose names include the characters *yao* [藥] or *i* [醫]) appear in a total of twenty-five *sūtras* translated into Chinese in the T'ang period or earlier. These citations are listed in the following order:

A. Bodhisattva King of Healing Mentioned without Supreme Healer.
B. Bodhisattva Supreme Healer Mentioned without King of Healing.
C. The Two Bodhisattva Brothers Mentioned Together.
D. Some Other Bodhisattvas of Healing.

There is a purpose for this long and rather tedious list, and that is to show from textual evidence the long-standing popularity of the Bodhisattvas of Healing in the Mahāyāna Buddhist traditions. Also, I wish—by means of the numerical weight of these references—to support my belief that Bhaiṣajya-rājā was perhaps the first and certainly the most popular of the Healing Bodhisattvas.

In relation to the Bodhisattva Bhaiṣajya-rājā, I began to compile a list of textual citations for the term *bhaiṣajya-rājā,* used as an epithet ("king of healing") or as a term for a substance ("king of medicines"), in order to indicate the early and continued popularity of this term, eventually adopted as the name of the foremost Bodhisattva of Healing. The preliminary list of textual citations for this term grew to such unwieldy proportions that it is best to merely report on its long-standing popularity in Buddhist *sūtras.*

The order of these lists, and those of appendix III, is based on the date of transmission of the text to China. Where listed in the *Hōbōgirin*, Sanskrit titles (often reconstructed) of the *sūtras* are included. The end of the T'ang is the cut-off point for these lists; by that time the Buddhist pantheon was well-nigh complete. Where several translations of a given text exist, I have listed references for only one, unless significant differences warrant mention of the variants.

I should note that the comprehensive indices to the *Taishō* Canon are invaluable, and without them appendices II and III could not have been compiled. However, the indices are not always entirely accurate in their citation of passages, and in addition through continued reading in various *sūtras*, I have found a number of references which were not noted in the indices. Therefore, though I have sought to be as inclusive as possible in these two appendices, there may be a few references overlooked.

A. BODHISATTVA KING OF HEALING MENTIONED WITHOUT SUPREME HEALER

1. Buddhayaśas (late fourth-early fifth century), trans. *Hsü-k'ung-tsang p'u-sa ching (Ākāśagarbhabodhisattvasūtra).* T. XIII, 405, pp. 649C-650A.
2. Kumārajīva (early fifth century), trans. *Fo-shuo hua-shou ching (Kuśalamūlasamparigrahasūtra).* T. XVI, 657, pp. 145B, 147B, 154A.
3. ______. *Miao-fa lien-hua ching (Saddharmapuṇḍarīkasūtra).* T. IX, 262. Numerous citations in chapters one, ten, thirteen, twenty-three, and twenty-seven.
4. Anon. (mid-fifth century), trans. *Fo-shuo to-chi-hui cheng-fa ching (Saṅghāṭīsūtradharmaparyāya).* T. XIV, 424, pp. 976C, 987A.
5. Saṅghavara (early sixth century), trans. *Wen-shu shih-li so-shuo pan-jo t'o-lo-ni ching (Saptaśatikāprajñāpāramitāsūtra).* T. VIII, 233, p. 732C.
6. Bodhiruci (sixth century), trans. *Fo-shuo fo-ming ching (Buddhanāmasūtra).* T. XIV, 440, pp. 123A, 125A, 145B, 182C.
7. Jñānagupta (mid-late sixth century), trans. *Chung-chung tsa-chou ching.* T. XXI, 1337, p. 637C.
8. I-ching (eighth century), trans. *Chin-kuang-ming tsui-sheng-wang ching (Suvarṇaprabhāsa* [*uttamarāja*] *sūtra).* T. XVI, 665, p. 403B.
9. Amoghavajra (mid-eighth century), trans. *Ta-chi ta-hsü-k'ung-tsang p'u-sa so-wen ching (Gaganagañja*[*paripṛcchā*]. T. XIII, 404, 628B.

10. ______. *Fa-hua man-t'o-lo wei-i hsing-se fa ching.* T. XIX, 1001, p. 603B. Here he is described as having a complexion like the sun at dawn, his form—visualized in a lunar disc—emitting an all-pervading radiance.
11. Dānapāla (late tenth century), trans. *Ta-chi-hui cheng-fa ching.* T. XIII, 424, pp. 976C ff.
12. Ratnolkādhāraṇī (late tenth century), trans. *Ta-fang-kuang tsung-t'ai pao-kuang-ming ching.* T. X, 299, p. 892B.

B. BODHISATTVA SUPREME HEALER MENTIONED WITHOUT KING OF HEALING

1. Bodhiruci (sixth century), trans. *Fo-shuo fo-ming ching (Buddhanāmasūtra).* T. XIV, 440, p. 130A.
2. Upaśūnya (mid-sixth century), trans. *Seng-chia-che ching (Saṅghāṭisūtradharmaparyāya).* T. XIV, 423. pp. 968A ff.

C. THE TWO BODHISATTVA BROTHERS MENTIONED TOGETHER

1. Anon. (ca. second century), trans. *Fo-shuo wei-tseng yu ching (Abhutadharmaparyāya).* T. XVI, 688, p. 782A.
2. Kumārajīva (early fifth century), trans. *Miao-fa lien-hua ching (Saddharmapuṇḍarīkasūtra).* T. IX, 262. Numerous references in chapter twenty-seven.
3. ______. *K'ung-ch'üeh-wang ching (Mahāmāyūrīvidyārājñīsūtra).* T. XIX, 988, p. 482A.
4. Dharmamitra (early fifth century), trans. *Kuan Hsü-k'ung-tsang p'u-sa ching.* T. XIII, 409, p. 679B.
5. Kālayaśas (early-mid fifth century), trans. *Kuan Yao-wang Yao-shang erh-p'u-sa ching.* T. XX, 1161, numerous references throughout the text.
6. Chü-sha-ching-sheng (mid-fifth century), trans. *Chih-ch'an ping pu-pi yao-fa.* T. XV, 620, p. 342A. Though technically speaking not a *sūtra,* I have included this text because of its intrinsic interest; it discusses methods for the curing of disease by meditation. The devotee is instructed to meditate on the two Bodhisattvas, who will rain down upon him sublime medicines and speak to him on various topics related to meditative practices.
7. Dharmaruci (early sixth century), trans. *Ju-lai chuang-yen chih-hui kuang-ming ju i-ch'ieh fo-ching-chieh ching (Sarvabuddhaviṣayāvatāra-jñānālokālaṃkarāsūtra).* T. XIII, 357, p. 239A.
8. Gautama Prajñāruci (mid-sixth century), trans. *Pu-pi ting ju yin ching (Niyatāniyata*[*gaṭi*]*mudrāvatārasūtra).* T. XV, 645, pp. 699B–C.

9. Bodhiruci (sixth century), trans. *Wu-tzu pao-ch'ieh ching (Anakṣarra-karaṇdaka[vai]rocanagarbhasūtra)*. T. XVII, 828, p. 871A.
10. Jñānagupta (late sixth century), trans. *Fo-hua-yen ju ju-lai te-chih pu-ssu-i ching-chieh ching (Tathāgataguṇajñānācintyaviṣayāvatāranirdeśa)*. T. X, 303, p. 918A.
11. Hsüan-tsang (mid-seventh century), trans. *Chi-chao shen-pien san-mo-ti ching (Praśāntaviniścayapratikārya[samādhi]sūtra)*. T. XV, 648. p. 723A.
12. Bhagavaddharma (mid-seventh century), trans. *Ch'ien-shou ch'ien-yen kuan-shih-yin p'u-sa kuang-ta t'u-man wu-ai ta-fei-hsin t'o-lo-ni ching*. T. XX, 1066. p. 106A.
13. Prajñā (late eighth-early ninth century), trans. *Ta-cheng pen-sheng hsin ti kuan ching*. T. III, 159, p. 291B.

D. SOME OTHER BODHISATTVAS OF HEALING

1. I-ching (eighth century), trans. *Chin-kuang-ming tsui-sheng-wang ching (Suvarṇaprabhāsa[uttamarāja]sūtra)*. T. XVI, 665, p. 403B. In a passage which mentions the Bodhisattva King of Healing, there also appear the Bodhisattva Donor of Medicines and the Bodhisattva Disperser of Afflictions and Diseases.

APPENDIX III

References to the Buddha of Healing in the Chinese Buddhist Canon

IN THIS APPENDIX all references which I have found to names of the Buddha of Healing in T'ang and pre-T'ang *sūtras* are listed. Included in all of these names is the word *yao* [藥] or *i* [醫], the Chinese equivalents for *bhaiṣajya* (*i* in some cases may be the equivalent for *vaidya*, physician). Here again, the purpose of such a list is to indicate by textual citation the importance of the Buddha of Healing in the Mahāyāna traditions.

These citations are listed in the following order: A. Names of the Buddha of Healing Which Include the Word *"King,"* (*Rāja*, or *Wang* [王]). B. Names of the Buddha of Healing Which Include Both the Words "King" (*Rāja*, or *Wang*) and "Master" (*Guru*, or *Shih* [師]). C. Names of the Buddha of Healing Which Include the Word "Master" (*Guru*, or *Shih*), Excluding Those in B.

The citations in category A make clear the close relationship of the Buddha of Healing to the earlier Bodhisattva known as King of Healing, while the fact that categories A and B overlap further strengthens the belief that worship of the Buddha of Healing may have emerged from earlier worship of that popular Bodhisattva of Healing.

I should make clear that these lists do not include the special scriptures on the Buddha of Healing; there, the Buddha is generally called the Master of Healing, the Lapis Lazuli Radiance Tathāgata. Also, the six brothers of the Buddha of Healing, who are introduced into Chinese Buddhist texts in the mid-T'ang, are not included in these lists.

Originally, I had intended to include a list of all references to the word *bhaiṣajya-guru* (*yao-shih* or *i-shih*), in the Chinese

Buddhist Canon. My preliminary survey located the word in well over thirty texts, and I found that it is used (reasonably enough) in a literal sense to refer to great physicians. For example, a "master of healing" is questioned about a diagnosis in the *Hsien-yü ching* (T. IV, 202, p. 404A; translated by Hui-chüeh and others ca. 445). Also, in the *Pu-ming p'u-sa-hui,* a text found in Bodhiruci's T'ang collection of the *Ratnakūṭa* (T. XI, 310, p. 636C):

He is like a master of healing who, though he holds a sack of medicines for practicing his art, is unable to heal the diseases of his own body. People who are well learned in the Dharma and [still] have the disease of [karmic] afflictions are just like this.

A. NAMES OF THE BUDDHA OF HEALING WHICH INCLUDE THE WORD "KING" (RĀJA, OR WANG 王).

1. Anon. (ca. second century) trans. *Fo-shuo wei-tseng yu ching (Abhutadharmaparyāya).* T. XVI, 688, p. 782A. King of Healing Buddha.
2. Chih-ch'ien (mid-third century), trans. *Fo-shuo wei-mo-chieh ching (Vimalakīrtinirdeśasūtra).* T. XIV, 474, pp. 535C–536A. [Also in the translations of Kumārajīva (T. XIV, 475, pp. 556B–C) and Hsüan-tsang (T. XIV, 476, pp. 586A, 587A).] King of Healing Tathāgata.
3. Dharmarakṣa (late third-early fourth century), trans. *Cheng-fa lien-hua ching (Saddharmapuṇḍarīkasūtra).* T. IX, 263. Numerous references in chapter twenty. King of Healing Tathāgata.
4. Kumārajīva (early fifth century), trans. *Fo-shuo hua-shou ching (Kuśalamūlasaṃparigrahasūtra).* T. XVI, 657, p. 162B. King of Healing Buddha.
5. ______. *Ssu-i fan-t'ien so-wen ching (Viśeṣacintābrahmaparipṛcchāsūtra).* T. XV, 586, p. 51B. (Also in Dharmarakṣa's translation, T. XV, 585, p. 20C). King of Healing Tathāgata (mentions his Buddha-land in the East).
6. Buddhabhadra (early fifth century), trans. *Ta-fang-kuang fo-hua-yen ching ([Buddha]avataṃsakasūtra).* T. IX, 278, p. 764B. [Also, with some minor variations, in translations by Śikṣānanda (T. X, 279, p. 400A, 416B) and Prajñā (T. X, 293, pp. 775C, 801C).] King of Healing Buddha.
7. Dharmakṣema (early fifth century), trans. *Ta-fang-teng ta-chi ching ([Mahāvaipulyamahā]sanipātasūtra).* T. XIII, 397, p. 108C. Supreme King of Healing Buddha.
8. Dharmāgatayaśas (late fifth century), trans. *Wu-liang-i ching.* T. IX, 276, p. 384C. King of Healing Buddha.
9. Bodhiruci (sixth century), trans. *Fo-shuo fo-ming ching (Buddhanāmasūtra).* T. XIV, 440, pp. 117C, 143C, 151B, 165C, 175C,

180C. King of Healing Buddha. Also: King of Healing, the King of the Sublime Voice Buddha (p. 117C); Great King of Healing (p. 118B). [In an earlier version by an anonymous translator, only King of Healing Buddha is listed, T. XIV, 442, p. 315B.]

10. ______. *Pu-k'ung p'o-so shen-pien chen-yen ching (Amoghapāśakalparājasūtra).* T. XX, 1092, p. 229B. Unhindered King of Healing Tathāgata.
11. Anon. (mid-sixth century), trans. *Hsien-tsai hsien-chieh ch'ien-fo-ming ching (Bhadrakalpikasūtra).* T. XIV, 447, pp. 377C, 379C, 384C. King of Healing Buddha.
12. Anon. (mid-sixth century), trans. *Wei-lai hsing-su-chieh ch'ien-fo-ming ching.* T. XIV, 448, p. 390C. King of Healing Tathāgata. Also, King of Healing, the Kingly Voiced Tathāgata (p. 396C).
13. Jñānagupta (late sixth century), trans. *Ta-chi p'i-yu wang ching.* T. XIII, 422, p. 316C. Unhindered King of Healing Buddha.
14. Amoghavajra (eighth century), trans. *Ta-chi Hsü-k'ung-tsang p'u-sa so-wen ching (Gagaṇagañja[paripṛcchā]sūtra).* T. XIII, 404, p. 633A. King of Healing Buddha (identified as Buddha of the East).
15. Dharmarakṣa (early eleventh century), trans. *Ta-cheng p'u-sa-tsang cheng-fa ching (Bodhisattvapiṭakasūtra).* T. XI, 316, p. 790C. King of Healing Buddha.

B. NAMES OF THE BUDDHA OF HEALING WHICH INCLUDE BOTH THE WORDS "KING" (RĀJA, OR WANG 王), AND "MASTER" (GURU, OR SHIH 師)

1. Chih-ch'ien (mid-late third century), trans. *Fo-shuo pa-chi-hsiang shen-chou ching (Aṣṭabuddhakasūtra).* T. XIV, 427, p. 72B. Master of Healing, Fully Endowed King Tathāgata.
2. Dharmarakṣa (late third-early fourth century), trans. *Cheng-fa lien-hua ching (Saddharmapuṇḍarīkasūtra).* T. IX, 263, p. 103A. Master who is King of Healing Buddha.
3. Wan-t'ien-i (mid-late sixth century), trans. *Tsun-sheng p'u-sa so-wen i-ch'ieh chu-fa ju-wu-liang-men t'o-lo-ni ching.* T. XXI, 1343, p. 849C. Master of Healing, the Completely Endowed King, Tathāgata.
4. Jñānagupta (mid-late sixth century), trans. *Fo-pen-hsing-chi ching (Abhiniṣkramaṇasūtra).* T. III, 190, p. 719A. Master of Healing, the Kingly Buddha.
5. ______. *Wu-ch'ien-wu-pai fo-ming shen-chou chu-chang mieh-tsui ching (Buddhanāmasahasrapañcaśatacatustripañcadaśasūtra).* T. XIV, 443, p. 328C. Master of Healing, the King of Lapis Lazuli Radiance Tathāgata. Also, Master of Healing, the Kingly Tathāgata (pp. 340B, 341A).

C. NAMES OF THE BUDDHA OF HEALING WHICH INCLUDE THE WORD "MASTER" (GURU, OR SHIH 師), EXCLUDING THOSE IN B.

1. Kumārajīva (early fifth century), trans. *K'ung-ch'ueh wang-chou ching (Mahāmāyuri[vidyārajñī]sūtra).* T. XIX, 988, p. 482C. Buddha of the East, Master of Healing of Lapis Lazuli Radiance.
2. Anon. (mid-sixth century), trans. *Hsien-tsai hsien-ch'ien-fo-ming ching (Bhadrakalpikasūtra).* T. XIV, 447, pp. 382A, 387B. Supreme Master of Healing Buddha. Also, Master of Healing Buddha (p. 384C).
3. Divākara (late seventh century), trans. *Fang-kuang ta-chuang-yen ching (Lalitavistarasūtra).* T. III, 187, p. 567A. Master of Healing Buddha.
4. Buddhapāli (late seventh century), trans. *Fo-ting tsun-sheng t'o-lo-ni ching ([Sarvadurgatipariśodhana]uṣṇīṣavijayadhāraṇīsūtra).* T. XIX, 967, p. 410B. Master of Healing, the Lapis Lazuli Radiance Tathāgata.

The many special texts translated into Chinese on the Buddha of Healing—as listed fully in the bibliography—generally refer to him as "Master of Healing, the Lapis Lazuli Radiance Tathāgata."

APPENDIX IV

Chinese Character List

[For complete bibliographic information, see relevant notes, Appendices II and III, and the Selected Bibliography.]

A. TEXTS CITED

1. *Besson Zakki*	別尊雜記
2. *Cheng-fa hua ching* (T. 263)	正法華經
3. *Chi-chao shen-pien san-mo-ti ching* (T. 648)	寂照神變三摩地經
4. *Ch'ien-shou ch'ien-yen kuan-shih-yin p'u-sa kuang-ta t'u-man wu-ai ta-fei-hsin t'o-lo-ni ching* (T. 1066)	千手千眼觀世音菩薩廣大圓滿無礙大悲心陀羅尼經
5. *Chih-ch'an ping pu-pi yao-fa* (T. 620)	治禪病秘要經
6. *Chin-kuang-ming tsui-sheng-wang ching* (T. 665)	金光明最勝王經
7. *Chung-chung tsa-chou ching* (T. 1337)	種種雜咒經
8. *Ch'u san-tsang chi-chi* (T. 2145)	出三藏記集
9. *Fang-kuang ta-chuang-yen ching* (T. 187)	方廣大莊嚴經
10. *Fa-hua man-t'o-lo wei-i hsing-se fa ching* (T. 1001)	法華曼荼羅威儀形式法經
11. *Fa-yün chih-lüeh*	法運志畧

12. *Fo-hua-yen ju ju-lai te-chih pu-ssu-i ching-chieh ching* (T. 303) 佛華嚴入如來德智不思議境界經
13. *Fo-pen-hsing-chi ching* (T. 190) 佛本行集經
14. *Fo-shuo fo-ming ching* (T. 440) 佛說佛名經
15. *Fo-shuo hua-shou ching* (T. 657) 佛說華手經
16. *Fo-shuo kuan-fo san-mei-hai ching* (T. 643) 佛說觀佛三昧海經
17. *Fo-shuo kuan Mi-lo p'u-sa shang-sheng Tu-shi-t'ien ching* (T. 452) 佛說觀彌勒菩薩上生兜率天經
18. *Fo-shuo kuan P'u-hsien p'u-sa hsing-fa ching* (T. 277) 佛說觀普賢菩薩行法經
19. *Fo-shuo kuan-t'ing ching* (T. 1331) 佛說灌頂經
20. *Fo-shuo kuan Yao-wang Yao-shang erh-p'u-sa ching* (T. 1161) 佛說觀藥王藥上二菩薩經
21. *Fo-shuo pa-chi-hsiang shen-chou ching* (T. 427) 佛說八吉祥神咒經
22. *Fo-shuo to-chi-hui cheng-fa ching* (T. 424) 佛說大集會正法經
23. *Fo-shuo tso fo-hsing-hsiang ching* (T. 692) 佛說作佛形像經
24. *Fo-shuo Wei-mo-chieh ching* (T. 474) 佛說維摩詰經
25. *Fo-shuo wei-tseng yu ching* (T. 688) 佛說未曾有經
26. *Fo-ting tsun-sheng t'o-lo-ni ching* (T. 967) 佛頂尊勝陀羅尼經
27. *Hsien-tsai hsien-chieh ch'ien-fo-ming ching* (T. 447) 現在賢劫千佛名經
28. *Hsien-tsai shih-fang ch'ien-wu-pai fo-ming ping-tsa fo t'ung hao* 現在十方千五百佛名并雜佛同號

29. *Hsien-yü ching* (T. 202)	賢愚經
30. *Hui-shang p'u-sa wen ta-shan-ch'uan ching* (T. 345)	慧上菩薩問大善權經
31. *I-ch'ieh-ching yin-i* (by Hui-lin, T. 2128)	一切經音義
32. *I-ch'ieh-ching-yin-i* (by Hsüan-ying)	一切經音義
33. *Ju-lai chuang-yen chih-hui kuang-ming ju i-chieh fo-ching-chieh ching* (T. 357)	如來莊嚴智慧光明入一切佛境界經
34. *Kakuzen-shō*	覺禪鈔
35. *Kao-seng-chüan* (T. 2059)	高僧傳
36. *Kuan Hsü-k'ung-tsang p'u-sa hui* (T. 409)	觀虛空藏菩薩經
37. *Kuan-shih-yin kuan ching*	觀世音觀經
38. *Kuan Wu-liang-shou-fo ching* (T. 365)	觀無量壽佛經
39. *K'ung-ch'üeh-wang-chou ching* (T. 988)	孔雀王呪經
40. *Li-tai san-pao chi* (T. 2034)	歷代三寶記
41. *Miao-fa lien-hua ching* (T. 262)	妙法蓮華經
42. *Pu-k'ung-p'o-so shen-pien chen-yen ching* (T. 1092)	不空羂索神變真言經
43. *Pu-ming p'u-sa hui* (T. 310)	普明菩薩會
44. *Pu-pi ting-ju ting-ju yin ching* (T. 645)	不必定入定入印經
45. *P'u-sa tsang* (T. 310)	菩薩藏
46. *Seng-chia-che ching* (T. 423)	僧伽吒經
47. *Shou-leng-yen san-mei ching* (T. 642)	首楞嚴三昧經
48. *Ssu-i fan-t'ien so-wen ching* (T. 586)	思益梵天所問經
49. *Ta-ch'eng fang-pien hui* (T. 310)	大乘方便會
50. *Ta-cheng pen-sheng hsin-ti kuan ching* (T. 159)	大乘本行心地觀經

51. *Ta-cheng p'u-sa tsang cheng-fa ching* (T. 316) 大乘菩薩藏正法經
52. *Ta-chih tu-lun* (T. 1509) 大智度論
53. *Ta-chi-hui cheng-fa ching* (T. 424) 大集會正法經
54. *Ta-chi p'i-yu wang ching* (T. 422) 大集譬喻王經
55. *Ta-chi Ta-hsü-k'ung-tsang p'u-sa so-wen ching* (T. 404) 大集大虛空藏菩薩所問經
56. *Ta-fang-kuang fo-hua-yen ching* (T. 278) 大方廣佛華嚴經
57. *Ta-fang-kuang tsung-t'ai pao-kuang-ming ching* (T. 299) 大方廣總持寶光明經
58. *Ta-fang-teng ta-chi-ching* (T. 397) 大方等大集經
59. *Ta-fo-ting ju-lai mi-yin hsiu-teng liao-i che-p'u-sa wan-hsing shou-leng-yen ching* (T. 945) 大佛頂如來密因修證了義諸菩薩萬行首楞嚴經
60. *Tsun-sheng p'u-sa so-wen i-ch'ieh chu-fa ju-wu-liang-men t'o-lo-ni ching* (T. 1343) 尊勝菩薩所問一切諸法入無量門陀羅尼經
61. *Wei-lai hsing-hsiu-chieh ch'ien-fo-ming ching* (T. 448) 未來星宿劫千佛名經
62. *Wei-mo-chieh so-shuo ching* (T. 475) 維摩詰所說經
63. *Wen-shu shih-li so-shuo pan-jo t'o-lo-mi ching* (T. 233) 文殊師利所說般若波羅蜜經
64. *Wu-ch'ien-wu-pai fo-ming shen-chou chu-chang mieh-tsui ching* (T. 440) 五千五百佛名神咒除障滅罪經
65. *Wu-liang-i ching* (T. 276) 無量義經
66. *Wu-tzu pao-ch'ieh ching* (T. 828) 無字寶篋經
67. *Yao-shih i-kuei i-chu* (T. 924C) 藥師儀軌一具
68. *Yao-shih ju-lai hsien-kuan chien-lüeh i-kuei* 藥師如來現觀簡略儀軌

69. *Yao-shih ju-lai kuan hsing i-kuei fa* (T. 923) 藥師如來觀行儀軌法
70. *Yao-shih ju-lai nien-sung i-kuei* (T. 924A) 藥師如來念誦儀軌
71. *Yao-shih ju-lai nien-sung i-kuei* (T. 924B) 藥師如來念誦儀軌
72. *Yao-shih ju-lai pen-yüan ching* (T. 449) 藥師如來本願經
73. *Yao-shih ju-lai pen-yüan ching hsü* (T. 449) 藥師如來本願經序
74. *Yao-shih liu-li-kuang ch'i-fo pen-yüan kung-te ching* (T. 451) 藥師琉璃光七佛本願功德經
75. *Yao-shih liu-li-kuang ju-lai hsiao-tsai ch'u-nan nien-sung i-kuei* (T. 922) 藥師琉璃光如來消災除難念誦儀軌
76. *Yao-shih liu-li-kuang ju-lai pen-yüan kung-te ching* (T. 450) 藥師琉璃光如來本願功德經
77. *Yao-shih liu-li-kuang-wang ch'i-fo pen-yüan kung-te ching nien-sung i-kuei* (T. 925) 藥師琉璃光王七佛本願功德經念誦儀軌
78. *Yao-shih liu-li-kuang-wang ch'i-fo pen-yüan kung-te ching nien-sung i-kuei kung-yang fa* (T. 926) 藥師琉璃光王七佛本願功德經念誦儀軌供養法
79. *Zuzō-shō* 圖像抄

B. NAMES

1. An Shih-kao 安士高
2. Chang Sheng-wen 張勝温
3. Ch'ang-shun 長順
4. Chih Tun 支遁
5. Chiu-t'o 救脱
6. Chu Fa-k'uang 竺法曠
7. Chung-tsung 中宗

8. Chü-sha-ching-sheng 沮渠京聲
9. Fa-hsing 法行
10. Fo-t'u-teng 佛圖澄
11. Hai-yü 海馭
12. Hsüan-tsang 玄奘
13. Hsüan-ying 玄應
14. Hsiao-wu 孝武
15. Hui-chien 慧簡
16. Hui-chü 慧矩
17. Hui-chüeh 慧覺
18. Hui-kuo 慧果
19. Hui-lin 慧琳
20. Hsü Yün 虛雲
21. I-ching 義淨
22. Kūkai 空海
23. Ming-tse 明則
24. Pao-chih 寶誌
25. Seng-han 僧含
26. Sha-lo-pa 沙囉巴
27. Sun Ching-feng 孫景風
28. Wu-tse-t'ien 武則天
29. Yü Fa-k'ai 于法開
30. Yü Tao-sui 于道邃

C. TERMS AND PHRASES CITED

1. ch'ang-che 長者
2. hsing-chu 行處
3. hua-fo 化佛
4. liu-li; pi-liu-li 琉璃；吠琉璃
5. Nan-mo hsiao-tsai yen-shou Yao-shih-fo 南無消災延壽藥師佛
6. ying 應
7. ying-kung 應供
8. Shingon (Chen-yen) 真言

Selected Bibliography

BUDDHIST TEXTS IN ASIAN LANGUAGES

1. Texts on the Healing Buddhas and Bodhisattvas

Amoghavajra, trans. *Yao-shih ju-lai nien-sung i-kuei.* T. XIX, 924A.

______. *Yao-shih ju-lai nien-sung i-kuei.* T. XIX, 924B.

Anon., trans. *Yao-shih i-kuei i-chu.* T. XIX, 924C.

Anon., trans. *Yao-shih liu-li-kuang ju-lai hsiao-tsai ch'u-nan nien-sung i-kuei.* T. XIX, 922.

Dharmagupta, trans. *Yao-shih ju-lai pen-yüan ching.* T. XIV, 449. With a preface by Hui-chü.

Dharmarakṣa, trans. *Cheng-fa lien-hua ching.* T. IX, 263, chapter ten.

Dutt, Nalinaksha, ed. *Gilgit Manuscripts.* vol. I. Srinagar, Kashmir: 1939 (Skt. edition of the *Bhaiṣajya-guru-sūtra*).

Hsüan-tsang, trans. *Yao-shih liu-li-kuang ju-lai pen-yüan kung-te ching.* T. XIV, 450.

I-ching, trans. *Yao-shih liu-li-kuang ch'i-fo pen-yüan kung-te ching.* T. XIV, 451.

Kālayaśas, trans. *Fo-shuo kuan yao-wang yao-shang liang-p'u-sa ching.* T. XXI, 1161.

Sha-lo-pa, trans. *Yao-shih liu-li-kuang-wang ch'i-fo pen-yüan kung-te ching nien-sung i-kuei.* T. XIX, 925.

______. *Yao-shih liu-li-kuang-wang ch'i-fo pen-yüan kung-te ching nien-sung i-kuei kung-yang-fa.* T. XIX, 926.

Śrīmitra, trans. *Fo-shuo kuan-t'ing ching.* T. XXI, 1331, chapter twelve.

Sun Ching-feng, ed. and trans. *Yao-shih ju-lai hsien-kuan chien-lüeh i-kuei.* Shanghai: 1940.

Vajrabodhi, trans. *Yao-shih ju-lai kuan hsing i-kuei fa.* T. XIX, 923.

Vira, Raghu, and Chandra, Lokesh, eds. *Gilgit Buddhist Manuscripts* (Facsimile Editions). Pt. 8. New Delhi: 1974 (*Śata-piṭaka series,* vol. 10:8).

2. Related Texts

Kumārajīva, trans. *Miao-fa lien-hua ching.* T. IX, 262.

______. *Wei-mo-chieh so-shuo ching.* T. XIV, 475.

Wogihara, U. and Tsuchida, C. eds. *Saddharmapuṇḍarīkasūtram.* Tokyo: 1933–1935.
[For Chinese Buddhist texts briefly consulted that mention the Healing Buddhas and Bodhisattvas, see Appendices II and III.]

B. BUDDHIST TEXTS IN WESTERN LANGUAGES

Anonymous, *Shingon Buddhist Service Book.* Koyasan: 1975.
Bendall, Cecil and Rouse, W. H. D., trans. *Śāntideva's Śikṣāsamuccaya.* Delhi: 1971.
Benveniste, E. *Textes Sogdiens: Mission Pelliot en Asie Centrale.* vol. III. Paris: 1940.
Conze, Edward, trans. *The Perfection of Wisdom in Eight Thousand Lines.* Bolinas, Calif.: 1973.
Cowell, E. B., ed. *Buddhist Mahāyāna Texts.* Oxford: 1894.
Emmerick, R. E., trans. *The Sūtra of the Golden Light.* London: 1970.
Evans-Wentz, W. Y., trans. *The Tibetan Book of the Dead.* Oxford: 1927.
George, Christopher S., trans. *The Caṇḍamahāroṣaṇa Tantra.* New Haven: 1974.
Hakeda, Yoshito S., trans. *The Awakening of Faith, Attributed to Asvaghosha.* New York: 1967.
______. *Kūkai: Major Works.* New York: 1973.
Hare, E. M., trans. *Woven Cadences of the Early Buddhists.* London: 1944.
Horner, I. B., trans. *The Book of the Discipline.* 4 vols. London: 1938–1951.
Horner, I. B., trans. *The Middle Length Sayings.* 3 vols. London: 1954–1959.
Hurvitz, Leon, trans. *Scripture of the Lotus Blossom of the Fine Dharma.* New York: 1976.
Katō, Bunnō, *et al.*, trans. *The Threefold Lotus Sūtra.* New York and Tokyo: 1975.
Lamotte, Étienne, trans. *L'Enseignement de Vimalakīrti.* Louvain: 1962.
Lessing, Ferdinand D. and Wayman, Alex, trans. *Mkhas grub rje's Fundamentals of the Buddhist Tantras.* The Hague: 1968.
Liebenthal, Walter, trans. *The Sūtra of the Lord of Healing.* Peking: 1936.
Norman, K. R., trans. *The Elder's Verses.* 2 vols. London: 1969, 1971.
Pe Maung Tin, trans. *Buddhaghosa's Visuddhimagga, The Path of Purity.* London: 1971.
Rhys Davids, Caroline, trans. *Kuddaka-Patha, The Minor Anthologies of the Pāli Canon.* vol. I. London: 1938.
______. *Psalms of the Early Buddhists.* London: 1964.
______, and Rhys Davids, T. W., trans. *Dialogues of the Buddha.* vols. II and III. London: 1910, 1921.

———, and Suriyagoda Sumangala Thera, trans. *The Book of Kindred Sayings.* vol. I. London: 1917.
———, and Woodward, F. H., trans. *The Book of Kindred Sayings.* vol. II. London: 1922.
Rhys Davids, T. W., trans. *Dialogues of the Buddha.* vol. I. London: 1889.
———. *The Questions of King Milinda.* 2 vols. New York: 1903.
Thurman, Robert A. F., trans. *The Holy Teaching of Vimalakīrti.* University Park, Penn.: 1976.
Wayman, Alex and Wayman, Hideko, trans. *The Lion's Roar of Queen Śrīmāla.* New York: 1974.
Wayman, Alex, trans. *Bhaiṣajya-guru—The Seven Brothers.* Draft translation manuscript from *Rin Lhan.* vol. *Ga,* folios 121a-2 to 127 a-6.

C. SECONDARY SOURCES

Bagchi, P. C. *Le Canon Bouddhique en Chine.* 2 vols. Paris: 1927, 1938.
Barua, Dipak Kumar. *Vihāras in Ancient India: A Survey of Buddhist Monasteries.* Calcutta: 1969.
Basham, A. C. *The Wonder That Was India.* New York: 1959.
Bharati, Agehananda. *The Tantric Tradition.* London: 1965.
Bhattacharyya, Benoytosh. *The Indian Buddhist Iconography.* 3rd ed. Calcutta: 1968.
Blofeld, John. *Mantra: Sacred Words of Power.* New York: 1977.
———. *The Tantric Mysticism of Tibet.* New York: 1970.
Chapin, Helen B. and Soper, Alexander Coburn. *A Long Roll of Buddhist Images.* Ascona, Switzerland: 1972.
Chandra, Lokesh. *The Three Hundred Icons.* New Delhi: n.d.
Conze, Edward. "List of Buddhist terms." *The Tibet Journal* I (1975).
———. *Materials for a Dictionary of the Prajñā-Pāramitā Literature.* Tokyo: 1967.
Davidson, J. LeRoy. *The Lotus Sutra in Chinese Art.* New Haven: 1954.
Dayal, Har. *The Bodhisattva Doctrine in Sanskrit Buddhist Literature.* London: 1932.
Demiéville, Paul. "Byō." In *Hōbōgirin.* Fascicule III. Tokyo: 1937.
Dutt, Nalinaksha. *Early Monastic Buddhism.* Calcutta: 1960.
Dutt, Sukumar. *Buddhist Monks and Monasteries of India.* London: 1962.
Edgerton, Franklin. *Buddhist Hybrid Sanskrit Dictionary.* New Haven: 1953.
Filliozat, Jean. *La Doctrine Classique de la Médicine Indienne, ses Origines et ses Paralèlles Grecs.* Paris: 1949.
———. "La mort volontaire par le feu et la tradition bouddhique indienne." *Journal Asiatique* 251 (1963).

Gaeffke, Peter. "The snake-jewel in ancient Indian literature." *Indian Linguistics* XIV (1954), pp. 581–594.

Gemological Institute of America. *Colored Stones.* 2 vols. Los Angeles: 1975.

Geiger, Wilhelm, trans. *Mahāvaṃsa or The Great Chronicle of Ceylon.* London: 1964.

Gernet, Jacques. "Les suicides par le feu chez les bouddhistes chinoises de Ve au Xe siècle." *Mélanges publiés par l'Institut des Hautes Études Chinoises* II. Paris: 1960.

Giles, Lionel. *Descriptive Catalog of the Chinese Manuscripts from Tun-huang in the British Museum.* London: 1957.

Gonda, J. "The Indian mantra." *Oriens* XVI (1963).

Harada, Yoshito. "Ancient glass in the history of cultural exchange between east and west," *Acta Asiatica* 3 (1962), pp. 57–69.

Hirakawa, Akira. "The rise of Mahāyāna Buddhism and its relation to the worship of *stūpas.*" *Memoirs of the Research Department of the Toyo Bunko* 22. Tokyo: 1963.

Jan, Yün-hua. "Buddhist self-immolation in medieval China." *History of Religions* 4 (1964–1965).

Jayne, W. A. *The Healing Gods of Ancient Civilizations.* New Haven: 1925.

Karmay, Heather. *Early Sino-Tibetan Art.* Warminster, England: 1975.

Kerenyi, C. *Asklepios.* New York: 1959.

Lamotte, Étienne. *Histoire du Bouddhisme Indien.* Louvain: 1958.

______. "La concentration de la marche héroique (*Śūraṃgamasamādhi-sūtra*)." *Mélanges Chinois et Bouddhiques* XIII. Brussels: 1965.

______. "Sur la formation du Mahāyāna." *Asiatica.* Leipzig: 1954.

Lancaster, Lewis A. "An early Mahāyāna sermon about the body of the Buddha and the making of images." *Artibus Asiae* 36 (1974), pp. 287–291.

______. "The oldest Mahāyāna sūtra: its significance for the study of Buddhist development." *Eastern Buddhist* n.s. 8 (1975), pp. 30–41.

Lessing, Ferdinand D. Draft manuscripts pertaining to Bhaiṣajya-guru, including extensive notes recorded after witnessing various rituals at the Yung-ho-kung in Peking, in the early 1930s.

______. *Yung-ho-kung.* Stockholm: 1942.

Luk, Charles (Lu K'uan-yu), trans. *Empty Cloud: The Autobiography of the Chinese Zen Master Hsü Yün.* Rochester, N.Y.: 1974.

______. *The Secrets of Chinese Meditation.* New York: 1969.

Majno, Guido. *The Healing Hand.* Cambridge, Mass.: 1975.

Matsubara, S. *Chūgoku Bukkyō Chokoku Shi Kenkyū.* Tokyo: 1966.

Miller, Roy Andrew. *"The Footprints of the Buddha": An Eighth Century Old Japanese Poetic Sequence.* New Haven: 1975.

Mizuno, Seiichi. *Asuka Buddhist Art: Hōryūji.* Tokyo: 1974.

Mochizuki, Shinkō, ed. *Bukkyō Daijiten.* 8 vols. Kyoto: 1954.

Nagao, Gadjin. "On the theory of the Buddha-body (*Buddha-kāya*)." *Eastern Buddhist* n.s. 6 (1973), pp. 25–53.

Nakamura, Hajime. "A critical survey of Mahāyāna and esoteric Buddhism chiefly based on Japanese sources." *Acta Asiatica* 6 (1964), 7 (1964).

Nakamura, Susumu W. "Pushapa-pūjā, flower offering in Buddhism." *Oriens* II (1958), pp. 117–180.

______. "Pradakshiṇa, a Buddhist form of obeisance," *Semitic and Oriental Studies* XI (1951), pp. 345–359.

Nicolas-Vandier, Nicole, *et al. Bannières et Peintures de Touen-houang Conservées au Musée Guimet.* 2 vols. Paris: 1974–1976. (Louis Hambis, ed. *Mission Paul Pelliot.* vols. XIV–XV).

Oldenberg, Serge. *Materials for a Buddhist Iconography from Khara-Khoto.* St. Petersberg: 1914.

Olschak, Blanche Christine and Wangyal, Thubten. *Mystic Art of Ancient Tibet.* New York: 1973.

Ono, Gemmyō, ed. *Bussho Kaisetsu Daijiten.* 12 vols. Tokyo: 1936.

Ooka, Minoru. *Temples of Nara and Their Art.* Tokyo: 1973.

Pelliot, Paul. "Le Bhaiṣajyaguru." *B.E.F.E.O.* 3 (1903).

______. *Les Grottes de Touen-houang.* 6 vols. Paris: 1912–1924.

Prip-Møller, Johannes. *Chinese Buddhist Monasteries.* Copenhagen: 1937; reprinted Hong Kong: 1967.

Rahula, Walpola. *History of Buddhism in Ceylon.* Colombo: 1956.

Saha, Kshanika. *Buddhism in Central Asia.* Calcutta: 1970.

Sastri, N. A. K., ed. *A Comprehensive History of India.* vol. II. Bombay: 1957.

Saunders, E. Dale. *Mudrā.* New York: 1960.

Sawa, Ryuken, ed. *Mikkyō Jiten.* Kyoto: 1975.

Schopen, Gregory. "*Sukhāvatī* as a generalized religious goal in Sanskrit Mahāyāna *sūtra* literature," *Indo-Iranian Journal* 19 (1977), pp. 177–210.

______. "The phrase '*sa pṛthivīpradeśaś caityabhūto bhavet*' in the *Vajracchedikā:* notes on the cult of the book in Mahāyāna." *Indo-Iranian Journal* 17 (1975), pp. 147–182.

Sircar, D. C., trans. *The Inscriptions of Aśoka.* Delhi: 1967.

Soothill, W. E. and Houdous, Lewis. *A Dictionary of Chinese Buddhist Terms.* Taipei, Taiwan: 1970.

Soper, Alexander Coburn. "Aspects of light symbolism in Gandhāran sculpture." *Artibus Asiae* XII (1949), XIII (1950).

______. *Literary Evidence for Early Buddhist Art in China.* Ascona, Switzerland: 1959.

Stablein, William. "A medical-cultural system among the Tibetan and Newar Buddhists: ceremonial medicine." *Kailash* I (1974).

Stein, Mark Aurel. *Serindia.* 5 vols. Oxford: 1921.

______. *The Thousand Buddhas.* 2 vols. London: 1921.

Suzuki, D. T. *Studies in the Laṅkāvatāra Sūtra.* London: 1930.
Takubo, Shūyo. *Shingon Daranizō no Kaisetsu.* Tokyo: 1967.
Tucci, Giuseppe. *Tibetan Painted Scrolls.* 3 vols. Rome: 1949.
de Visser, M. W. *Ancient Buddhism in Japan.* 2 vols. Leiden: 1935.
de la Vallée Poussin, Louis. *Catalogue of the Tibetan Manuscripts from Tun-huang in the India Office Library, with an Appendix on the Chinese Manuscripts,* by Kazuo Enoki, London: 1967.
Waddell, L. A. *Lamaism, or the Buddhism of Tibet.* Cambridge, England: 1967.
Waley, Arthur. *A Catalogue of Paintings Recovered from Tun-huang by Sir Mark Aurel Stein.* London: 1931.
Wayman, Alex. "Aspects of meditation in the Theravāda and Mahīśāsaka sects." *Studia Missionalia* 24. Rome: 1975.
______. "Buddhism." *Historia Religionum.* vol. III. Leiden: 1971.
______. *The Buddhist Tantras: Light on Indo-Tibetan Esotericism.* New York: 1973.
______. "Buddhist tantric medicine theory on behalf of oneself and others." *Kailash* I (1973).
______. "The concept of poison in Buddhism." *Oriens* X (1957).
______. "Contributions regarding the thirty-two characteristics of the great person." *Sino-Indian Studies* V (1957) [Liebenthal Festschrift].
______. "Notes on the three myrobalans." *Phi Theta Annual* 5 (1954–1955).
______. "The significance of mantras, from the Veda down to Buddhist tantric practice." *Adyar Library Bulletin* (1975) [Centenary Issue].
Welch, Holmes. *The Practice of Chinese Buddhism.* Cambridge, Mass.: 1967.
Wright, Arthur F. "Fo-t'u-teng: a biography." *Harvard Journal of Asiatic Studies* XI (1948).
Yoritomi, Motohiro. *Jōyō Shingon no Kaisetsu.* Tokyo: 1975.
Zürcher, Erik. *The Buddhist Conquest of China.* 2 vols. Leiden: 1970.

Index

Pao-chi, 35
Pāramitās ("perfections"), six, 45, 126, 134, 146 n.25, 176, 216 n.6. *See also Dāna; Śīla; Kṣānti; Vīrya; Dhyāna; Prajñā*
Paramiti, 50 n.26
Pārapariyā, 6
Parittā, 12–13, 22 n.30
Pas, Julian F., 37–38
Path, Noble Eightfold, 22 n.37, 100, 135, 148 n.38
Pearl, 129, 138, 145, 171 n.7
Pelliot, Paul, 57
Phur-bu, 106
Piśaca, 119
Poisons: interior, 11, 90, 109 n.25, 148 n.42; physiological, 11
Prajñā ("insight"), 16, 147 n.36; perfection of, 134, 216 n.6
Prajñā-pāramitā (Buddha or Bodhisattva), 98, 111 n.42
Pratyekabuddha, 62, 128, 147 n.28, 153, 164, 177, 180, 187, 192, 203
Precepts, ten wholesome, 40, 118, 145 n.10, 159, 190, 198. *See also* Acts, ten negative
Preta, 104, 119; realm of. *See* Woesome paths
Pūjā, 84–89, 108 n.11, 122, 149, 161, 162, 166, 200, 201, 202, 204, 205, 209, 210, 211, 212, 214
Pure Land School, 36

Quartz crystal (*sphāṭika*), 65, 187

Radiant Gem of Golden Hue, Perfected in the Sublime Practices (Buddha), 71, 182–185; calling name of, 182–183; *dhāraṇī* of, 184–185; realm of (Wholly Complete Incense Heap), 71, 182, 183–184, 185; vows of, 71, 182–183, 184
Rajomaṇḍala. *See Maṇḍala*
Rākṣasa, 119, 158, 197
Ratnakūṭa-sūtras, 24
Rebirth, 88, 118, 119, 138; into Bhaiṣajya-guru's realm, 155, 160, 195; into the Bodhisattva family, 135; into a Buddha realm, 41, 92, 121, 143, 159, 180, 181, 188, 189, 210, 213; as *deva*, 176, 179, 186; Hall of, 91; as human, 157, 158, 159, 164, 176, 179, 182, 186, 191, 196, 197, 198, 203; as a male, 62, 154, 159, 179, 193, 199; into Western Paradise, 67, 91, 159, 198
Requisites for life, four, 3
Rin Lhan, 105
Rope, five-colored, 87, 169, 208

Saddharma-puṇḍarīka-sūtra, 17, 25, 38, 40, 41, 46, 52, 53, 54, 61, 68, 81, 86, 99, 108; Bodhisattvas of Healing discussed, 17–19; parable of physician, 17–19
Śakra. *See* Indra
Śakrābhilagna, 129, 147 n.29
Śākyamuni, 5, 26, 29, 34, 38–39, 69, 85, 86, 90, 115; in assembly with Seven Healing Buddhas, 93, 97, 103; as healer, 4, 8–9, 10, 11–12, 13, 15–19, 22 n.30, 32, 48, 69, 70, 88, 93; past lives of, 8–9, 32–33, 82; as revealer, 27–28, 29–31, 33–34, 40–47, 52, 66–67, 68, 82, 92; in trinity with Amitābha and Bhaiṣajya-guru, 90–91
Samāhitabhūmi, 32
Samādhi, 10, 119, 120, 123, 124, 127, 130, 132, 135, 144, 147 n.36, 188,